TOO FAT
OR TOO THIN?

TOO FAT
OR TOO THIN?

A Reference Guide
to Eating Disorders

Cynthia R. Kalodner

GREENWOOD PRESS
Westport, Connecticut • London

Library of Congress Cataloging-in-Publication Data

Kalodner, Cynthia R.
  Too fat or too thin? : a reference guide to eating disorders / Cynthia R. Kalodner.
    p. cm.
  Includes bibliographical references and index.
  ISBN 0–313–31581–7 (alk. paper)
  1. Eating disorders. 2. Anorexia nervosa. 3. Bulimia. I. Title.
[DNLM: 1. Anorexia Nervosa. 2. Bulimia. 3. Eating Disorders. WM 175 K14e 2003]
RC552.E18K356   2003
616.859 26—dc21   2002041596

British Library Cataloguing in Publication Data is available.

Library of Congress Catalog Card Number: 2002041596
ISBN: 0–313–31581–7

First published in 2003

Greenwood Press, 88 Post Road West, Westport, CT 06881
An imprint of Greenwood Publishing Group, Inc.
www.greenwood.com

Printed in the United States of America

The paper used in this book complies with the
Permanent Paper Standard issued by the National
Information Standards Organization (Z39.48–1984).

10 9 8 7 6 5 4 3 2 1

Copyright Acknowledgments

The author and publisher gratefully acknowledge permission to reprint the following:
Journal of Behavior Therapy & Experimental Psychiatry, Vol. 18(1), Chiodo: "Invited Case
Transcript Bulimia . . ." Quotes from pp. 41–2, 46. © 1987. Reprinted with permission of
Elsevier Science; Excerpts from *Full Lives: Women Who Have Freed Themselves from Food
and Weight Obsession* by Linsey Hall. 1993. Reproduced with permission of Gürze Books;
Excerpts from *Anorexia Nervosa and Recovery*, Karen Ways. Copyright © 1993. Repro-
duced with permission of Haworth Press; Excerpt from "Walking in the Woods" by
Thomas Holbrook from the book *Making Weight: Men's Conflicts with Food, Weight,
Shape, and Appearance*. Copyright © 2000. Reproduced with permission of Gürze Books,
Psychological Medicine, Vol. 12 (1982): 625–635, Abraham, S. F., and Beumont, P. J.:
"How Patients Describe Bulimia or Binge Eating." Descriptions of material on pp.
628–633. Reproduced with permission of Cambridge University Press.

I dedicate this book to my now seven-year-old daughter, Elena Rose—I hope you will have a strong sense of who you are and what is imporant in life.

Contents

Acknowledgments

Writing a book was not something I planned to do, but I was convinced to do so by Emily Birch, an acquisitions editor at Greenwood Press. Though I worked with her only briefly, I am glad that she extended the offer and made this book happen. Debby Adams served as the editor; she was patient when I was behind schedule, but helped to keep my work on track throughout the writing stage. I also thank the staff of Impressions Book and Journal Services, Inc., for handling all the technicalities necessary to bring the book to fruition.

My colleagues at West Virginia University and Towson University, notably Dr. Jeff Messing and Dr. Maria Fracasso, supported the time it took to work on this book. Special thanks to Dr. Janelle Coughlin, one of my doctoral advisees, who made significant contributions throughout this book, especially to chapter 7. I enjoy our ongoing collaborations. Her work in the area of media literacy is cutting edge and very exciting. I thank my graduate assistant, Stacy Waterman, for her invaluable assistance and attention to detail in work on the references, library research, and proofreading.

Finally, I acknowledge my mother and father, who somehow prevented me from developing an eating disorder. I am not sure how, since all the risk factors were present. A close relationship may be part of it, and I thank them for creating that. I wrote a good part of this book in hospital waiting rooms, while my father recovered from a stroke and later a cardiac arrhythmia. Wile my mother spent long hours in his room, I typed away and promised that I would finish this book so both my parents would be able to see it. I achieved success!

However, it is my husband and children to whom I owe the greatest thanks. Roberto Martin, along with Elena and Noah Kalodner-Martin, supported my efforts throughout this book—from start to finish—and that wasn't easy. Writing requires long periods of quiet, not an easy thing to find with two young children. They understood my commitment to finishing something that I started.

1

Introduction

Is thinner really better? Is there really only one body size or shape that is beautiful? Am I morally weak or ugly because I don't look like a model? Does this make me unworthy of friendship, attention, or love? Does it make sense that my self-worth should be measured by my ability to fit into a size four skirt?

(Radcliffe, 1993, p. 140)

Today I never worry about what or how much I eat. I just eat naturally, and for the most part, healthfully. I usually exercise three times a week, but if for some reason I don't manage to exercise, I don't feel anxious or guilty. I rarely weigh myself, nor is weight a problem for me. In other words, I have not only recovered from my eating disorder, I have freed myself from the diet/weight conflict.

(Kano, 1993, p. 110)

TINKERBELL AND BARBIE: WHAT DO THEY MEAN FOR EATING DISORDERS?

In the Disney movie Peter Pan, there is a scene in which Tinkerbell (the little fairy that follows Peter Pan everywhere) lands on a mirror and looks down at her body. She makes a face of disgust when she sees the size of her hips, and it is clear that she believes her hips are too wide. This is a movie seen by young children. My daughter asked me about this scene one day, and I responded, "Tinkerbell is looking at herself in the mirror. What do you think she is thinking?" My four-year-old daughter told me that Tin-kerbell didn't like her hips.

One of the most popular dolls in American culture, with almost $2 bil-lion in sales each year, is Mattell's Barbie. Mattel estimates that two dolls are sold every second. Annual sales surveys indicate that Barbie is always on the top ten list of toy sales, usually first or second (Nussbaum, 1997). Over 90 percent of all American girls from three to eleven years old own one or more Barbies (even my daughter has a few). Toys are important objects in the sense that they reflect the values of the society in which they exist (Maine, 2000). The average American girl has at least one Bar-bie by the time she is three years old, and collects seven Barbies during her childhood (Lord, 1994).

Barbie is an "aspirational role model" that almost no one can achieve; there is a chance less than 1 in 100,000 that someone could have a body like Barbie's (Pederson & Markee, 1991). If Barbie were a real person, she would be 5'9" tall and would weigh 110 pounds. Her body measurements would be 39–18–33. Her heels, permanently molded in a high-heeled position, would be a child's size 3. At her height, a minimum expected weight is 145 pounds; at 110, she would be at a weight that poses a medi-cal risk. She has no body fat or belly. If she were a real person, she would not menstruate. Her rib cage is indented in such a way that she would have had to have plastic surgery and the removal of ribs. In the fall of 1997, Mattel announced that Barbie was in need of a make-over, which would include a more realistic shape. However, only 1 of the 24 new Bar-bies was changed.

Maine (2000) compared Barbie to a Lands' End sizing chart for a woman's size 10. Here I include comparisons between Barbie's size and Lands' End sizing for girls large, girls slim, and a woman's small:

	Barbie	Girls Large	Girls Slim	Woman's Small
Bust	39"	32	31	34–35
Waist	18"	26	24	26–27
Hips	33"	34	$32^1/_2$	$28–29^1/_2$

As you can see from reviewing this chart, Barbie's bust is considerably larger than any of the sizes for girls or women, and her waist is much smaller. Barbie's hourglass shape of large bust, narrow waist, and wide hips is just not the same as the shapes of girls or women.

Barbie, Tinkerbell, and countless others (celebrities such as models, performers, and some of those in the political spotlight) reinforce the societal message about the value of thinness. These messages may become internalized and have tremendous implications for females and, increasingly, for males. These influences effect children, adolescents, adults, and the elderly.

Children and adolescents form ideas about the negative aspects of being larger and begin to worry at a young age that they might get fat. Alarmingly, this concern about weight and body shape is evident in young children; 21 percent of five-year-old girls worried about their weight (Davison, Markey, & Birch, 2000). Young girls are more weight dissatisfied than are boys (Cusumano & Thompson, 2001), and body dissatisfaction increases as the child gets older (see Smolak & Levine, 2001). Dieting among young children is not uncommon; in large surveys of nine- and ten-year-old children, 42 percent of the nine-year-old black girls and 37 percent of the nine-year-old white girls reported that they were trying to lose weight. The corresponding percentages for the 10 year olds are 44 percent and 37 percent (Schreiber, Robins, Striegel-Moore, Obarzanek, Morrison, & Wright, 1996).

Plastic surgery in children and adolescents has increased 80 percent from 1996 and 138 percent from 1994 (Sarwer, 2001); almost 25,000 people under the age of eighteen underwent cosmetic procedures in 1998 (last year the data are available). Liposuction is the sixth most frequently performed procedure in adolescents (it is the most common in adults). Sarwer (2001) suggests that the increase in plastic surgery is reflective of the high levels of body dissatisfaction in children and adolescents, but he warns that there is little research to document the effects of surgical intervention on the psychological well-being of those who elect to use these techniques.

As adolescents get older, weight and body concerns often intensify. The Centers for Disease Control and Prevention in Atlanta sponsored a large study of high school students, and findings indicated that girls in grades 9–12 were much more likely to be attempting to lose weight (42.5%–45.3%) than male students (14.5%–16%; Serdula, Collins, Williamson, Anda, Pamuk, & Byers, 1993). Males were more often interested in gaining weight, an issue that is discussed later in this book. Studies of college students indicate a wide range of eating disturbances and disorders; between 19 percent and 23 percent of female students have symptoms of eating disorders (Mintz, O'Halloran, Mulholland, & Schneider, 1997; Mulholland & Mintz, 2001).

The American Psychiatric Association (2000) estimates that there is a .5 percent lifetime prevalence of anorexia nervosa for females. The prevalence for males is one-tenth that of females. Approximately 1 percent to 3 percent of females meet the criteria for bulimia nervosa. In addition, for every one male with bulimia, there are ten females with bulimia. However, both anorexia and bulimia may be underdiagnosed in males.

It is noteworthy that there are no nationally representative data regarding the prevalence and basic demographic descriptions of eating disorders (Garvin & Striegel-Moore, 2001; Striegel-Moore & Smolak, 2001). Some researchers assert that due to the tremendous cost of conducting large epidemiological studies, it is not economical to focus solely on the prevalence of eating disorders, but rather studies should be done to assess a variety of psychological problems and the factors for each of these disorders (Garvin & Striegel-Moore, 2001). More information about the available statistics concerning eating disorders and symptoms of eating disorders is found in this book.

There is a much higher prevalence of eating disorders in women relative to men, with 90 percent of cases of anorexia and bulimia occurring in females (APA, 2000). Reports of eating disorders in males do exist, and some researchers have noted that eating problems in males are becoming more prevalent (Andersen, Cohn, & Holbrook, 2000). Until recently, eating disorders were typically described as a Western cultural phenomenon facing primarily middle- to upper-class white females. There is evidence, however, that symptoms of eating disorders exist among various ethnic and cultural minority groups in the United States and in the whole world (APA, 2000; Smolak & Striegel-Moore, 2001).

MEDIA ATTENTION TO EATING DISORDERS

Eating disorders fascinate and intrigue people. Television talk shows featuring people who have anorexia nervosa or bulimia nervosa continue to bring attention to eating disorders. In some cases, these shows have "ballooned into circus sideshows" and sometimes seem like "a spectator sport for the non-afflicted public" (Levenkron, 2001, p. 11). Oprah covered the story of Rudine, a woman with severe anorexia nervosa who died in 1995 weighing only 38 pounds. Maury Povich hosted the twins Michaela and Samantha Kendall who both had anorexia nervosa; Michaela died in 1994 and Samantha died in 1997.

Magazines also include many articles about people with eating disorders (Bishop, 2001). In a review of forty-seven articles about eating disorders published in popular magazines from 1980 until 2000, Bishop (2001) found that people with eating disorders are described as suffering alone, self-absorbed, fixated in images of thinness in the media, driven by perfectionism, and have a strong need to be in control. The person with an eating disorder in the articles was a female (except in two cases), Caucasian (in all but three cases), and from an affluent background. Many of the articles were autobiographical accounts.

Why is there so much media attention to eating disorders? Are we afraid that our mothers, daughters, sisters, aunts, or friends (boys and men, too) might develop this problem? Or, maybe we have interest because we have a personal issue with weight and body image. Maybe we are interested in eating disorders because we are afraid of being fat. Perhaps it is reflective of societal obsession with thinness and the individuals who commit themselves to the pursuit of the thinnest bodies. Or, maybe it is the disbelief that people will vomit and exercise for hours after eating.

Eating disorders have a kind of peculiar status among other mental health problems (Streigel-Moore & Smolak, 2001). They have been treated in a depreciatory manner by both the general public and by physicians (Garfinkel & Dorian, 2001). Eating disorders are glamorized in the media, made to seem like problems of the rich and famous, and considered a way to lose weight. Women joke about catching anorexia for a while to help them lose weight. Eating disorders have been characterized as "the self-induced problems of spoiled women" (Garfinkel & Dorian, 2001, p. 20). Sometimes, they are considered a kind of moral issue; in this view, eating disorders are a lack of willpower. However, all this fails to acknowledge the emotional and physical issues associated with eating disorders.

OBESITY

In addition to eating disorders, there is a need for attention to obesity in the United States. Although obesity is not an eating disorder (it does not appear in the American Psychiatric Association's book of mental disorders [DSM-IV-TR; 2000]), it is an associated serious health concern defined by excess weight. Data from a large national study indicate that 63 percent of adult men and 55 percent of adult women are obese (Must, Spadano, Coakley, Field, Colditz, & Dietz, 1999). Heinberg, Thompson, and Matzon (2001) indicate that this translates to an estimated 50 million people in the United States. Obesity is also highly prevalent in young children; recent data suggest that 20 percent of children in the United States are obese (Dounchis, Hayden, & Wilfley, 2001). There are significant health consequences of obesity, including high blood pressure, cardiovascular disease, diabetes, stroke, some cancers, osteoarthritis, sleep apnea, and gallstones (Heinberg et al., 2001).

The increase in obesity has led to a focus on obesity prevention programs. Reducing dietary fat through dieting is typically viewed as desirable from the perspective of those trying to reduce obesity (Liebman,

Cameron, Carson, Brown, & Meyer, 2001). However, research has demonstrated that dieting among college students is associated with eating-related psychopathology, meaning that those who diet have higher scores on measures of drive for thinness, bulimia, and body dissatisfaction than nondieters (Liebman et al., 2001). This finding, and others that link dieting to binge eating and other problematic eating patterns, cause those individuals working in the eating disorders field to approach obesity prevention cautiously. Professionals associated with the eating disorders field express concern that obesity prevention programs may cause eating disorders. This has been described as a "thorny relationship between professionals in the fields of eating disorders prevention and obesity prevention" (Striegel-Moore & Smolak, 2001, pp. 6–7). This book is focused on eating disorders, though it is clear that both eating disorders and obesity are associated with significant body dissatisfaction and unhealthy behaviors and attitudes toward food.

BODY TRAPS

We can understand the continued attention to eating and weight concerns when we learn about what Judith Rodin (1992) called "body traps." In her book, she describes the "double binds caused by ignorance about our bodies on the one hand and preoccupation with them on the other" (p. 12). These body traps, which she asserts are shared by almost every woman, even those who appear to have bodies close to ideal, cause people to obsess about their bodies and continue to attempt to look a certain way. She reviews several of these traps in the book; the vanity, shame, competition, food, dieting-rituals, fitness, and success traps all focus on how people think that they must look good, in spite of the high costs that can be psychologically damaging. For example, the fitness trap is about the balance between healthy physical exercise and compulsive overexercise associated with eating disorders and disturbances. It is quite clear that there are physical and psychological benefits from regular physical exercise. When does it become too much? Rodin indicates that exercise dependency occurs when people depend on exercise and suffer the effects of withdrawal when they cannot exercise. They may also feel guilty, ashamed, or irritable when they do not exercise. This is a sign that exercise is not healthy anymore. All the body traps described share this balance between what is good and healthy and how it becomes problematic when there is too little or too much of it.

Breaking body traps comes in three ways—by changing yourself, changing other people, and changing society. Rodin (1992) indicates that when a person treats her (or his) body with respect by giving it what it needs, including moderate exercise, healthful foods, sensual pleasures and relaxation, her (or his) body will respond by treating the person better. She believes that people will look healthier and feel better when they break the body traps. Changing other people and society is important since body traps are found everywhere. Rodin (1992) recommends that people stay away from environments that make them feel badly about themselves. This may involve changing behaviors, such as reading magazines that contain pictures of models who are too thin. Despite the fact that the culture has an established beauty standard with rules for how bodies should look, Rodin asserts that changes in societal tastes and attitudes can be made, but that this kind of change is gradual and requires activism. Maine's (2000) book, *Body Wars*, is an activist's guide to fighting the societal issues that create an environment that facilitates the development of body image problems in women.

EATING DISORDERS DISCUSSED IN CONGRESS

Eating disorders have been discussed in the U.S. Senate and House of Representatives several times since 1987. On June 20, 1997, a bill entitled the "Eating Disorders Information and Education Act of 1997" was introduced. A review of all eating disorders legislation can be found at www.eatingdisorderscoalition.org.

A section of the Eating Disorders Act follows:

The Congress finds the following:

(1) Eating disorders include anorexia nervosa, bulimia nervosa, and binge eating disorder, as well as eating disorders not otherwise defined.
(2) Anorexia nervosa and bulimia each can result in death, cardiac impairments, depression, substance abuse, osteoporosis, infertility, amenorrhea, anemia, and other medical conditions.
(3) Medical authorities are uncertain to what extent eating disorders are caused by physiological factors, by psychosocial factors, or both.
(4) Such disorders primarily affect women. As many as 7% of women may be experiencing eating disorders, and the rate of new cases is increasing. As many as 80% of women may during their lifetimes display symptoms of eating disorders.
(5) There are effective treatments for some eating disorders.

This proposal included the development of a program to provide information and education of the public on the prevention and treatment of eating disorders. Congress was asked to provide a toll-free telephone line to provide education and to serve as a referral source for eating disorders prevention and treatment services. A part of this bill was included in the 1998 Committee Report of the Departments of Labor, Health and Human Services, and Education, and Related Agencies Appropriation Bill. Once the goals of this bill were included in the report, the National Women's Health Information Center responded by creating the Bodywise project and including eating disorders in their women's health hotline. For Bodywise materials on the Web go to www.4woman.gov/BodyImage.

A more recent act, the "Eating Disorders Awareness, Prevention, and Education Act of 2003" involves the use of funds for programs to: (1) improve identification of students with eating disorders; (2) increase awareness of such disorders among parents and students; and (3) train educators with respect to effective eating disorder prevention and assistance methods. Among other things, this act directs the Secretary of Education to carry out a program to broadcast public service announcements to improve public awareness and to promote the identification and prevention of eating disorders.

The Eating Disorders Coalition for Research, Policy, and Action (see www.eatingdisorderscoalition.org) is a cooperative of professional and advocacy-based organizations committed to federal advocacy on behalf of people with eating disorders, their families, and professionals working with these populations. This means that they work to bring eating disorders to the attention of lawmakers and politicians. Their mission is "To promote, at the federal level, further investment in the healthy development of children and all at risk for eating disorders, recognition of eating disorders as a public health priority, and commitment to effective prevention and evidence based and accessible treatment of these disorders." For example, The Eating Disorders Coalition held a congressional briefing on July 24, 2001, entitled "Not just a passing phase: The truth about children and eating disorders."

The goals of the eating disorders coalition are to

1. Increase resources for research, education, prevention, and improved training;
2. Promote federal support for improved access to care;
3. Promote the national awareness of eating disorders as a public health problem;
4. Promote initiatives that support the healthy development of children.

The Eating Disorders Coalition continues to be active in the political arena and has recently announced that major new federal obesity legislation, the IMPACT bill (S. 1172), now incorporates concrete language and support for addressing eating disorders. EDC Policy Director Dr. Jeanine Cogan says:

After months of working with the Senate, the legislation's sponsors moved from a bill that originally approached obesity in a vacuum to one that mentions eating disorders everywhere that obesity is mentioned. By including eating disorder language in this bill, Congress recognizes eating disorders as an important health priority. This is unprecedented in Congress and a huge victory for people victimized by eating disorders.

Thus, it can be seen that eating disorders and disturbances are a part of the culture in which we live. Toys and movies reflect the popular cultural emphasis on thinness, and talk shows and magazines continue to focus on eating disorders. The Congress and groups with political agendas also bring a focus to the problems associated with eating and body image concerns.

PURPOSE OF THE BOOK

The purpose of this book is to provide practical information about eating disorders and disturbances. The major types of eating disorders are anorexia nervosa, bulimia nervosa, and eating disorders not otherwise specified. In this book, the term *eating disorders* refers to these three disorders. Most people have heard about anorexia nervosa or bulimia nervosa. Many people know someone who struggles with one of these eating disorders or have seen a movie about someone who has anorexia nervosa or bulimia nervosa. Although anorexia and bulimia are the most well-known eating disorders, eating disorders not otherwise specified affects a larger group of people. Eating disorders not otherwise specified is a special category for those people who do not quite fit the specific criteria for either anorexia nervosa or bulimia nervosa but who have an eating problem. Binge eating disorder is like bulimia nervosa in many ways and is an example of an eating disorder not otherwise specified.

This book also describes eating disturbances, which are defined as problems associated with eating and body image but are not severe enough to warrant a diagnosis of any eating disorder. There are a large number of people who have these eating disturbances that do not have a clinical name. They engage in disordered eating but do not meet the criteria for an eating disorder. This may also be called "restrained," "dysfunctional," or "emotional" eating (BodyWise, 2000) and includes people who are on a diet all the time, those who may binge eat or even purge sometimes, or those who have another unusual eating problem. Sometimes people with eating disturbances develop eating disorders.

Eating disorders are serious psychological disorders that predominately affect females during adolescence and adulthood. Eating disorders often exist with other psychological issues, such as depression and anxiety. All eating disorders and disturbances have several things in common, including extreme concerns about body weight and shape and an unrealistic perception of body image. Most people with eating disorders and those with eating disturbances have dieted to lose weight, and many used unhealthy strategies to avoid gaining weight (such as purging, fasting, or overexercising).

In the simplest definition of anorexia, people see themselves as overweight, even though they weigh much less than the healthiest weight for their body size. Anorexia nervosa is well known for low weight; the movies portray people with anorexia as extremely thin. Additionally, a key issue is the compulsive pursuit of thinness.

Bulimia nervosa is the eating disorder associated with binge eating and purging (though not all people with bulimia vomit). The key issue in bulimia is the feeling of being out of control in binge eating episodes and using binge eating as a way to cope with various emotions. Individuals with bulimia also have a problem with viewing their body in an unrealistic way.

In eating disorders not otherwise specified, a person may be very thin, binge eat, purge, or have some combination of these problems. Binge eating disorder is the most common of the eating disorders not otherwise specified and is known for binge eating without the use of any strategy such as purging, fasting, or excessive exercise to compensate for the calories consumed in the binges.

EATING DISORDERS: BEHAVIORAL, COGNITIVE, AND EMOTIONAL SYMPTOMS

Before introducing a list of symptoms, it is useful to identify some of the behavioral, cognitive or attitudinal, and emotional components of eating disorders and disturbances. Although the following list is not meant to be exhaustive, it delineates the most commonly cited symptoms related to eating disturbances and disorders. Some of the symptoms of eating disorders are common to those with anorexia nervosa, bulimia nervosa, and eating disorders not otherwise specified. A person with any kind of eating disorder would not have all of these symptoms but would probably have many.

Behavioral Components

Some common behaviors found among those who are attempting to lose weight and maintain weight loss include weighing, measuring, and counting the fat grams and caloric content of food. Individuals who weigh themselves frequently and consistently may also be obsessed with their body weight. Binge eating, the consumption of extreme amounts of food in a short period of time, combined with a feeling of loss of control, is another measurable eating-related disturbance. Further, when one attempts to maintain a low body weight or to compensate for a binge eating episode through purging types of behaviors including self-induced vomiting and/or misuse of diuretics, enemas, or laxatives, this is indicative of unhealthy eating behaviors. Although excessive exercise and fasting are not as commonly thought of as behaviors associated with eating disorders, these nonpurging behaviors are included as criteria for eating disorders when they are used to compensate for binges. In summary, the following behaviors related to eating disturbances might be present: *purging behaviors, restricting behaviors, binge eating behaviors, frequent weighing of self, counting calories or fat*, and *weighing and measuring food*.

Cognitive Components

There is considerable overlap in the cognitive or attitudinal criteria for eating disorders. The tendency for one to base self-evaluation on their body weight and an intense preoccupation with weight gain are common body image concerns found among individuals with eating disorders and disturbances. Body dissatisfaction and a desire for thinness are recognizable characteristics, along with the drive for thinness. Another cognitive component is internalization or acceptance of the standards of beauty and thinness that are highly glorified by society; internalization has been associated with increased rates of weight-related cognitions, including weight preoccupation and body dissatisfaction. Perfectionism, or an excessive desire to perform and achieve at superior levels, has also been identified as an important psychological construct associated with eating disorders. In summary, the following cognitions related to body image disturbances might be present: *preoccupation with weight, self-evaluation based on body weight, desire for thinness, body dissatisfaction, acceptance of cultural standards of thinness*, and *perfectionism*.

Emotional Components

Depression and anxiety are common emotional issues in people with eating disorders and disturbances. One of the many ways that anxiety may present itself is through an intense fear of weight gain or becoming fat, even when one is not in danger of being overweight. Another important emotional factor that has been associated with body image disturbance is ineffectiveness, or an individual's general feelings of inadequacy and worthlessness. Further, feelings of esteem tend to decrease as level of eating disturbance increases. While all individuals who have body image disturbances are not depressed, it is reasonable to suggest that feelings of worthlessness, coupled with low self-esteem, deserve careful clinical attention. When guilt, a common emotional reaction to one's unhealthy attempts to achieve a lower body weight, is introduced, the implications for depression are strengthened. In summary, the following emotions related to eating and body image disturbances might be present: *anxiety, fear of weight gain, ineffectiveness, worthlessness, low self-esteem,* and *guilt.*

SYMPTOMS OF EATING DISORDERS AND DISTURBANCES

Here is a list of things that might be noticed in individuals who have an eating problem.

Behavioral Symptoms
- Dramatic weight loss in a relatively short period of time
- Wearing big or baggy clothes or dressing in layers to hide body shape and/or weight loss
- Frequent trips to the bathroom immediately following meals (sometimes accompanied with water running in the bathroom for a long period of time to hide the sound of vomiting)
- Visible food restriction and self-starvation
- Visible binge eating and/or purging
- Use or hiding use of diet pills, laxatives, ipecac syrup, or enemas
- Hiding food in strange places (closets, cabinets, suitcases, under the bed) to avoid eating or to eat at a later time
- Flushing uneaten food down the toilet (can cause sewage problems)

Cognitive Symptoms
- Obsession with weight or with weight problems (even if "average" weight or thin)
- Obsession with calories and fat content of foods
- Obsession with continuous exercise

- Isolation, that is, fear of eating around and with others
- Preoccupied thoughts of food, weight, and cooking
- Self-defeating statements after food consumption
- Perfectionist personality

Emotional Symptoms
- Low self-esteem; feeling worthless; individuals often putting themselves down and complaining of being "too stupid" or "too fat" and saying they don't matter
- Need for acceptance and approval from others
- Mood swings; depression

A caveat: This book provides information about eating disorders, including definitions of the disorders, as well as information on various treatments and medical issues. It is not, however, a tool for diagnosing illnesses, prescribing treatments, or a substitute for counseling and psychotherapy for people who have an eating concern. People who are concerned about their own health or the health of someone they love are strongly encouraged to seek psychological or medical services.

In chapter 2, the continuum of eating disorders and disturbances is presented as a way to think about anorexia nervosa, bulimia nervosa, eating disorders not otherwise specified, and the people who struggle with eating and body image problems but do not meet the criteria for an eating disorder. Since some individuals may progress from a less serious problem to a more severe one over time, this conceptualization provides a background for understanding how eating disturbances and disorders may develop and change as time passes. In this chapter, there is a focus on eating disorders not otherwise specified that are as serious as anorexia nervosa and bulimia nervosa in some important ways. Binge eating disorders is a type of eating disorder not otherwise specified or discussed in this chapter.

Chapters 3 and 4 focus on anorexia nervosa and bulimia nervosa, respectively. These chapters provide information on the characteristics of these eating disorders, client descriptions of key facets of the eating disorder (such as the drive for thinness or binge eating), and short case descriptions of people who have these types of eating disorders. The history of each eating disorder is presented, along with current information about the prevalence of each eating disorder. Sections on eating disorders in males and in other cultures are included. There is a section with a list of fictional and autobiographical works describing anorexia nervosa and bulimia nervosa. Each chapter has a section on recovery from these eating disorders.

Chapter 5 focuses on medical care and the physical health and medical issues associated with eating disorders and disturbances. The first part of the chapter concerns the issues related to seeking medical care and highlights the reasons why medical treatment may not happen as quickly as it should for people who have an eating disorder; often, patients don't tell their doctor about their eating disorders, and sometimes doctors may miss the signs of eating disorders. Eating disorders are associated with a variety of physical health problems and medical complications due to starvation, vomiting, and use of laxatives or diuretics. This chapter contains definitions of the medical terms needed to understand the health hazards of eating disorders, such as electrolyte imbalances, cardiac irregularities, and dehydration. The health considerations of eating disorders and disturbances include issues that affect the entire body. The central nervous system, cardiovascular, skeletal, muscular, reproductive, endocrine, hematological, and gastrointestinal systems are impacted by starvation, malnutrition, and purging. Starting from the mouth and working through the body, we will see the impact of eating disordered behavior on the body and some of the subsystems within it.

Chapter 6 focuses on psycho-educational issues that are relevant to all types of eating disturbances and disorders. Psycho-education is used to provide information that can prevent a person from developing an eating problem, assist someone who does have a problem (though professional help is required to recover from an eating disorder), and teach about the issues related to eating problems and disorders. Psycho-education includes information on the causes of eating problems; the cultural context for these eating disorders and disturbances; the set-point theory and the physiological regulation of weight; the effects of starvation on behavior; restoring regular eating patterns; vomiting, laxatives, and diuretics in controlling weight; determining a healthy body weight; physical complications; and relapse prevention techniques. There is a great deal of practical information in this chapter, including a list of Internet resources on eating disorders.

Chapter 7 is a review of the sociocultural model of eating disorders, which is based on the finding that sociocultural pressures are often an important contributor to the development of eating disorders. In particular, the media is a source of powerful perpetuating influence and further develops the sociocultural pressures to be thin. Sociocultural pressures on young women and men to be thin and attractive are a factor in the development of eating disturbances and disorders.

Chapter 8 concerns prevention of eating disorders and disturbances and focuses on how developmental transitions are associated with developing eating disturbances and disorders. In addition, there is a section that addresses athletes, who are a special population considered by many to be at-risk for developing eating disorders and disturbances. Prevention is a key issue in the field of eating disorders because treatment of eating disorders may take a long time and be very expensive. Primary, secondary, and tertiary prevention are defined, and examples of each are included. In addition, descriptions of prevention programs appropriate for different developmental stages are reviewed.

Chapter 9 describes treatment for eating disorders. Eating disorders are problems that often require collaboration between mental health professionals (psychologists, social workers, counselors, and nutritionists) and physicians (especially primary care practitioners, pediatricians, and psychiatrists). There are a tremendous number of treatment options for people with eating disorders. There are a variety of different treatments, including nutritional rehabilitation, psychosocial treatments (counseling and psychotherapy), and medication. Individual counseling of various sorts, group counseling, and family therapy are often part of the treatment of individuals with eating disorders. Anorexia nervosa, bulimia nervosa, and eating disorders not otherwise specified are disorders that share many features; therefore, it makes sense that there are similarities in treatment that address these common themes regardless of the type of eating disorder. Chapter 9 describes treatment using a stepped model, which starts with the shorter-term interventions and moves through more intensive kinds of therapy, including inpatient hospitalization. Treatment goals for each eating disorder are also included in this chapter.

QUOTATIONS FROM FULL LIVES

At the beginning of this chapter and every other chapter in this book, you will find the words of a person who has recovered from an eating disorder. These quotes come from a book called *Full Lives: Women Who Have Freed Themselves from Food and Weight Obsession* (Hall, 1993). What is most interesting about these quotations is that they come from women who are best-selling authors, respected psychotherapists, and directors of national associations dedicated to preventing or treating eating disorders, and each of them has recovered from an eating disorder. The quotes selected do not speak to the "how to" aspect of overcoming an eating disorder, but rather the "why to" do it. These women have experienced firsthand the difficulties associated with eating disorders: weight obsession, the pursuit of thinness, body image hatred, and body shame. They have dieted, binged, and purged. But, more important, they recovered.

REFERENCES

American Psychiatric Association (APA). (2000). *Diagnostic and statistical manual of mental disorders* (4th ed—TR.). Washington, DC: Author.

Andersen, A., Cohn, L., & Holbrook, T. (2000). *Making weight: Men's conflicts with food, weight, shape, and appearance.* Carlsbad, CA: Gurze Books.

Bishop, R. (2001). The pursuit of perfection: A narrative analysis of how women's magazines cover eating disorders. *Howard Journal of Communication, 12,* 221–240.

Cusumano, D.L., & Thompson, J.K. (2001). Media influence and body image in 8–11 year old boys and girls: A preliminary report on the Multidimensional Media Influence Scale. *International Journal of Eating Disorders, 29,* 37–44.

Davison, K.K., Markey, C.N., & Birch, L.L. (2000). Etiology of body dissatisfaction and weight concerns in 5-year-old girls. *Appetite, 35,* 143–151.

Dounchis, J.Z., Hayden, H.A., & Wilfley, D.E. (2001). Obesity, body image and eating disorders in ethnically diverse children and adolescents. In J.K. Thompson & L. Smolak (Eds.), *Body image, eating disorders and obesity in youth* (pp. 67–98). Washington, DC: American Psychological Association.

Garfinkel, P.E., & Dorian, B.J. (2001). Improving understanding and care for the eating disorders. In R.H. Striegel-Moore & L. Smolak (Eds.), *Eating disorders: Innovative directions in research and practice* (pp. 9–26). Washington, D.C: American Psychological Association.

Garvin, V., & Striegel-Moore, R.H. (2001). Health services research for eating disorders in the United States: A status report and a call to action. In R.H. Striegel-Moore & L. Smolak (Eds.), *Eating disorders: Innovative directions in research and practice* (pp. 135–152). Washington, DC: American Psychological Association.

Hall, L. (1993). *Full lives: Women who have freed themselves from food and weight obsession.* Carlsbad, CA: Gurze Books.

Heinberg, L.J., Thompson, J.K., & Matzon, J.L. (2001). Body image dissatisfaction as a motivator for healthy lifestyle change: Is some distress beneficial? In R.H. Striegel-Moore & L. Smolak (Eds.), *Eating Disorders: Innovative directions in research and practice* (pp. 215–232). Washington, DC: American Psychological Association.

Levenkron, S. (2001). *Anatomy of anorexia.* New York: W.W. Norton.

Liebman, M., Cameron, B.A., Carson, D.K., Brown, D.M., & Meyer, S.S. (2001). Dietary fat reduction behaviors in college students: relationship to dieting status, gender and key psychosocial variables. *Appetite, 36,* 51–56.

Lord, M.G. (1994). *Forever Barbie: The unauthorized biography of a real doll.* New York: William Morrow.

Maine, M. (2000). *Body wars: Making peace with women's bodies.* Carlsbad, CA: Gurze Books.

Mintz, L.B., O'Halloran, M.S., Mulholland, A.M., & Schneider, P.A. (1997). The questionnaire for eating disorder diagnoses: Reliability and validity of operationalizing *DSM-IV* criteria into a self-report format. *Journal of Counseling Psychology, 44,* 63–79.

Mulholland, A. M., & Mintz, L. B. (2001). Prevalence of eating disorders among African American women. *Journal of Counseling Psychology, 48,* 111–116.

Must, A., Spadano, J., Coakley, E. H., Field, A. E., Colditz, G., & Dietz, W. H. (1999). The disease burden associated with overweight and obesity. *Journal of the American Medical Association, 282,* 1523–1529.

Nussbaum, D. (1997). "The hunt is on for the toy that will make parents panic" *New York Times,* December 7, 1997, sec. 3, pp. 1, 10.

Pederson, E. L., & Markee, N. L. (1991). Fashion dolls: Representations of ideals of beauty. *Perceptual and Motor Skills, 73,* 759–769.

Rodin, J. (1992). *Body traps.* New York: William Morrow and Company, Inc.

Sarwer, D. (2001). Plastic surgery in children and adolescents. In J. K. Thompson & L. Smolak (Eds.), *Body image, eating disorders, and obesity in youth: Assessment, prevention and treatment* (pp. 341–366). Washington, DC: American Psychological Association Press.

Schreiber, G. B., Robins, M., Striegel-Moore, R., Obarzanek, E., Morrison, J. A., & Wright, D. J. (1996). Weight modification efforts reported by Black and White preadolescent girls: National Heart, Lung, and Blood Institute Growth and Health Study, *Pediatrics, 98,* 63–70.

Serdula, M. K., Collins, M. E., Williamson, D. F., Anda, R. F., Pamuk, E. & Byers, T. E. (1993). Weight control practices of U.S. adolescents and adults. *Annals of Internal Medicine, 119,* 667–671.

Smolak, L., & Levine, M. P (2001). Body image in children. In J. K. Thompson & L. Smolak (Eds.), *Body image, eating disorders, and obesity in youth: Assessment, prevention and treatment* (pp. 41–66). Washington, DC: APA.

Smolak, L., & Striegel-Moore, R. H. (2001). Challenging the myth of the golden girl: Ethnicity and eating disorders. In R. H. Striegel-Moore & L. Smolak (Eds.), *Eating disorders: Innovative directions in research and practice* (pp. 111–132). Washington, DC: American Psychological Association.

Striegel-Moore, R. H. & Smolak, L. (2001). Introduction. In R. H. Striegel-Moore & L. Smolak (Eds.), *Eating disorders: Innovative directions in research and practice* (pp. 3–7). Washington, DC: American Psychological Association.

2

⸺⸺⸺

Eating Disorders and Disturbances: The Continuum of Eating Disturbances

I did not think of myself as having an eating disorder, yet I could intimately understand the pain of these women. I was clearly not anorexic or bulimic, yet I definitely used food to sooth myself, was uncomfortable with my body, and shared the same struggle for wholeness.

(Radcliffe, 1993, p. 138)

Anorexia nervosa and bulimia nervosa are eating disorders, well known in popular culture since the media has identified and publicized them through articles, movies, and books. However, when considering eating disorders, limiting discussion to anorexia and bulimia is inaccurate since there are other eating disorders and problems that do not fit the criteria for anorexia or bulimia. In this book, the term *eating disorders* refers to psychiatric illnesses with specific criteria; these include anorexia nervosa, bulimia nervosa, and eating disorder not otherwise specified, which is a special category used for people who have eating disorders that meet most, but not all, of the criteria for anorexia or bulimia.

Eating disorder not otherwise specified is a very heterogeneous category, with six different types. The "not otherwise specified" part of the name might be misunderstood as somehow less serious or not as important as anorexia or bulimia, however, as we will see later in this chapter, eating disorders not otherwise specified are clinically significant eating disorders that require treatment. People with an eating disorder not otherwise specified do not have less body dissatisfaction than do people with anorexia or bulimia. Furthermore, there may be a progression from eating disorders not otherwise specified to anorexia or bulimia (Herzog & Delinsky, 2001).

In addition to the three major types of eating disorders, there is a large group of people who are dissatisfied with body image and practice unhealthy eating practices, but they may not fit the criteria for any eating disorder. They engage in disordered eating, but do not meet the criteria for an eating disorder. These people have *eating disturbances*. In fact, there are many, many people who are dissatisfied with their body, have a fear of gaining weight, and may be anxious or stressed about weight and body shape. People with eating disturbances may skip meals, restrict food choices to a few acceptable things, and avoid foods that contain fat. They may binge eat occasionally and self-induce vomiting but do not have an eating disorder.

ASYMPTOMATIC, SYMPTOMATIC, AND EATING DISORDERS

One way to think about the definition of various types of eating disorders and disturbances is to use the terms "asymptomatic," "symptomatic," and "eating disordered" (Mintz, O'Halloran, Mulholland, & Schneider, 1997). Those who are asymptomatic do not have any symptoms of any eating disorder. Those who are symptomatic have symptoms of eating disorders, but do not meet the criteria for anorexia, bulimia, or eating disorder not otherwise specified; in the language of this book, they have eating disturbances. Finally, those who have anorexia nervosa, bulimia nervosa, or eating disorders not otherwise specified are considered to have an eating disorder.

THE CONTINUUM OF EATING DISTURBANCES

The eating disorders continuum is a way to think about the various kinds of eating problems. The continuum of eating disorders places normal eating at one end of the spectrum (asymptomatic), eating disorders at the opposite end, and eating disturbances at intermediate points. On the normal end of the continuum, people have normal eating behaviors whereas those on the eating disordered end have significant eating and body image problems. The groups between normal and eating disordered display some eating disordered behaviors such as dieting, binge eating, and various methods of purging. The phrase "continuum" was first used in regard to eating disorders in 1971 (Nylander), and it continues to be a useful way to explain eating disturbances and eating disorders.

BRIDGE—BUILDING THE RELATIONSHIP BETWEEN BODY IMAGE AND DISORDERED EATING GRAPH AND EXPLANATION

BRIDGE (Russell & Ryder, 2001a) is a graphical presentation of the relationship between body image attitudes and disordered eating behaviors that can provide a framework for connecting attitudes (such as body satisfaction or dissatisfaction) and behaviors (such as exercise, healthy eating, binge eating) on the continuum of eating disturbances and disorders. The BRIDGE concept is consistent with the continuum concept since it does not dichotomize between normal and abnormal behaviors and attitudes, but rather presents a continuum of attitudes and behaviors (see Figure 2.1). The developers of BRIDGE highlight the need to be concerned about a wide range of disordered eating behaviors and attitudes and emphasize the importance of discussing eating disorders in the context of a continuum (Russell & Ryder, 2001).

The graph shows how an eating disorder may develop when unhealthy attitudes and behaviors meet. The horizontal axis is a continuum of body image that ranges from healthy to unhealthy. It is the axis of attitudes and feelings about bodies; the healthiest attitudes are on the left near the intersect point on the graph. As you move to the right on the horizontal line, attitudes become increasingly unhealthy. At the extreme, a person may not see himself or herself accurately, seeing the body as larger than it is. The vertical axis ranges from healthy to unhealthy in terms of different behaviors. The healthiest behaviors start at the bottom of the graph near the intersect point and become less healthy as you go up the vertical line. Anorexia and bulimia are at the extreme of this axis.

The shaded areas on the graph represent the intersection of attitudes and behaviors. The "Body Awareness and Acceptance" ellipse holds the part of the horizontal and vertical axes associated with the healthiest attitudes and behaviors. People who fall into this area have healthy attitudes about their bodies and engage in healthy behaviors. They are asymptomatic. They accept their bodies and understand that the way they look is only one part of who they are. Primary prevention programs are designed to promote these healthy attitudes and behaviors are recommended for people who fit into this ellipse (Russell & Ryder, 2001a, 2001b; see chapter 8 for more information on prevention of eating disorders).

The "Body Preoccupation" ellipse is much larger, and it encompasses restrictive dieting/overeating, binge eating, compulsive exercise, and disordered eating. The people who fall into this ellipse are overly concerned about their bodies and are engaging in behavior that is not healthy. This shaded area may include people who would benefit from secondary pre-

Figure 2.1
The Relationship between Body Image and Eating Disorders

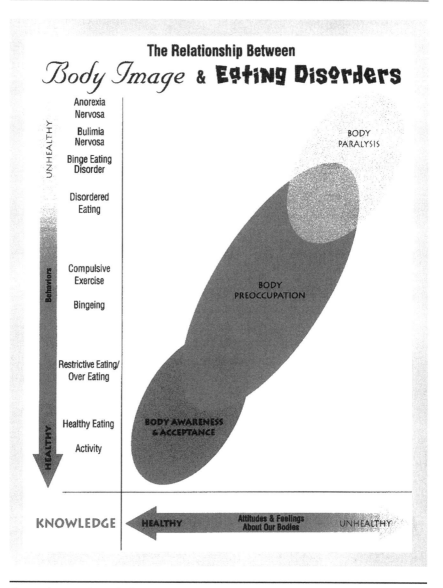

The Relationship Between
Body Image & **Eating Disorders**

vention or early intervention (such as psycho-education or counseling) to help them change their unhealthy attitudes and behaviors (Russell & Ryder, 2001a, 2001b). Some people in this area have eating disturbances.

The third ellipse is called "Body Paralysis" and is characterized by extremely disordered attitudes and behaviors. People in this ellipse are obsessed with their bodies to such an extent that it becomes the most important thing in life. This ellipse includes people who have anorexia or bulimia, or eating disorders not otherwise specified. These individuals need treatment or specialized services to help them recover from their eating disorders (Russell & Ryder, 2001a, 2001b).

A CLOSER LOOK AT THE EATING DISORDERS CONTINUUM—CROSS-SECTIONAL, RETROSPECTIVE, AND LONGITUDINAL RESEARCH

The continuum conceptualization provides a background for understanding how eating disturbances and disorders may develop and change as time passes. Individuals may progress from a less serious problem to a more severe one over time. Or, it is possible that some people may move from the more severe end of the continuum toward the normal end.

There are three kinds of research that can be used to study this issue: cross-sectional, retrospective, and longitudinal studies. Cross-sectional studies compare different groups of people along the continuum on eating attitudes and behaviors and other variables of interest. Retrospective studies are based on asking people who developed an eating disorder about events that happened to them before the beginning of their eating disorder. Longitudinal studies determine if there is a progression from one point on the continuum to another in the same individual as time passes. Different types of information can be obtained from studies of these sorts.

A Survey of the Cross-Sectional Research

Most of the cross-sectional studies were published in the late 1980s and early 1990s when the field was just beginning to explore the idea of the continuum of eating disorders. The older studies (i.e., Mintz & Betz, 1988; Scarano & Kalodner-Martin, 1994) are cross-sectional studies, since they involved collecting data from a large group, assigning the individuals to a group on the continuum based on their responses to a questionnaire, and then making comparisons between the groups on the continuum. Cross-sectional studies are a way to determine if there are differences between the groups on the continuum.

In one continuum from normal eating to bulimia nervosa (anorexia was not included in this work), six groups were used (Scarano & Kalodner-Martin, 1994). These include normal eaters, weight preoccupied, chronic dieters, purgers, subthreshold bulimia, and clinically diagnosed bulimia. In this continuum, the groups were defined as follows:

- Normal eaters do not binge eat, restrict eating, or use any method of purging.
- Weight preoccupied individuals express significant concern about body weight and shape, but they do not engage in any kind of binge eating, restricting, or purging.
- Chronic dieters engage in repeated dieting behavior at least once a week, including the use of diet pills, fasting, or overexercising.
- Purgers self-induce vomiting, fast, or use diuretics at least once a month.
- Individuals with subthreshold bulimia or bulimia are characterized by both binge eating and purging behaviors, but differ in the frequency of these behaviors; bulimia nervosa is defined by binge episodes at least eight times a month, while those with subthreshold bulimia do this less than eight times a month (Scarano & Kalodner-Martin, 1994).

In several studies based on this continuum with six groups, the groups differed from each other on a variety of eating attitudes and behaviors. For example, a measure of behaviors associated with bulimia showed a linear increase from normal eaters through those with bulimia. A linear increase means that with increasing levels of eating disturbances, there is also an increase in measures of eating related problems, such as binge eating or body image dissatisfaction (Mintz & Betz, 1988; Scarano, 1991; Scarano & Kalodner-Martin, 1994). Other findings that support the linear increase are (1) individuals who meet the criteria for bulimia were more weight preoccupied than those who meet the criteria for subthreshold bulimia, (2) purgers were more weight preoccupied than normal eaters and chronic dieters, and (3) body dissatisfaction increased from normal eaters through the group with bulimia in an incremental way. Similar patterns exist for thinking about appearance and food, feeling fat, and fearing becoming fat.

In another more recent cross-sectional study of the continuum, the three groups of asymptomatic, symptomatic, and eating disordered were used (Mintz, O'Halloran, Mulholland, & Schneider, 1997). A study of college students using this three-group continuum indicated that a continuum existed for the issues most closely associated with eating disorders, such as body dissatisfaction. Scores on a measure of body dissatisfaction increased from 37.9 to 75.9 to 76.2 for asymptomatic, symptomatic, and eating disordered groups respectively (Tylka & Subich, 1999). This kind of linear increase supports the idea that a continuum exists. However, Tylka and Subich also found that some variables did not differentiate between the three groups in this way. Some measures of psychological and behavioral variables (such as extraversion, openness to experience, agreeableness, and conscientiousness) did not distinguish the three groups in any meaningful way. These variables may be less relevant to the eating disorders continuum.

A Survey of the Retrospective Research

Shisslak and Crago (2001) reviewed the studies that used a retrospective model and summarized the findings by saying that people who develop eating disorders are more likely than other psychiatric patients to have experienced greater parental pressure, high expectations or abuse, more health problems, childhood obesity, more familial criticism about their weight, shape, or eating habits, and a more negative self-evaluation. In contrast, the death of someone close, a loss of relationship with a friend or family member, and work or school problems were not factors that were reported more often by those who developed an eating disorder than those who had another psychiatric problem.

An example of retrospective research is provided by Fairburn, Welch, Doll, Davies, & O'Connor (1997). In this study, 102 people with bulimia were compared with 204 control group participants, and 102 psychiatric patients with disorders other than eating disorders. All participants were British females between 16 and 35 years, and they were matched for age and social class. The participants with bulimia reported exposure to twenty-nine risk factors, but only 4 of the 58 were at greater levels than those who developed another psychiatric problem. This led the researchers to conclude that risk factors for bulimia are similar to those factors that lead to the development of psychiatric problems in general.

There has been no study of the groups on the continuum using a retrospective approach, thus it is unclear if asymptomatic, symptomatic, and eating disordered groups would provide different data on the factors that preceded the development of eating problems. It is also worth noting that retrospective studies are subject to the bias of recall of stressful events. For example, some events that participants may report occurred before their eating problems began, may actually have developed at the same time, or even as a result of the eating disorder. In addition, individuals vary in their perception of what is stressful; that is, what creates a great deal of stress for one person may not be as stressful to another. Even in light of these limitations, retrospective research adds to our understanding of the differences between groups of people who develop a problem and those who do not.

A Survey of the Longitudinal Research

Longitudinal studies can be used to study how individuals change from less severe to more severe eating disturbances in the same individual over time (Shisslak & Crago, 2001). This type of study is based on collecting data from a large sample of individuals and following their development to see who develops eating problems and what precedes or is associated with the development of eating disorders. According to Shisslak and Crago, twenty-six studies have been published that fit into this category; the first one was published in 1989 (Attie & Brooks-Gunn). Since longitudinal studies take much more time to complete (because you have to wait for people to get older and see how their attitudes and behavior change), and there can be problems with attrition (participants drop out of the study or cannot be reached to provide data), they are quite expensive to conduct.

Longitudinal research suggests that low self-esteem, weight concerns, dietary restraint, body dissatisfaction, depression, negative emotionality, early maturation and being overweight are risk factors for the development of eating disorders and disturbances (Shisslak & Crago, 2001). The four factors that are associated most strongly with the development of eating disorders are weight concerns, dietary restraint, body dissatisfaction, and early maturation, while the other factors are associated with the development of other psychiatric disorders as well. This is consistent with a two-track approach to the continuum that is discussed below.

An example of a longitudinal study of 800 children and their mothers is provided by Kotler, Cohen, Davies, Pine, & Walsh (2001). The procedures involved interviewing mothers and children between the ages of 1 and 10 (childhood), then again in adolescence (mean age 13.9), late adolescence (mean age 16.3), and early adulthood (mean age 22.1). It can be expected, at childhood, there were no children who met the criteria for anorexia or bulimia. In early adolescence, 1 (.2 percent) male and no females met the criteria for anorexia, and 7 (1.4 percent) females met the criteria for eating disorder not otherwise specified Type 1 (anorexia nervosa without the criteria of amenorrhea). There were 6 (1.2 percent) females and 1 male (.2 percent) with bulimia. In late adolescence, 4 (1 percent) males and no females met the criteria for anorexia, and 4 (1.1 percent) females met the criteria for eating disorder not otherwise specified as Type 1. There were 12 (3.2 percent) females and 2 (.5 percent) males with bulimia. In early adulthood, no males or females met the criteria for anorexia, and 2 (.5 percent) females met the criteria for eating disorder not otherwise specified as Type 1. There were 4 (1.1 percent) females and 4 (1.1 percent) males with bulimia. These data fit with the data that suggest there is a low prevalence of anorexia and bulimia.

Relevant to the notion of the continuum and understanding what factors may lead to the development of these eating disorders, Kotler at al. (2001) indicated that the adolescents who scored highest on a measure of symptoms of bulimia developed bulimia at a much higher rate than those with no symptoms when they were younger (7.9 percent more likely); having severe symptoms of anorexia or bulimia in early or late adolescence predicted severe symptoms of these disorders in young adulthood. In addition, certain childhood eating problems, such as conflicts over eating, struggles with meals, and unpleasant meals (as rated by mother) increased the risk for the later diagnosis of anorexia nervosa. Additional research of this type that includes more psychological assessments may add considerably to our understanding of the risk factors for the development of eating disorders and help understand how eating disturbances develop into eating disorders.

A longitudinal study based on twenty-one female college students who were symptomatic of eating disorders during their college years was conducted to see what happened to their eating attitudes and behaviors after they graduated from college (Hesse-Biber, Marina, & Watts-Roy, 1999). In this interview-based study, it was noted that 11 women experienced reductions in their eating problems, whereas 10 other women remained at risk of developing an eating disorder. The group that reduced eating problems reported better interpersonal relationships and more adaptive means for coping with stress, whereas the group that continued to experience eating-related difficulties described feelings of isolation and discontent with relationships with family and friends and had less satisfying relationships with men.

The results of a longitudinal study involving a ten-year long follow-up of 509 women and 206 men who completed a questionnaire about eating attitudes and behaviors when they were in college has implications for the continuum of eating disturbance and the natural progression among the continuum as people mature and become adults (Heatherton, Mahamedi, Striepe, Field, & Keel, 1997). The first questionnaire was collected in 1982, and the follow-up was in 1992. The ten years after college are ones in which people generally settle down, get married, have children, and establish careers. The researchers wanted to know how their eating attitudes and behaviors would change during that time. A large percentage of the initial respondents returned the follow-up questionnaire (82 percent of the women and 76 percent of the men). During the ten years, the women gained an average of 4 pounds, while men gained 12 pounds.

The groups on the continuum used in this research included nondieters, dieters, problem dieters, and those with subclinical eating disorders and clinical eating disorders. The percentage of women classified as having any sort of eating problem (problem dieter, subclinical, or clinical) dropped from more than 40 percent in 1982 to just over 15 percent in 1992. Thus, it was found that 46 percent of the women moved to a lower category of eating disorder, while 41 percent stayed in the same category and 14 percent moved to a more disordered category. Overall, this study found that body dissatisfaction, chronic dieting, and eating disorder symptoms declined for women in the 10 years after college. Rates of eating disorders dropped by more than half and the prevalence of binge eating and purging declined as well. Maturing into adulthood seems to help women stop dieting and abnormal eating. Some participants wrote notes to the researchers saying that dieting was much less important to them as they gained some distance from the college experience. So even though it may be normative for women to have some degree of problem eating while in college, it may also be normative for the problems to diminish as the person moves into adulthood. Unfortunately, some of the women continued to have eating related problems after college. About 1 person in 5 who met the clinical criteria for an eating disorder in college still met the criteria ten years later.

For men, the data suggest something quite different. Men gained more than ten pounds from 1982 to 1992, and they also reported increases in body weight concerns, desire to lose weight, and dieting behavior. These changes were associated with increases in attitudes consistent with eating problems. The data suggest that it was the men who were most concerned about being thin who actually got heavier in the ten years.

DOES THE CONTINUUM REALLY EXIST?

Whether eating disorders actually exist on a continuum has been the subject of a great deal of study. Based on many studies, it appears that there is a continuum of food and body image issues, but there may not be a continuum of the psychological aspects of eating disorders (Connors, 1996). There may be meaningful differences on psychological variables between those who have eating disorders and those who do not. In other words, there may be a continuum for some aspects of eating disorders, but not for others. The eating disorders continuum holds true for variables that are more closely related to eating and body image, rather than the psychological issues that may be associated with anorexia and bulimia.

The continuum of food and body image includes body dissatisfaction and negative body image, weight preoccupation, and dieting. The food and body image issues (which include intense concern with weight, appearance, and body shape) may be common among people who diet and those who have eating disorders. The second set of concerns refers to psychological issues such as problems with affect (mood), low self-esteem, and insecure relationships with parents. The second set of issues may be deeper and more complex and may be issues that affect those with the more serious eating disorders— not those who do not have a diagnosis of any eating disorder.

A summary of the state of the art of the continuum follows:

The data suggest that the normative levels of body dissatisfaction and dieting so prevalent in the current sociocultural context may be differentiated from clinically significant eating disorders on the basis of emotional disturbance. Body dissatisfaction and dieting behaviors could be viewed as spanning a continuum from slight to very intense. Individuals may have mild to moderate levels without other life impairment. Women with more symptoms of eating disorders seem to have high levels of body dissatisfaction and disturbed eating attitudes and behaviors in conjunction with other psychological problems, including greater levels of depression, feelings of ineffectiveness, self-criticism, impulsivity, emotional reactivity, and life impairment. (Connors, 1996, pp. 289–290)

This quote means that it may take eating and body image problems along with other psychological problems to lead to the development of eating disorders. Connors (1996) also indicates that when a person has both body dissatisfaction and certain psychological issues (such as depression or a high degree of self-criticism), an eating disorder may develop, but that when body dissatisfaction occurs without psychological issues, an outcome might be normative discontent dieting. The term normative discontent is a classic phrase because it is used so often in the literature. It was first used by Rodin, Silberstein, and Striegel-Moore in 1985 to describe the pervasiveness of women and their dissatisfaction with appearance. Authors continue to describe the problem differentiating between pathological concern associated with eating disorders and cultural norms of thinness (Herzog & Delinsky, 2001).

THE CONTINUUM AND IMPLICATIONS FOR TREATMENT OF EATING DISTURBANCES

The two aspects of the continuum (food/body issues and psychological concerns) are consistent with a two-track approach for counseling clients who have eating disturbances and disorders (Garner, Vitousek, & Pike, 1997). The first component to treatment is concerned with weight and body image, while the second track involves the psychological and emotional disturbances. Track one issues refer to weight preoccupation, body image, and eating, including binge eating and methods of purging. Track two refers to the psychological issues such as self-esteem, anxiety, depression, and family issues.

These two tracks can be used to describe treatment for all groups on the eating disorders continuum. The chapter on treatment of eating disorders (chapter 9) focuses specifically on treatment for those who have been diagnosed with an eating disorder. However, those who fall in the symptomatic part of the eating disorders continuum may require some type of intervention as well. Those with eating disturbances require secondary prevention (see chapter 8) to reduce the risk of developing an eating disorder. For example, people who fall into the category of weight preoccupied may benefit from track one interventions to target unhealthy attitudes toward weight and body image. If these attitudes are not modified, individuals are likely to begin to diet. Social pressures to be thin may be addressed in a media literacy kind of intervention for people who are in the weight-preoccupied group (see chapter 7). The two tracks of treatment may also be applied to repeat or chronic dieters. Treatment for repeat dieters should include psycho-education about the negative effects of chronic diets.

DO NORMAL EATERS NEED TREATMENT?

In the first article to address this topic, Polivy and Herman (1987) raised the idea that treatment may be necessary for "normal eaters"; they wrote about this in an article with the provocative title, "The Diagnosis and Treatment of Normal Eating." This highlights the fact that what is societally normal eating may be quite abnormal, depending on the definition of normal. Does normal mean normative, in that it is what most people are doing? If that is true, then what is normal may include concern with weight and use of repeated diets. People who are of normal weight may feel as if they are overweight. Chronic dieting is normal in some groups. The important point of this article is that just because behavior is normal does not mean that it is okay; in fact, chronic dieting is not healthy. Dieting is the single most common factor in developing an eating disorder (Ghaderi, 2001). Many professionals in the eating disorders field have addressed the problems associated with dieting as a risk factor for the development of eating disorders.

Since dieting is a common eating style, it may be that this seems like normal eating, though it is quite a bit like disordered eating and therefore it may require treatment. Physiologically normal eating requires eating in response to hunger, which means that people must be able to accurately determine if they are truly hungry. Normal eating, simply put, is eating when you are hungry and stopping when you are full and satisfied. To learn (or relearn) to respond to hunger and satiety (being full), one must perceive them accurately. Dieters learn to ignore these normal cues; as part of their diets, they learn not to eat when hungry and to stop eating before they are full. Ignoring hunger and satiety cues creates a kind of distorted regulation of eating. Dieters fear that when they eat naturally the result will be uncontrollable binge eating and weight gain. However, uninhibited eating does not lead to overeating and binge eating. Sometimes dieters who stop dieting actually lose weight by stopping their diets. The reversion to physiologically (rather than cognitively) controlled eating ends obsessions with dieting and allows dieters to recognize that normal eating is not a threat to well-being. In *Full Lives*, Hutchinson (1993) said, "It was dieting, and not some intrinsic neurosis, that made me into a compulsive overeater. Therefore, it was dieting, not compulsive overeating, from which I really needed to recover" (p. 97).

Dieting behaviors are associated with a drive for thinness and body dissatisfaction. Reduction in dietary fat is one way in which people may attempt to lose weight. This is a strategy that is viewed as positive; there is an inherent assumption that fat avoidance is desirable and consistent with improved health. However, fat avoidance behaviors have also been associated with high levels of eating pathology and psychosocial problems (Liebman, Cameron, Carson, Brown, & Meyer, 2001).

DOES DIETING LEAD TO BINGE EATING?

Polivy and Herman (1985) were among the first to study the relationship between dieting and binge eating. Their initial work provided a great deal of evidence that suggests that dieting causes binge eating. Recently, Stice (2001) summarized a great deal of research on the temporal relationship between dieting and binge eating, indicating that in prospective longitudinal studies dieting does seem to predate bulimic behaviors. This may be due to the "abstinence-violation effect," which means that although someone may create a set of rules about eating and restrict intake of food, when these rules are broken, it may lead to overeating or binge eating. The abstinence-violation effect means going on a diet, breaking a rule of the diet, and then binge eating.

Several experiments in which subjects were put on diets and then developed binge eating behaviors provide additional support for the idea that dieting causes binge eating. The famous Keys study (of starvation in male volunteers; see chapter 6) showed that when people are placed on a restrictive diet, they "exhibited a persistent tendency to binge, gorging at meals to the limit of their physical capacity" (Polivy & Herman, 1985, p. 195). Successful dieting demands that physiological controls, which by themselves are conducive to a "desirable" weight level, be replaced with cognitive controls designed specifically to achieve a lower weight in line with the dieter's personal aspirations (Polivy & Herman, 1985, p. 198).

Why does dieting precede binge eating? A physiological reason is that binge eating might be the body's attempt to restore weight to a more appropriate level. This relates to the idea of set point, which holds that a person has a range of weight that is determined for them biologically. When a person gets much lower than the set point, the body may respond by developing a binge eating style. However, there may be other reasons to explain this relationship. As indicated earlier, dieting is a cognitive (thinking) kind of activity. Cognitive factors may be more important determinants of intake on a given occasion than are physical factors. In the final comment of the article, Polivy and Herman (1985) suggest that dieting is the disorder that we should be attempting to cure.

EATING DISORDER NOT OTHERWISE SPECIFIED

Serious eating problems exist in individuals who do not meet the criteria of anorexia or bulimia. In addition to understanding anorexia and bulimia, it is important to attend to those eating disorders that are assigned to the category eating disorder not otherwise specified. This is a poorly defined large "catch-all" category (Striegel-Moore & Smolak, 2001) with 25 percent–60 percent of people presenting for treatment fitting in the "not otherwise specified" group (Andersen, Bowers, & Watson, 2001). Individuals with an eating disorder not otherwise specified can be quite distressed and need attention to the eating issues and associated psychological concerns.

As you can see, the types are defined by "falling just short of full criteria" (Herzog & Delinsky, 2001, p. 36). Type One includes females who meet all the criteria for anorexia except the individual has regular menses. Type Two is for people who meet all criteria for anorexia except that, despite significant weight loss, the individual's weight is in the normal range. Type Three includes people who meet all criteria for bulimia except that binge eating and purging or other ways to control weight gain occur at a frequency of less than twice a week or for less than three months. In Type Four, individuals of normal weight vomit after eating a small amount of food or use other inappropriate compensatory behavior. Type Five is for people who repeatedly chew and spit out food (they do not swallow it). Type Six is called binge eating disorder and is described below.

People may move from one type of eating disorder not otherwise specified to another, and from an eating disorder not otherwise specified to anorexia or bulimia. For example, in Marya Hornbacher's (1998) book *Wasted,* about her personal struggle with eating, she wrote, "I became bulimic at the age of nine, anorexic at the age of fifteen. I couldn't decide between the two and veered back and forth from one to the other until I was twenty, and now, at twenty-three, I am an interesting creature, an eating disorder not otherwise specified" (p. 2).

Eating disorder not otherwise specified is a category that concerns researchers and clinicians for several reasons. First, the large number of people who are diagnosed with eating disorders not otherwise specified makes one wonder if the criteria for anorexia and bulimia may be too restrictive. Second, insurance companies may restrict coverage for people with this diagnosis, assuming that it is less serious than anorexia or bulimia (Andersen et al., 2001). Third, some clinicians who treat eating disorders have expressed uncertainty of the methods that they should use with eating disorders not otherwise specified since the research is based on anorexia and bulimia, but rarely mentions eating disorders not otherwise specified. In fact, the Practice Guidelines for the Treatment of Patients with Eating Disorders does not make specific treatment recommendations for people with eating disorders not otherwise specified (APA, 2000b).

If there were changes that broadened the diagnostic criteria for anorexia and bulimia, there could be a significant reduction in the number of people assigned to an eating disorder not otherwise specified. Redefining anorexia and bulimia would result in an increase in the cases of both of these disorders. For example, one criterion for the diagnosis for anorexia requires an absence of menstruation for three months. Forty-seven percent of a group of eating disorders not otherwise specified fit into this category, thus with a revision in the criteria for anorexia, they would no longer be considered eating disorders not otherwise specified. When adjustments to the criteria for anorexia and bulimia were made, only 18 percent of people with a diagnosis of eating disorder not otherwise specified remained in this category. Since the majority of influence of reducing eating disorders not otherwise specified is due to changes in the criteria for anorexia nervosa, this is described in the chapter on anorexia.

INCIDENCE AND PREVALENCE OF EATING DISTURBANCES AND DISORDERS

Epidemiology concerns the number of people who are diagnosed with a specific disorder. In this book, we are concerned with the number of people who have eating disorders or disturbances of various types. Both incidence and prevalence data are available to provide estimates of the number of people who have eating disorders or disturbances. Incidence is defined as the frequency of the occurrence of a disorder; it may refer to the number of new cases of a disorder. Prevalence is defined as the number of cases of a disorder in a specific population at a specific point in time.

Eating disturbances and disorders occur in children, adolescents, adults, and the elderly, but the majority of the research has focused on people between the ages of twelve and twenty-two. In the sections that follow, data are presented to demonstrate the number of children, adolescents, and young adults with eating disturbances. In chapters 3 and 4, data are provided on the frequency of occurrence of anorexia and bulimia. Briefly, anorexia has a lifetime prevalence of .05 percent and the prevalence reported for bulimia ranges from 1 percent to 3 percent (APA, 2000a). For bulimia nervosa, the prevalence rate is 1 to 3 percent (APA, 2000a).

Eating disorders not otherwise specified occurs in 4 percent to 6 percent of the general population (Herzog & Delinsky, 2001), thus, the prevalence of eating disorders not otherwise specified is approximately twice that of anorexia and bulimia. In addition, eating disorder not otherwise specified is the appropriate diagnosis for more than 50 percent of patients with eating disorders who present for treatment (APA, 2000b). Major epidemiological studies of eating disorders have shown that by adopting subthreshold criteria, defined as meeting all but one of the diagnostic criteria for anorexia or bulimia, the number of cases of anorexia or bulimia would more than double (Garfinkel, 1996; Garfinkel, Lin, Goering, Spegg, Goldbloom, Kennedy, Kaplan, & Woodside, 1995). Those who meet all but one of the diagnostic criteria for bulimia do not differ from those who have been diagnosed with bulimia in terms of demographic characteristics, psychiatric comorbidity, family history, or early childhood experiences (Garfinkel, 1996; Garfinkel et al., 1995). Since those with an eating disorder not otherwise specified may engage in all the same disturbed eating behaviors as those with the diagnosis of anorexia or bulimia, it is an important group that requires attention.

As for eating disturbances, studies suggest that unhealthy eating and weight related behaviors and body image dissatisfaction exists in vast numbers of young females, as well as college students and adults. In addition, there is also increasing emphasis on eating disturbances in males (Andersen, Cohn, & Holbrook, 2000).

COLLEGE STUDENTS

College students have been the subjects in a great deal of prevalence research. For example, a group of researchers using the same instrument in four different studies of the prevalence of eating disorders in college students revealed that the prevalence of bulimia ranged from 0 percent to 3 percent, eating disorder not otherwise specified ranged from 2 percent to 5 percent and symptomatic eating issues ranged from 19 percent to 23 percent (Mintz, O'Halloran, Mulholland, & Schneider, 1997; Mulholland & Mintz, 2001). In a prevalence study of African American women enrolled in a predominately Caucasian university, 2 percent met criteria for eating disorders, 23 percent were symptomatic, and 75 percent were asymptomatic (Mulholland & Mintz, 2001). In a sample of 330 female undergraduates enrolled in psychology classes at a public university, Tripp and Petrie (2001) reported 7.6 percent met criteria for an eating disorder, 72.7 percent were symptomatic, and only 19.7 percent were asymptomatic. Likewise, using a different measure, Franko and Omori (1999) reported that in their sample of 207 female students enrolled in psychology classes, 2.4 percent fell into a group they called "probable bulimic," 6.7 percent were dieters, 23 percent were called intense dieters, 17 percent were termed casual dieters, and 51 percent were not dieters.

CHILDREN AND ADOLESCENTS

In the introduction to a book entitled *Body Image, Eating Disorders and Obesity in Youth* published in 2001, Thompson and Smolak reviewed the most recent prevalence data for children and adolescents. Three recent large surveys of children have been conducted to assess the number of children and adolescents who have symptoms of eating disturbances.

Dieting prevalence was studied by the Heart, Lung and Blood Institute (Schreiber, Robins, Striegel-Moore, Obarzanek, Morrison, & Wright, 1996) in a study of over 2,000 black and white 9- and 10-year-old girls.

Among the 9-year-olds, 42 percent of the black girls and 37 percent of the white girls reported that they were trying to lose weight. For the 10 year olds, the corresponding percentages are 44 percent and 37 percent.

Another study that is cited often because of the large number of participants and the data available from adolescents of varying ethnic backgrounds yielded higher percentages of adolescents who report weight loss attempts of varying kinds (Serdula, Collins, Williamson, Anda, Pamuk, & Byers, 1993). Of Caucasian female adolescents, 47.4 percent were trying to lose weight, while 30.4 percent of African American and 39.1 percent of Hispanic American adolescents were also trying to lose weight. For males, the percentages were Caucasian 16.2 percent, African American 10 percent, and Hispanic 16.7 percent. Interestingly, this survey also assessed desire to gain weight and found that 26 percent of boys wanted to gain weight, along with 6.6 percent of the girls.

Field and colleagues (1999) studied a very large sample of more than 16,000 9- to 14-year-old boys and girls (93 percent of the sample was white) and found that the 44 percent of the older girls were trying to lose weight. However, they also found that 20 percent of the 9-year-old girls were trying to lose weight. Girls reported that they exercised to lose weight rather than dieted. Of the boys in this study, 17 percent of the 9-year-olds and 19 percent of the 14-year-olds were trying to lose weight.

These studies suggest that there are a large number of children and adolescents who are dissatisfied with their bodies and attempting to lose (or, in some cases, gain) weight. It is important to remember that these high rates of dieting may not indicate that these individuals have eating disorders. Rather, the data suggest that many adolescents and some children have weight concerns that may be associated with unhealthy behaviors. Some of these individuals may develop symptoms of eating disorders.

After reviewing the information on prevalence on the various types of eating disorders, one might ask the question: Why is it so difficult to provide precise figures that represent the prevalence of these problems? It is impossible to come up with exact percentages for several reasons. First of all, the current percentages provided by the American Psychiatric Association are based on documented, or reported, cases of eating disorders. These numbers represent people who are receiving treatment for their eating disorder. It is very likely that many cases go unreported or undiagnosed, which could make this number inaccurate. Second, oftentimes, young women are asked to fill out questionnaires to indicate whether they meet criteria for an eating disorder. As with any kind of self-report questionnaire, this may not be the most accurate method of determining who has an eating disorder. For example, people who have an eating disorder may be uncomfortable filling out questionnaires or may be ashamed to answer the questions honestly. Another reason is that the numbers may not accurately reflect the prevalence of the disorder in different populations. Whenever we read about percentages or prevalence rates, we should ask the question: What group did they use to get this information? For example, if we know that a group of athletes were used, with an equal percentage of African American, Hispanic, Native American, Asian American, and white females, we may have a pretty good idea that the results represent athletes from various racial backgrounds. If, on the other hand, a group of white swimmers were used, we can say that those numbers represent that population only. Some groups may be more at-risk than other groups. For example, sorority members and athletes may be more prone to develop eating problems than other populations. For this reason, we must always be aware of the group upon which results are based.

BINGE EATING DISORDER

Binge eating disorder, in the eating disorder not otherwise specified category, involves recurrent episodes of binge eating in the absence of regular use of purging, fasting, or excessive exercise, which are also characteristic of bulimia (see criteria). Binges are characterized by some of the following: rapid eating, eating until uncomfortably full, eating when not hungry, eating alone to avoid embarrassment about how much food is eaten, and feeling disgusted, depressed, or guilty when overeating. People with binge eating disorder are concerned about their binge eating, including concern about the long-term effects of binge eating on the body. In addition, in order to have binge eating disorder, the binges must occur an average of two times a week for at least six months. Finally, binge eating disorder is not diagnosed when the person meets the criteria for anorexia or bulimia.

Binge eating disorder is also more prevalent than anorexia or bulimia. The overall prevalence of binge eating disorder taken from weight-control programs is 15 percent to 50 percent (with a mean of 30 percent; APA, 2000a). Less is known about the prevalence of this disorder in the general population. In samples taken from the general community, the prevalence of binge eating disorder ranged from .7 percent to 4 percent (APA, 2000a), though some researchers believe that the number is much greater. Some researchers say that there is no doubt that binge eating will be increasingly recognized as a clinical problem and will be the object of additional research.

There has been more attention to binge eating disorder than any of the other types of eating disorder not otherwise specified. Although binge eating disorder is not common in adolescents or college students, a few paragraphs are included to define and describe this eating disorder. Binge eating disorder may be associated with depression and anxiety (APA, 2000a). It appears that binge eating disorder often begins following a significant weight loss from dieting. Some people report that they feel numb or spaced out by the binge episodes. Binge eating disorder is associated with obesity; this makes sense when you remember that this is a disorder of binge eating without any kind of purging or other way to compensate for the calories consumed in the binges. Many people with binge eating disorder have been struggling with weight issues for many years and have repeatedly dieted and experienced failure in their ability to lose weight and keep the weight off. Females are 1.5 times as likely to have binge eating disorder than males but note that the female/male ratio in binge eating disorder is much closer to even than in either anorexia or bulimia. The onset of binge eating disorder occurs more frequently in adults than in adolescents (APA, 2000a). Binge eating disorder appears to be a chronic kind of disorder, which means that it recurs in the lifetime.

Case of Binge Eating Disorder

Mr. Cohen is a thirty-seven-year-old man who weighed 272 pounds at 5 feet 9 inches tall. He sought therapy for weight loss related to a job promotion. Mr. Cohen indicated that he had gained 60 pounds in a year and he "ate all the time." He explained that he dieted and could lose weight in the past, but now he could not generate the willpower. Mr. Cohen thought that having someone weigh him each week would help him to start to lose some weight. Mr. Cohen had some interesting things to say about guilt. "My guilt drives me here, but why do I feel so guilty? Why is it so out of proportion to what I have done? It is not that terrible to overeat and yet I feel it is." Through counseling, it was difficult to discover what triggered Mr. Cohen's overeating. It seemed as though he ate when he was frustrated and also ate when he felt like he had made a significant achievement. He did manage to lose some weight and began to feel better. The weekly weigh-in and attention in psychotherapy may have been helping. But, after New Year's Day, Mr. Cohen reported a food binge—after he cashed his paycheck, he kept $100 and "everything just seemed to go blank...all of my good intentions just seemed to fade away I...just said 'what the hell' and started eating and what I did then was an absolute sin." He ate a cake, several pieces of pie, and several boxes of cookies, which he ate while he drove his car around town. He ate quickly, in a kind of frenzy. Then he visited a series of restaurants, eating a little bit in each. When he described this binge, he said that he didn't enjoy it but that he couldn't stop it. He said that a part of him just blacked out (Stunkard, 1993, pp. 18–21).

These food binges described in this case were part of Mr. Cohen's food problems. They also became a part of the history of binge eating disorder, since the therapist that he saw was Dr. Albert Stunkard, who is now well known for his work in binge eating disorder.

SUMMARY

The eating disorders continuum is a way to think about the various kinds of eating problems. The continuum of eating disorders and disturbances places normal eating at one end of the spectrum (asymptomatic), eating disorders at the opposite end, and eating disturbances at intermediate points. The continuum continues to be a useful way to explain the difference between eating disturbances and eating disorders and how people may move from eating disturbances to disorders. BRIDGE (Building the Relationship between Body Image and Disordered Eating Graph and Explanation) is a graphical presentation that links attitudes and behaviors on the continuum of eating disturbances and disorders. In addition to understanding these well-known eating disorders, it is important to attend to those eating disorders that are assigned to the category called eating disorder not otherwise specified. Anorexia nervosa, bulimia nervosa, and eating disorder not otherwise specified (including binge eating disorder) are all disorders of eating.

DSM-IV-TR Criteria for Eating Disorder Not Otherwise Specified

The Eating Disorder Not Otherwise Specified category is for disorders of eating that do not meet the criteria for any specific eating disorder. Examples include:

1. For females, all of the criteria for anorexia nervosa are met except that the individual has regular menses.
2. All of the criteria for anorexia nervosa are met except that, despite significant weight loss, the individual's weight is in the normal range.
3. All of the criteria for bulimia nervosa are met except that the binge eating and inappropriate compensatory mechanisms occur at a frequency of less than twice a week or for a duration of less than 3 months.
4. The regular use of and inappropriate compensatory behavior by an individual of normal body weight after eating small amounts of food (e.g., self-induced vomiting after the consumption of two cookies).

5. Repeatedly chewing and spitting out, but not swallowing large amounts of food.
6. Binge eating disorder: recurrent episodes of binge eating in the absence of the regular use of and inappropriate compensatory behaviors characteristic of bulimia nervosa. (APA, 2000, p. 594 Reprinted with permission from the *Diagnostic and Statistical Manual of Mental Disorders, Fourth Edition, Text Revision.* Copyright 2000 American Psychiatric Association.)

DSM-IV-TR Criteria for Binge Eating Disorder

A. Recurrent episodes of binge eating. An episode of binge eating is characterized by both of the following:

    (1) eating, in a discrete period of time (e.g., within any 2-hour period), an amount of food that is definitely larger than most people would eat during a similar period of time and under similar circumstances

    (2) a sense of lack of control over eating during the episode (e.g., a feeling that one cannot stop eating or control what or how much one is eating)

B. The binge-eating episodes are associated with three (or more) of the following:

    (1) eating much more rapidly than normal

    (2) eating until feeling uncomfortably full

    (3) eating large amounts of food when not feeling physically hungry

    (4) eating alone because of being embarrassed by how much one is eating

    (5) feeling disgusted with oneself, depressed, or very guilty after overeating

C. Marked distress regarding binge eating is present.
D. The binge eating occurs, on average, at least 2 days a week for 6 months.
E. The binge eating is not associated with regular use of inappropriate compensatory behavior (e.g., purging, fasting, excessive exercise) and does not occur exclusively during the course of anorexia nervosa or bulimia nervosa. (APA, 2000, p. 787 Reprinted with permission from the *Diagnostic and Statistical Manual of Mental Disorders, Fourth Edition, Text Revision.* Copyright 2000 American Psychiatric Association.)

REFERENCES

American Psychiatric Association (APA). (2000a). *Diagnostic and statistical manual of mental disorders* (4th ed.—TR.). Washington, DC: Author.

American Psychiatric Association (APA). (2000b). Practice guidelines for the treatment of patients with eating disorders (revision). *American Journal of Psychiatry, 157*(1), 1–39.

Andersen, A. E., Bowers, W. A., & Watson, T. (2001). A slimming program for eating disorders not otherwise specified. *The Psychiatric Clinics of North America, 24* (2), 271–280.

Andersen, A., Cohn, L., & Holbrook, T. (2000). *Making weight: Men's conflicts with food, weight, shape, and appearance.* Carlsbad, CA: Gurze.

Attie, I., & Brooks-Gunn, J. (1989). The development of eating problems in ado-lescent girls: A longitudinal study. *Developmental Psychopathology, 25,* 70–79.

Connors, M. E. (1996). Developmental vulnerabilities for eating disorders. In L. Smolak, M. P. Levine, & R. H. Striegel-Moore (Eds.)., *The developmental psychopathology of eating disorders* (pp. 285–310). Mahwah, NJ: Lawrence Erlbaum.

Fairburn, C. G., Welch, S. L., Doll, H. A., Davies, B. A., & O'Connor, M. E. (1997). Risk factors for bulimia nervosa: A community-based case-control study. *Archives of General Psychiatry, 54,* 509–517.

Field, A., Camargo, C, Taylor, C. B., Berkey, C., Frazier, L., Gillman, M., & Colditz, G. (1999). Overweight, weight concerns, and bulimic behaviors among girls and boys. *Journal of the American Academy of Adolescent Psychiatry, 38,* 754–760.

Franko, D. L., & Omori, M. (1999). Subclinical eating disorders in adolescent women: A test of the continuity hypothesis and its psychological corre-lates. *Journal of Adolescence, 22,* 389–396.

Garfinkel, P. E. (1996). Should amenorrhoea be necessary for the diagnosis of anorexia nervosa? *British Journal of Psychiatry, 152,* 1052–1058.

Garfinkel, P. E., Lin, E., Goering, P., Spegg, C., Goldbloom, D. S., Kennedy, S., Kaplan, A. S., & Woodside, D. B. (1995). Bulimia nervosa in a Canadian community sample: Prevalence and comparison of subgroups. *American Journal of Psychiatry, 152* (7), 1052–1058.

Garner, D. M., Vitousek, K. M., & Pike, K. M. (1997). Cognitive-behavioral therapy for anorexia nervosa. In D. M. Garner & P. E. Garfinkel (Eds.), *Handbook of treatment for eating disorders* (2nd ed., pp. 94–144). New York: Guilford Press.

Ghaderi, A. (2001). Review of risk factors for eating disorders: Implications for primary prevention and cognitive behavioural therapy. *Scandinavian Journal of Behaviour Therapy, 30,* 57–74.

Heatherton, T. F., Mahamedi, F., Striepe, M., Field, A. E., & Keel, P. (1997). A 10-year longitudinal study of body weight, dieting, and eating disorder symptoms. *Journal of Abnormal Psychology, 106* (1), 117–125.

Herzog, D. B., & Delinsky, S. S. (2001). Classification of eating disorders. In R. H. Striegel-Moore & L. Smolak (Eds.), *Eating disorders: Innovative directions in research and practice* (pp. 31–50). Washington, DC: American Psychological Association

Hesse-Biber, S., Marino, M, & Watts-Roy, D. (1999). A longitudinal study of eat-ing disorders among college women: Factors that influence recovery. *Gender & Society, 13,* 385–408.

Hornbacher, M. (1998). *Wasted: A memoir of anorexia and bulimia.* New York: Harper Collins.

Hutchinson, M. G. (1993). To be recovered and fat. In L. Hall (Ed.), *Full lives: Women who have freed themselves from food and weight obsession* (pp. 95–106). Carlsbad, CA: Gurze Books.

Kotler, L. A., Cohen, P., Davies, M, Pine, D. S., & Walsh, B. T. (2001). Longitudinal relationships between childhood, adolescent, and adult eating disorders. *Journal of the American Academy of Child and Adolescent Psychiatry, 40,* 1434–1440.

Liebman, M., Cameron, B. A., Carson, D. K., Brown, D. M., & Meyer, S. S. (2001). Dietary fat reduction behaviors in college students: Relationships to dieting status, gender, and key psychosocial variables. *Appetite, 36,* 51–56.

Mintz, L. B., & Betz, N. E. (1988). Prevalence and correlates of eating disordered behaviors among undergraduate women. *Journal of Counseling Psychology, 35* (4), 463–471.

Mintz, L. B., O'Halloran, M. S., Mulholland, A. M., & Schneider, P. A. (1997). The questionnaire for eating disorder diagnoses: Reliability and validity of operationalizing *DSM-IV* criteria into a self-report format. *Journal of Counseling Psychology, 44,* 63–79.

Mulholland, A. M., & Mintz, L. B. (2001). Prevalence of eating disorders among African American women. *Journal of Counseling Psychology, 48,* 111–116.

Nylander, J. (1971). The feeling of being fat and dieting in a school population: Epidemiologic interview investigation. *Acta Sociomedica Scandinavica, 3,* 17–26.

Polivy, J., & Herman, C. P. (1985). Dieting and binging: A causal analysis. *American Psychologist, 40* (2), 193–201.

Polivy, J., & Herman, C. P. (1987). Diagnosis and treatment of normal eating. *Journal of Consulting and Clinical Psychology, 55* (5), 635–644.

Radcliffe, R. R. (1993). Hunger for more. In L. Hall (Ed.), *Full lives: Women who have freed themselves from food and weight obsession* (pp. 132–143), Carlsbad, CA: Gurze Books.

Rodin, J., Silberstein, L. R., & Striegel-Moore, R. H. (1985). Women and weight: A normative discontent. In T. B. Sonderegger (Ed.), *Psychology and Gender: Nebraska Symposium on Motivation, 1984* (pp. 267–307). Lincoln: University of Nebraska Press.

Russell, S., & Ryder, S. (2001a). BRIDGE (Building the Relationship Between Body Image and Disordered Eating Graph and Explanation): A tool for parents and professionals. *Eating Disorders: The Journal of Treatment and Prevention, 9,* 1–14.

Russell, S., & Ryder, S. (2001b). BRIDGE 2 (Building the Relationship Between Body Image and Disordered Eating Graph and Explanation): Interventions and transitions. *Eating Disorders: The Journal of Treatment and Prevention, 9,* 15–27.

Scarano, G. M. (1991). Self-worth determinations and self-efficacy expectations: Their relations to eating disorders among college women. Unpublished master's thesis, The University of Akron, Ohio.

Scarano, G. M., & Kalodner-Martin, C. R. (1994). A description of the continuum of eating disorders: Implications for intervention and research. *Journal of Counseling and Development, 72,* 356–361.

Schreiber, G. B., Robins, M., Striegel-Moore, R., Obarzanek, E., Morrison, J. A., & Wright, D. J. (1996). Weight modification efforts reported by Black and White preadolescent girls: National Heart, Lung, and Blood Institute Growth and Health Study, *Pediatrics, 98,* 63–70.

Serdula, M. K., Collins, M. E., Williamson, D. F., Anda, R. F., Pamuk, E. & Byers, T. E. (1993). Weight control practices of U.S. adolescents and adults. *Annals of Internal Medicine, 119,* 667–671.

Shisslak, C. M., & Crago, M. (2001). Risk and protective factors in the development of eating disorders. In J. K. Thompson & L. Smolak (Eds.), *Body image, eating disorders, and obesity in youth: Assessment, prevention and treatment* (pp. 103–125). Washington, DC: APA.

Stice, E. (2001). Risk factors for eating pathology: Recent advances and future directions. In R. H. Striegel-Moore & L. Smolak (Eds.), *Eating disorders: Innovative directions in research and practice* (pp. 51–74). Washington, DC: American Psychological Association.

Striegel-Moore, R. H., & Smolak, L. (2001). Introduction. In R. H. Striegel-Moore & L. Smolak (Eds.), *Eating disorders: Innovative directions in research and practice* (pp. 3–7). Washington, DC: American Psychological Association.

Stunkard, A. J. (1993). A history of binge eating. In C. G. Fairburn & G. T. Wilson (Eds.), *Binge Eating: Nature, assessment and treatment* (pp. 15–34). New York: Guilford.

Thompson, J. K. & Smolak, L. (2001). Introduction: Body image, eating disorders and obesity in youth—The future is now. In J. K. Thompson & L. Smolak (Eds.), *Body image, eating disorders and obesity in youth: Assessment, prevention, and treatment* (pp. 1–18). Washington, DC: American Psychological Association.

Tripp, M. M., & Petrie, T. A. (2001). Sexual abuse and eating disorders: A test of a conceptual model. *Sex Roles, 44,* 17–32.

Tylka, T. L. , & Subich, L. M. (1999). Exploring the construct validity of the eating disorder continuum. *Journal of Counseling Psychology, 46*(2), 268–276.

3

---oooo---

Anorexia Nervosa

A person with anorexia spends all of her time, energy, and thought in pursuit of something—namely being very thin—that accomplishes absolutely nothing of eternal value.

(Reiff, 1993, p. 200)

I could finally admit—if only to myself—that being thin meant absolutely nothing in the grand scheme of things. I had been thin, thinner than most people ever dream of being, and what had it gotten me? Not much. Rotten teeth, cold hands and feet, and embarrassing questions from curious people.

(Rubel, 1993, pp. 41–42)

Anorexia nervosa is a major eating disorder associated with refusal to maintain a minimally normal weight. The word "anorexia" is derived from the Greek for lack of appetite or avoidance of food (Blinder & Chao, 1994). Although lack of appetite is a misnomer, people who have anorexia nervosa do avoid food. They are quite thin—too thin—and they want to be thinner. In fact, they think they are fat and have an intense fear of gaining weight or becoming fat. It is common for individuals with anorexia to deny the seriousness of low body weight.

What, exactly, is anorexia nervosa? Most people have heard of anorexia, but it is important to know the criteria used to determine if a person has this eating disorder. The *Diagnostic and Statistical Manual of Mental Disorders-IV-TR* (APA, 2000a) provides the criteria for defining anorexia nervosa. The specific criteria used to define each kind of psychiatric or psychological disorder are contained in this book. In the case of anorexia, there are four criteria. The first, most important, and well-known facet of anorexia is low weight. People who have anorexia refuse to maintain a body weight that is normal for their age and height. They weigh much less than is healthy for them. Criterion B refers to the intense fear of gaining weight. This may be called a "drive for thinness," and it is an essential part of understanding anorexia nervosa. People with a strong drive for thinness report feeling guilty after overeating, terrified of gaining weight, and preoccupied with the desire to be thinner. They worry that they will become fat, even though their weight is quite low. It is not possible to convince people with anorexia that they will not get fat if they eat a balanced meal. Criterion C refers to the perception that people with anorexia have about their bodies. They do not see their body accurately; a person with anorexia sees an image with more weight than is actually there. This "fatter than reality" image is a major concern; it is a primary issue in life.

A final criterion concerns the absence of menstrual cycles. This is a criterion for females who have already begun to menstruate. This is called amenorrhea; a person is considered to meet this criterion if she has not had a menstrual cycle three months in a row. For younger girls, the beginning of the menstrual cycles may be delayed by the development of anorexia. Although this criterion does not apply to males, it has been noted that the male reproductive system is affected by anorexia nervosa. As females have reduced estrogen, males have diminished levels of testosterone. Many males with anorexia have reduced sexual interest and potency (Herzog & Delinski, 2001).

There are two types of anorexia: restricting and binge-eating/purging. These types are defined in the *Diagnostic and Statistical Manual of Mental Disorders-IV-TR* (APA, 2000a). Individuals with anorexia nervosa may alternate between these types during the course of their illness. The type of anorexia that is most well known is the restricting type. In the restricting type, the person does not binge eat or use any method of purging (i.e., self-induced vomiting or the misuse of laxatives, diuretics, or enemas). People with the restricting type restrict their diet quite significantly or fast for periods of time and may exercise to lose weight. For example, a person with restricting anorexia may eat only salad and certain fruit, and drink only diet soda and coffee. A person may fast, which means not eating any food at all for a certain period of time. People with restricting anorexia may exercise a great deal. An example of excessive exercising might be a five-mile run, an aerobics class, and an hour on a Stairmaster or other exercise machine in one day!

By contrast, in the binge-eating/purging type, the person will regularly engage in binge eating or purging behavior. The binges of a person with anorexia may be like the binges associated with bulimia nervosa. The methods of purging could include vomiting or the misuse of laxatives, diuretics, or enemas. There is a detailed description of the binge experience and methods of purging in chapter 4 on bulimia. This binge-eating type of anorexia is important to understand because people who binge eat and purge are usually thought of as individuals with bulimia. However, if a person is of low weight has not had a menstrual cycle in three months, she meets the criteria for anorexia. Individuals *can* binge and purge and meet the criteria for anorexia nervosa.

Diagnostic Criteria for Anorexia Nervosa

A. Refusal to maintain body weight at or above a minimally normal weight for age and height (e.g., weight loss leading to maintenance of body weight less than 85% of that expected; or failure to make expected weight gain during period of growth, leading to body weight less than 85% of that expected).
B. Intense fear of gaining weight or becoming fat, even though underweight.
C. Disturbance in the way in which one's body weight or shape is experienced, undue influence of body weight or shape on self-evaluation, or denial of the seriousness of the current low body weight.
D. In postmenarcheal females, amenorrhea, i.e., the absence of at least three consecutive menstrual cycles. (A woman is considered to have amenorrhea if her periods occur only following hormone, e.g., estrogen administration.)

Restricting Type: during the current episode of Anorexia Nervosa, the person has not regularly engaged in binge-eating or purging behavior (i.e., self-induced vomiting or the misuse of laxatives, diuretics, or enemas)

Binge-Eating/Purging Type: during the current episode of Anorexia Nervosa, the person has regularly engaged in binge-eating or purging behavior (i.e., self-induced vomiting or the misuse of laxatives, diuretics, or enemas). (APA, 2000, p. 589 Reprinted with permission from the *Diagnostic and Statistical Manual of Mental Disorders, Fourth Edition, Text Revision*. Copyright 2000 American Psychiatric Association.)

When a psychologist or psychiatrist is assessing an individual for an eating disorder, it is appropriate to begin with the criteria for anorexia. If the individual does not meet these criteria, the next ones to consider are those for bulimia. Finally, the criteria for eating disorders not otherwise specified are used if the person does not meet the criteria for either anorexia or bulimia. It is clear that eating and body weight are issues of concern of all three of these eating disorders. Furthermore, anorexic-like eating disturbances may exist in people who do not meet these criteria.

HOW A PERSON WITH ANOREXIA NERVOSA
DESCRIBES THE DRIVE FOR THINNESS

Following is a word for word description of how someone with anorexia nervosa describes her attitude toward her body, her need to be thin, and her restrictive attitudes and behaviors toward food.

Yvette said, "I'm very rigid. I'm five-foot-nine, and I like being 110, I like weighing 110, and I like weighing 110 *every day*. And I don't eat *anything* that's not good for me. I *never* have sugar—*ever!* I haven't in years. I never have anything—*anything*—that's not good for me. I'm very vegetarian and I don't eat a lot. I really don't. I just eat what I need. And I know how many calories I eat. I know exactly what I did. When I'm doing things, I don't think about food, but I know exactly what I am eating. Always. I'm very aware of nutrition and what is going in my mouth. And I *never* eat anything that's not good for me. I'm very rigid. I don't eat unless I really want to. I like being thin. And empty, too."

Later, Yvette said, "I don't menstruate. I haven't menstruated, well naturally, since 1978. I take estrogen replacement therapy, which is critical, because of osteoporosis and stuff. I don't know whether it's my body weight or the fact that I don't have any fat. Because I am in good shape. And I think if I would stop working out, I would probably menstruate. I feel that my working out—I know for a fact—is my therapy. And has been that way for *years* and *years*. I've been a swimmer since 1974 and I do, oh, two and a half miles a day easily. And I'm also a runner. I run very early in the morning before no one else is awake. And I think that while I'm working out, that is, my meditation time. It's *very* important to me. I would rather be *dead* than not have that. That's all there is, as far as I'm concerned. It's a real quality of life. I get up *very* early around four. I get up early. Then I greet the dawn and I go through a series of stretches, and I jog two miles, and then I swim. Then I go to work. And I work pretty well" (Way, 1993, pp. 19–20).

Yvette was one of the twenty-one interviewed in Way's (1993) book *Anorexia Nervosa and Recovery*. As you can see from reading Yvette's words, thinness and losing weight are the only things that mattered to her. In other parts of the interview, Yvette indicated that she was extremely isolated and had no relationships in her life. She said that she controlled her life by being extremely organized and structured about her activities. Anorexia nervosa became the single most important thing in her life.

Way (1993) noted that the twenty-one women in her book repeatedly explained that when a person has anorexia, "thinness is the obsession and losing weight is the fix. When you're anorexic, watching the numbers go down on the scale is the only thing in the world that matters to you. It's the center of your life, the only meaning to your existence. Pursuing it takes all your time, all of your energy. Once the obsession takes hold, no tactics seem too extreme or off-limits. You'll do anything—lie, cheat, pretend, sneak, and deny—to keep the weight loss going.... To fill the emptiness in your life" (Way, 1993, p. 21).

Way (1993) indicates that watching the numbers go down on the scale every day becomes a sort of high for the person with anorexia. "It's what she most looks forward to every morning when she wakes up: how much less she will weigh when she steps on the scale, as soon as her feet hit the floor" (p. 23). "When she examines her naked body in the mirror, she does not see how thin she is. She does not see her sharply defined rib cage, or her jutting hipbones, nor the stiff ligaments of her knees, nor the stark outline of her skeleton and her skull, when she is so clear and so abhorrent to everyone else. She sees only 'fat'—the hips, thighs, and buttocks that she has to lose in order to be acceptable" (p. 24). "She subconsciously distorts her body image so that she can continue to achieve, so that she can continue to feel successful and 'good' about herself, with one clear, conscious goal securely in her mind if she loses enough weight, she will reach the coveted, ultimate state of thinness. And then finally she will be accepted and approved of. Finally, she will be worthy of being loved—by herself, and the world at large. Someday. But someday never comes" (p. 24).

CASE EXAMPLES OF ANOREXIA NERVOSA

Following are two short descriptions of people who have been diagnosed with anorexia. The cases provide information about each individual and highlight the fact that there are two kinds of anorexia.

Cassidy is a young girl who has always been thin. She wore smaller clothes than her friends and sometimes got hand-me-downs from her younger cousins. At age eleven, when her body started to mature, she noticed that she was getting bigger, and this made her feel uncomfortable. She compared herself to her friends at school and noticed that she wasn't the skinniest one anymore. Her obsessions with thinness began slowly, and she started to watch what she ate. When asked if she wanted dessert, she said, "No thank you, I am full" after dinner and no one thought that she was starting to restrict her food. She lost weight very slowly, but as she did lose weight, she got excited about it. She saw her body getting smaller, but not small enough. She continued to limit her food intake carefully so that no one would notice and make her eat more. Certain foods were taboo, and she wouldn't eat them at all. The taboo list included chips, cheese, and chocolate. As she continued to lose weight, she added foods to her taboo list. She never ate foods on the list, and she continued to eat small amounts at mealtimes. Her menstrual cycle, which was just beginning to start, stopped. She was 5 feet tall and weighed 90 pounds when she was diagnosed with anorexia nervosa, restricting type.

Maria is a fifteen-year-old adolescent who began to diet after hearing one of her friends make a comment that everyone is getting fat. Although Maria had not really thought about her body very much, she started to think about the coming summer and bathing suits at the community pool. She looked at pictures of models in bathing suits in magazines and decided that since her body did not look like those in the magazine, she needed to lose a few pounds. She started her plan to lose weight by exercising in the morning and skipping lunch. No one in her family noticed these changes. After a while, she started to lose weight. Although she liked weighing herself every morning, she was only happy when she weighed less than the day before. She continued to lose weight over a six-week period, and weighed 100 pounds. At 5 feet 7 inches tall, she is below 15 percent of her expected weight. She continued to diet and exercise, but began to have strong cravings for food that she had not allowed herself to eat. Although she was intensely afraid of gaining weight, she lost control of herself one afternoon, and ate several chocolate chip cookies, a pint of ice cream, and then a bagel with cream cheese. She knew that if she kept this food inside, she would gain weight. She believed somehow that she would be very fat from this amount of food, and she resorted to vomiting to get rid of the calories. Once she binged the first time, she lost control more often, and she always followed her binges with vomiting. She continued to restrict her daily intake to nonfat yogurt, salad, and an occasional apple or orange, and continued to lose weight. Soon, her family began to notice her weight loss and made comments about it. She didn't believe them when they said that she was getting too skinny. Looking in the mirror, she saw fat. She didn't think anything was wrong with her losing a few more pounds. Her menstrual cycle became irregular, and after a while, she didn't get a period at all anymore. Ironically, she never did make it to the pool that summer because she always thought she looked too fat in a bathing suit. She fits the criteria for anorexia nervosa, binge-eating/purging type.

FAMOUS PEOPLE WITH ANOREXIA NERVOSA

There is a Web site (www.anorexicweb.com/Starvingfor attention/ starvingforattent.html) that provides a long list of celebrities who have struggled with eating disorders. Although not all this information is easily verifiable, some celebrities have gone public with eating struggles as a way to discourage others from developing eating problems. For example, the late Princess Diana, actresses Ally Sheedy, Tracy Gold, and Jane Fonda, as well as gymnasts Cathy Rigby and Nadia Comaneci have all talked about their eating problems in interviews. Some famous people have died due to complications associated with anorexia, including Karen Carpenter, gymnast Christy Heinrich, and ballerina Heidi Guenther.

HISTORICAL CASES OF ANOREXIA NERVOSA

There is a long history of anorexia or disorders that share symptoms of anorexia (Blinder & Chao, 1994; Silverman, 1997). Some of this is based in early religious literature about holy people who didn't consume any food. However, this literature does not present the obsession with thinness, fear of weight gain and body image disturbance that are criteria for anorexia today.

A French psychiatrist, Dr. Louis-Victor Marce, described a set of symptoms that sounds like what we now call anorexia. He called it "gastric nerve disorder" and did not use the word anorexia in his writing. In his paper published in 1860, he described young girls who thought they could not or should not eat. They willingly refused food and died of hunger. Marce advised colleagues to pay attention to the psychological and physical well-being of these patients. He believed that this disorder was a psychological one, and not physical in nature. His recommendations for treatment included sending the girls away from home and force feeding. In his words, treatment for "this hypochondriacal delirium...cannot be advantageously encountered so long as the subjects remain in the midst of their own family" (Marce, 1860, p. 264). Further, Marce said that it is "indispensable to change the habitation and surrounding circumstances, and to entrust the patients to the care of strangers." His advice about force feeding is "if the refusal of food continues notwithstanding these efforts, it becomes necessary to employ intimidation, and even force." As for outcome of treatment, Marce indicated that "when, by the aid of these precautions, the amount of nourishment has been raised to proper proportions, the patients will be seen to undergo a great change, their strength and condition to return, and their intellectual state to be modified in a most striking manner." He also warned against the possibility of relapse, noting that it is common for people with this disorder to revert to previous difficulties with eating.

In 1873, two other physicians published papers about anorexia, and the word anorexia was used in both of their papers. Charles Lasegue and William Gull are usually credited with being the first to define anorexia nervosa. They both described the treatment of anorexia. Lasegue used the words *L'anorexie hysterique* to describe the disorder. He documented eight women with the disorder, describing the symptoms as amenorrhea, wasting, drying of the skin, a heart murmur, anemia, and fatigue. From his perspective, anorexia was the result of an emotional trauma. He described the anxiety that would be present in the family and friends of the patient but that the patient would not be concerned. He advised that the clinician wait until the patient became anxious about herself, and then he may be able to treat her (Blinder & Chao, 1994).

William Gull is the first to use the words anorexia nervosa to describe the disorder (Silverman, 1997). He believed that the lack of appetite was due to a nerve problem in the vagus nerve, thus he used nervosa to clarify the reason for the lack of appetite. Gull used criteria very similar to the current ones to diagnose anorexia; his criteria were amenorrhea, decreased body weight, decreased respiration, and increased motor activities. His treatment recommendations included force feeding, warm baths, electric shock, and sending the patient away from home because family and friends were not helpful in recovery. Gull described three starving teenage patients and said that patients should be fed without concern for what the patient wants. He indicated that milk, cream, soup, eggs, fish, and chicken should be fed every two hours. Interestingly, he advised that relatives are the worst people to provide care; rather it is persons who have moral control over the patients who should provide care.

Another historical note to anorexia nervosa was made by Fenwick (cited in Silverman, 1992). Fenwick was a physician who wrote about anorexia in 1880, providing a great deal of clarity about the physical features of anorexia, along with suggestions for physical rehabilitation and warnings for the physician. Then in 1888, in the course of sixty-three days, eleven articles on anorexia appeared in *Lancet*. This flurry of reports about treatment for anorexia increased attention to this eating disorder. Recommendations of removal of persons with anorexia from their home environment, rest, massage, and overfeeding were made.

A fascinating report, published in 1936 by Dr. John Ryle, described in detail the treatment protocol for anorexia (Rye, 1936, cited in Silverman, 1997). He wrote, "The first essential, after diagnosis, is to explain to the patient and the parents separately the nature of the disease in the simplest and most direct terms. A strong assurance should be given that recovery will take place when the starvation habit is corrected and the appetite is restored by giving the stomach a sufficient intake of nourishing food to maintain, not only the general bodily requirement, but also its own efficiency, of which appetite is a normal expression.... In some cases it may be necessary to sit with the patient until each meal is finished. Firmness, kindness, and tact must be employed in just proportions, and the nurse must never let herself be wheeled into concessions.... It should be remembered that some patients are capable of not only declining food but also of hiding or disposing of it, and even inducing vomiting in the lavatory when the nurse's back is turned."

Modern contributions to understanding anorexia were made by Hilde Bruch (1962, 1973, 1979), Arthur Crisp (1967, 1980), and Gerald Russell (1970). These three individuals all made significant contributions to the current understanding of anorexia. Without these influences, it is doubtful that our current conceptualization of anorexia and the treatment for anorexia would be the same. Reading Hilde Bruch's book *The Golden Cage* (1979) is an excellent way to learn about the psychological aspects of anorexia nervosa. She wrote about anorexia as a struggle for autonomy, competence, control, and self-respect. She described the pursuit of thinness as a critical part of anorexia. She used three disturbances to describe anorexia:

(1) a disturbance of body image, in which the person with anorexia overestimated her own body size,

(2) interoceptive disturbance in which the patient could not interpret hunger cues, and

(3) a disorder of personal control, in which the patient had a sense of ineffectiveness (a sense that nothing can be accomplished along with feelings of insecurity).

These are still considered major issues in anorexia. In fact, Interoceptive Awareness and Ineffectiveness are two subscales on the Eating Disorder Inventory-2 (Garner, 1991), one of the most frequently used measures of the psychological issues evident in eating disorders (Kashubeck-West, Mintz, & Saunders, 2001).

Crisp (1967, 1980) wrote about anorexia as a way to cope with fears and conflicts associated with psychobiological maturity. The notion is that a person does not want to mature and the eating disorder becomes a way for her to regress to a prepubertal shape, hormone status, and experience. Russell is noted for the stating that a central component of anorexia is the morbid fear of fatness. Russell (1970) added that the starvation state must be a primary focus of treatment of anorexia and indicated that it was this that perpetuated the cycle of starvation and weight loss.

PREVALENCE OF ANOREXIA NERVOSA

The American Psychiatric Association (2000a) estimates that there is a .5 percent lifetime prevalence of anorexia in females. Nielsen (2001) reports a prevalence rate of .28 percent. In other words, for every 200 females, one may have anorexia. Ninety percent or more of all cases of anorexia nervosa are in females (APA, 2000a). There is limited information about the prevalence in males, though it may be that anorexia in males have been underrecognized and underdiagnosed (Andersen, Cohn, & Holbrook, 2000).

There is controversy over the answer to the question, Is there an increase in the prevalence rates for anorexia? Some investigators report that there is an increase in the prevalence of anorexia nervosa; several studies (of five varied sites in the United States and Scotland, Sweden, and Switzerland) show that there is an upward trend in the frequencies of anorexia based on case registries over time (Dorian & Garfinkel, 1999). Likewise, a threefold increase in the incidence of anorexia was found for women in their twenties and thirties (Pawluch & Gorey, 1998). However, Nielsen's review of the data (2001) indicates that there is not clear support for an increase in anorexia.

Anorexia typically begins between the ages of fourteen and eighteen (APA, 2000a). Almost all cases of anorexia develop between the ages of eleven and twenty-two (Levenkron, 2001). These ages include puberty and the transitions associated with junior high, high school, and college. Finally, although anorexia may be most common during adolescence and early adulthood, it is important to note that it is not restricted to this age group; however, anorexia in females over forty years old is rare (APA, 2000a). Interestingly, Pawluch and Gorey (1998) indicated that there is a shifted distribution of anorexia, such that women older than twenty are being diagnosed with eating disorders. Women who have eating disorders in middle to late adulthood may have first exhibited symptoms of eating disorders at an earlier stage in their life.

Anorexia has been documented in children of both sexes prior to puberty (Lask & Bryant-Waugh, 1997). Reports indicate that anorexia may be on the increase among children (Lask, 2000). When it appears in young children, the symptoms are similar to those in the older population, that is, the children report that they think that they are fat even though they are underweight and are afraid to gain weight. Anorexia in children is often associated with other psychological problems, such as depression or anxiety.

There are also related eating disorders that affect children. One is called food avoidance emotional disorder, in which a child does not meet the full criteria for anorexia, but they refuse to eat. These children also have a mood disturbance such as depression, anxiety, or phobias (Lask, 2000). Some children have selective eating patterns, which means that they will only eat a very narrow range of foods, usually high in carbohydrates (bread or cookies). Children with this eating style resist attempts to eat other foods though they do not seem to have impaired growth (Lask, 2000). Functional dysphagia is also a disorder of eating among children. This disorder is defined by a fear of swallowing food. This may be caused by some kind of traumatic event like a medical test involving the gastrointestinal tract, or by choking on food, or seeing someone choke on food. None of these disorders involve the fear of being fat that is part of the definition of anorexia (Lask, 2000).

Turning to elderly women, a recent article described the existence of anorexia nervosa in a ninety-two-year-old woman (Mermelstein & Basu, 2001). In the description of this elderly patient, it is clear that she meets the diagnostic criteria for the restricting type of anorexia (with the exception of amennorhea). She was a very low weight (98 pounds at 5 feet 9 inches), experienced a distortion of her body image and desired weight, had obsessive interest in food, and engaged in overexercise (she had a routine of running laps around the hospital floor). She also ate a great deal of prunes, as a kind of laxative, which she explained as a way to "relieve her bloating and return her stomach to its 'correct shape.' "

Overall, we can see that anorexia is not a common disorder, it occurs most often during adolescence and early adult life, and it affects women to a greater degree than men.

CULTURAL ISSUES AND ANOREXIA NERVOSA

Anorexia nervosa may still be thought of as a disease that affects rich, young, white girls, but this stereotype may need to change as we find increasing rates of anorexia in people who are not rich, young, or white. It is true that anorexia is found in individuals who live in societies that associate attractiveness with thinness (Nasser, 1997). Such societies tend to be highly industrialized and technologically advanced. Although this eating disorder seems to be more prevalent among the American and European populations, there appears to be an increase in eating disorders even in cultures where eating disorders are considered rare (Nasser, 1997). There are published reports of eating disturbances in Sweden, Germany, Switzerland, Scotland, the United Kingdom, Greece, South Africa, Zimbabwe, Egypt, Nigeria, Malaysia, China, Japan, India, Spain, and Chile

(Miller & Pumariega, 2001; Nasser, 1997; Nielsen, 2001). According to APA (2000a), anorexia nervosa is probably most common in the United States, Canada, Europe, Australia, Japan, New Zealand, and South Africa. One problem in the study of eating disorders from other cultures is that non-English publications may be left out of reviews, which has the effect of failing to note that eating disorders exist all over the world (Nielsen, 2001).

Anorexia is rare in Arab cultures, however, Abou-Saleh, Younis, and Karim (1998) described five cases of anorexia (three female and two male). It may be that eating disorders occur less frequently in Arab cultures because thinness is viewed as socially undesirable, while plumpness is a symbol of fertility and womanhood (Nasser, 1988). In the cases described, the theme of fear of fatness was present. However, it has been demonstrated that patients being treated for anorexia in Hong Kong do not present with fear of weight gain (Lee, Ho, & Hsu, 1993). These cultural differences raise the question of whether anorexia outside of the Western culture may be different than it is inside the culture.

While some cultural groups living in the United States (e.g., African Americans and Asian Americans) may have lower rates of anorexia nervosa than others (e.g., whites, Hispanics, Native Americans), the reality is that young women of various socioeconomic, racial, and cultural backgrounds develop anorexia (Kalodner, 1996; Smolak & Striegel-Moore, 2001). Smolak and Striegel-Moore's (2001) chapter, entitled "Challenging the Myth of the Golden Girl: Ethnicity and Eating Disorders," reviews the literature on this topic and concludes that "no ethnic group is completely immune to developing an eating disorder" (p. 114). This is a complicated area to study since the measures used have been developed and normed on white populations, and cultural definitions of beauty may vary between ethnic groups (see Smolak & Striegel-Moore, 2001).

ARE SOME CASES OF EATING DISORDERS NOT OTHERWISE SPECIFIED REALLY PEOPLE WITH ANOREXIA NERVOSA?

As mentioned in chapter 2, many people with eating problems are assigned to the eating disorders not otherwise specified category. Some researchers believe that the criteria for anorexia nervosa should be adjusted so that some people with a current diagnosis of eating disorders not otherwise specified would fit into the new criteria for anorexia or bulimia (Andersen, Bowers, & Watson, 2001). A study of people assigned to the eating disorders not otherwise specified category revealed that of

397 admissions to inpatient eating disorders units, 30 percent (119 people) were diagnosed eating disorders not otherwise specified. Researchers adjusted the criteria for anorexia nervosa and bulimia nervosa in the following ways. They created a category for anorexia that removed the criterion that requires three months of amenorrhea; this is eating disorder not otherwise specified Type 1. They also created a category of anorexia that removed the 85 percent weight loss criterion; this is eating disorder not otherwise specified Type 2. They also created a category for anorexia with neither amenorrhea nor the 85 percent weight loss criteria. A category of bulimia was developed that did not require the duration and frequency specified in the criteria of bulimia nervosa; this is eating disorder not otherwise specified Type 4. Lastly, they created a category for people who did not fit into any of these categories; this is a true eating disorder not otherwise specified category.

Of the 119 people originally assigned to the eating disorders not otherwise specified category, 47 percent met all the criteria for anorexia nervosa except they still had some menstrual activity. Another 28 percent met all the criteria for anorexia category except the 85 percent below expected weight. Only 3 percent fell into the category of anorexia with neither amenorrhea nor 85 percent weight loss. This means that more than three-quarters of the people assigned to eating disorders not otherwise specified could be reassigned to anorexia nervosa, if the criteria were adjusted. Only a small percentage of individuals were assigned to the bulimia nervosa category that removed the duration and frequency requirements.

The researchers used this study to highlight the problems with the diagnostic criteria of both anorexia and bulimia, though the data support the changes in the criteria of anorexia more strongly. They propose a new set of diagnostic criteria for anorexia (Andersen, Bowers & Watson, 2001, pp. 277–278) which include:

1. Substantial self-induced weight loss (or lack or normal weight gain). The weight loss is associated with physiological, psychological and social signs of starvation. The weight is not required to be 85% less than the weight expected, but it is not required if the weight loss is substantial.

2. "The presence of a morbid fear of fatness, a relentless drive for thinness that overrides personal awareness of weight loss consequences or both, or the admonitions of a clinician, parent, significant other, or responsible other person, such as a teacher or coach, to restore weight" (p. 277).

3. The weight loss, and the effects of this weight loss, are present for at least 3 months.

4. Self-esteem and mood are dependent on weight loss, despite the consequences and concern of others.

5. No clear other medical condition is causing this condition.

It is also indicated that it is common to find denial of thinness, distorted
body image, denial of sexuality, and depressed mood in people with
anorexia. The revised criteria retain the two subtypes of anorexia: restricting and binge-eating and purging. It is possible that in future editions of
the *Diagnostic and Statistical Manual* of the American Psychiatric Association there will be changes in the criteria for anorexia nervosa and bulimia
nervosa.

ANOREXIA NERVOSA IN MALES

Because anorexia, bulimia, and eating disorder not otherwise specified
(EDs) are much less common in males than females, there has been less
attention to eating problems in men. However, a community-based study in
Canada suggested that nearly one in six cases of various types of EDs were
males (Garfinkel, Lin, Goering, Spegg, Goldbloom, Kennedy, Kaplan, &
Woodside, 1995). Other studies have shown that 80 percent of males are
dissatisfied with their bodies in some way. Of the 80 percent, 40 percent
would like to weigh less and 40 percent would like to weigh more (Andersen et al., 2000). The stereotype that eating disorders are female illnesses
may be part of the reason why eating problems in males are underreported.
Males may not seek treatment for a problem they think is for women only.
Further, professionals may not identify an eating disorder in a male client as
quickly as they do in females. Some insurance companies have denied pay-
ment for treatment of anorexia in males (Andersen et al., 2000).

However, there has been a recent interest in cases of males with eating
disorders. For example, Andersen, Cohn, and Holbrook (2000) recently
published a book entitled *Making Weight*, which documents the importance
of eating problems in males and describes some of the unique issues for men
with eating disorders. Another book on the topic is *The Adonis Complex*
(Pope, Phillips, & Olivardia, 2000). One interesting finding is that what we
might describe as normal "guy behavior" such as pigging out or exercising,
might be ways to cover eating problems evident in bulimia and anorexia.
The male who exercises a great deal might be called a health nut, but he
may have the same drive for thinness that characterizes anorexia.

According to Andersen and his colleagues (2000), there are four reasons
why males develop anorexia that are less often found in females. These reasons include 1) to avoid ever being teased again for chubbiness like when

they were children, especially if they have particularly sensitive personalities, 2) to improve athletic performance, which occurs most frequently in sports with weight classes, like wrestling or boxing, but also in gymnastics, rowing, and long-distance running, 3) to avoid developing the medical illnesses their fathers have, especially heart disease, diabetes, or high blood pressure, and 4) to improve a gay relationship (pp. 33–34). Of course, these factors may explain the development of eating disorders in females as well, but Andersen and his colleagues point out that these are especially salient for the males with anorexia who they have seen in therapy. Consider these four reasons as you read the case of Thomas Holbrook.

The Case of Thomas Holbrook

Thomas Holbrook wrote his personal story about his own long struggle with anorexia nervosa (Holbrook, 2000). He is a psychiatrist who works with males with eating disorders at Rogers Memorial Hospital in Oconomowoc, Wisconsin, where he is the medical director of the only residential treatment program for males with eating disorders. In his story, he talks about being a skinny, socially slow child, who suffered a variety of health problems as a child, including casts to straighten his pigeon toes, rheumatic fever, and whooping cough. His mother seemed to be a perfectionist, who excelled in the arts, community leadership, and she was quite athletic. His father was an alcoholic who worked long hours. Holbrook remembers when his brother was called "the big guy" and he was called "the dink."

Holbrook was smaller than his peers, and was teased by them. When he was eleven, a sailing instructor referred to him as "toothpick Harry," which was humiliating to young Holbrook. He felt ashamed and developed a desire to get bigger and stronger. When he asked his dad to help with this, his father took him to an ex-professional wrestler who taught Holbrook boxing, wrestling, judo archery, and weightlifting. He began to work out at home, often chanting "you too, toothpick Harry." Academically, Holbrook did not do well in school, and began to exercise compulsively. He wanted to be strong and muscular, so he took supplemental protein amounts and ate meat compulsively. He says that for months he cooked seven pork chops each morning. His senior year of high school he went to Norway, and there he began running, which was the start of a lifelong obsession. He lost forty pounds that year, and when he began college, his running and eating became restrictive and ritualistic.

He finished college with a major in psychology and was accepted to medical school, but he always wondered if he was admitted by mistake. He continued to run and monitor his food intake carefully and continued to study medicine. When he graduated medical school, he did not feel like a competent new doctor. He continued to run, adding swimming, biking, and weight training to his schedule. As he established his own medical practice, he was still struggling with questions about his self-esteem. Crisis with his parents included a serious car accident in which his mother received a severe head injury that resulted in a loss of her physical strength and increased moodiness. Later, his father committed suicide, probably caused by increased drinking and tremendous financial problems.

Around this time, Holbrook developed knee problems and was advised to stop running. Surgery and physical therapy did not improve his knees, and he finally did stop running. Then he developed a fear of getting fat. He weighed himself daily, and restricted his diet severely. He began walking many miles and swam and biked. Though he had repeated overuse injuries, no one ever told him that he was exercising too much or questioned his restrictive eating.

As the story continues, Holbrook restricted his food intake, drank concoctions of egg whites, Carnation instant breakfast, and skim milk, and obsessed about protein and fat. He walked up to six hours a day. He drank more and more caffeine, which he believed made it possible for him to continue to work. Dinners developed into a binge of "a head of iceberg lettuce, a full head of raw cabbage, a defrosted package of frozen spinach, a can of tuna, garbanzo beans, croutons, sunflower seeds, artificial bacon bits, a can of pineapple, lemon juice, and vinegar" (p. 126). He had difficulty sleeping, often woke at 3:00 A.M. and began walking. He abused over-the-counter cold medications, muscle relaxants, and Valium.

The most alarming thing about this case is that during this whole time, he was seeing patients, most of whom had eating disorders. He says that it is incredible that he could be working with anorexic patients who were not any sicker than he was, certainly healthier in some ways, and be oblivious to his own condition. He did not identify his own behavior as anorexia nervosa! It is surprising that the professionals with whom he was working did not confront him about his bizarre behavior. No one seriously questioned him about his eating, weight loss, or exercise. His family members also did not question him about his eating and weight loss, though they did express concern about his health. He started to avoid social functions and says that he was "virtually friendless."

Holbrook finds it hard to believe that a physician aware of the symptoms of anorexia nervosa could be so blind to his own illness. He began to become sicker and had physical problems such as severe bowel pain with abdominal cramping and diarrhea. At its worst, he spent hours a day in the bathroom. He developed painful swelling on his hands and feet, and severe back spasms that resulted in several ambulance trips to the emergency room. He had very low vital signs (a pulse of less than forty), which he thought meant he was in shape. His skin was thin. He was tired all the time. He developed shortness of breath and could feel his heart pound. One day he fell when ice skating, and bruised his knee. When it swelled, he passed out (probably from stress on the heart) and was back in the emergency room. No one assessed his condition as anorexia! He even spent some time at a prestigious clinic with the hope of identifying the cause of his problems. He saw lots of specialists and aside from a comment that he had a high carotene level and orange-colored skin (caused by eating many, many carrots), they labeled his behavior as "in his head" and told him that it stemmed from his father's suicide twelve years before.

When he finally realized that he had anorexia, he began to identify in himself all the symptoms that he saw in his patients. He began to let others know that he had an eating disorder and even told his patients about his disorder. Some coworkers were helpful in his recovery, but even one of his colleagues believed that he could not really be anorexic. Once he stopped denying the problem, he began to work on recovery. He started eating three meals a day and slowly stopped exercising compulsively. He describes his struggles to eat regularly, but he continued to improve steadily. After ten years of recovery, Holbrook reports that eating is now something that he can do without thinking about it. He eats in restaurants without fear.

Exercising less was quite difficult, especially along with eating more and wondering if he was going to get fat. Like many people with anorexia, he was used to counting his exercise against the food he ate, so that he would swim an extra lap or two to counteract his food intake. This kind of thinking and behavior was difficult to change, and Holbrook consulted with a physical therapist to set limits to his exercise. He reports that he can now skip a day of exercise and doesn't push himself past the point of being tired. He also describes some of the feelings associated with recovery, which ranged from insecurity, ambivalence, fear of failure, and anxiety. Now he can be more at ease with people; he feels more confident and secure about who he is.

ANOREXIA NERVOSA IN FICTION AND AUTOBIOGRAPHIES

There are a number of novels that describe the development of anorexia and the process of recovery and treatment. These books provide a way to learn about the problems that could lead to an eating disorder. They are also powerful ways to develop an understanding of the thoughts and feelings of someone who is struggling with an eating problem. The first books described below are fictional accounts of eating disorders.

Perhaps the best and most well known of these is an excellent novel, *The Best Little Girl in the World* (Levenkron, 1979), which tells the story of Kessa. She is a high school student who develops anorexia nervosa partially as a result of her focus on her body that began in a dance class. In the book, Kessa describes her thoughts about her body so clearly that it is easy to see how her weight obsession develops and how she proceeds through inpatient treatment. This extremely popular book has also been made into a television movie of the same title.

In *My Sister's Bones*, Cathi Hanauer (1997) tells the story of a person who develops anorexia nervosa from the perspective of her sister. Billie tells the story of her older sister Cassie, who came home early from her first semester at Cornell. Cassie's dorm director called her parents to tell them that Cassie was not eating and isolating herself. Dynamics between Cassie and her father are described in detail in the book; dad is a surgeon who is a perfectionistic and demanding, especially regarding academic accomplishments. The story, which is really more about Billie's life (her boyfriend and relationships), is a way to see the life of someone who has anorexia from the eyes of a sibling who is concerned and confused by the eating disorder. There is a section on inpatient hospitalization, but Cassie does not do well there and is brought home by her father. A telling quote from the story was said by Billie: "If you love someone, you should do it without making them feel bad all the time. And I think about how he loves Cassie, too—and about how we all do. And I wonder if that's what made her sick, and if so, whether it'll be enough to save her again" (p. 235).

Second Star to the Right by Deborah Hautzig (1981) is about Leslie Hiller, a fourteen-year-old girl who develops anorexia. Although the serious eating problems don't surface in the book until page 42, the first chapters set the tone for the development of an eating disorder. Leslie begins a diet that doesn't end. She describes a voice inside herself that demanded that she refuse to eat. Arguments over food were a part of her daily life, and she avoided meals with her parents by scheduling activities in the early evenings. Later, when her parents insisted that she eat, she began to purge. The story follows her through visits to her doctor, during which the doctor recommended that she gain a few pounds (when she weighed eighty-six pounds). She weighed seventy-six when the doctor insisted that she go into the hospital. The remainder of the book tells about her time in the hospital, including the friends that she makes there and how she slowly gained weight.

AUTOBIOGRAPHIES AND BIOGRAPHIES

One autobiography called *Stick Figure* by Lori Gottlieb (2000) describes the development of anorexia from the perspective of an eleven-year-old girl. Lori, who presents her story in this book, is quite revealing about her desire to be thin, and the book chronicles her eating disorder and treatment. What is most telling in this book is the descriptions of her mother: "My mother is very pretty, but she doesn't like to think too much" (pp. 25–26) and "even though Mom acts like a kid, she loves dressing up like a beautiful woman" (p. 28). Lori learned from her mom and some of her friend's moms that talking about diets is important, that dessert is for boys and men, and that girls should leave the table wanting a little more. In the beginning of the book, Lori thinks that all of this is ridiculous, but these messages do become part of her eating disorder.

Inner Hunger by Marianne Apostolides (1998) is an exceptionally well written book about a young woman who begins her eating disorder with anorexia nervosa, but develops bulimia nervosa. Since most of her story is about bulimia, this book is discussed in the chapter on bulimia. It is noteworthy though, that she began by dieting and restricting, but was unable to refrain from eating and found binge eating and purging and her weight increased so that she did not meet the criteria for anorexia.

Bitter Ice by Barbara Lawrence (1999) is the true story of a wife's description of her husband's battle with anorexia nervosa. Titled *Bitter Ice* because of Tom's habit of eating ice rather than food, this book allows the reader to see what it is like to live with a person who compulsively exercises, spits out liquid and food, and abuses laxatives, saunas, and ice baths.

Ophelia Speaks by Sara Shandler (1999) is a compilation of short essays written by adolescent girls about a variety of topics of interest and relevance to girls age twelve to eighteen. A letter of invitation from the author of the book was sent to over 6,750 people who work with teenagers (such as public school principals, school psychologists, members of the clergy), with some suggested topics including body image or eating disorders, romantic relationships, friendships, drug use, death, depression, and others. These adults gave the packets to girls, and the author received over 800 responses. She compiled the responses into this very telling book. The single most written-about topic was eating disorders. The essays that addressed eating issues included phrases like "why does the Gap make size zero" (p. 14), "who designed Barbie?" (p. 15), "how did eating disorders become a plague in a land of plenty" (p. 15). This book is recommended reading since some essays are directly related to eating disorders, and the others include relationships with mothers, fathers, siblings, friends, academic pressures, depression and therapy are related to the development and recovery from eating disorders.

In addition, two autobiographies are recommended by Norcross, Santrock, Campbell, Smith, Sommer, & Zuckerman (2000) in their review of books that are rated by therapists as useful to clients. They are

> *Am I Still Visible* by Sandra Harvey Heater (1983) is about a preschool teacher who describes her life experience with anorexia.
>
> *Starving for Attention* by Cherry Boone O'Neill (1982) describes the author's experience with both anorexia and bulimia. This book is a frank discussion of the impact of eating disorders on life, career, and religion. Cherry Boone O'Neill is singer Pat Boone's daughter.

The Gurze Web site is an excellent place to find these and other books about anorexia and other eating disorders. (www.gurze.com)

RECOVERING FROM ANOREXIA NERVOSA

There is a body of research that provides information about recovery from anorexia. Before describing that literature, it is necessary to ask "How do you know when someone has recovered from this eating disorder?" Is it weight gain or achieving some normal weight? Or the return of menstruation? What about a reduction in the fear of weight gain? Or a more accurate view of one's own body? Most of the research has focused on the amount of weight gained and the return of menstruation, but very few have provided information on the patient's fear of weight gain or perceptions of body size or shape. It is unfortunate that the psychological aspects of recovery have rarely been reported in the recovery literature.

Once one develops anorexia, the course is quite variable. Some people seem to recover after a single episode, while others begin to gain weight and then relapse. Some people with anorexia develop bulimia. Some develop a chronic pattern of eating problems that lasts for many years. The percentage of individuals with anorexia who make a full recovery tends to be fairly moderate. Although some individuals improve over time, many continue to have food and body image problems and other psychological problems. The American Psychiatric Association (2000b) indicated that a review of a large number of follow-up studies at least four years after treatment demonstrated that about 44 percent have good outcomes (weight restored to within 15 percent of recommended weight for height and regular menses established), 24 percent have poor outcomes (weight never reached within the 15 percent weight recommended for height and menses not present or sporadic), 28 percent had intermediate outcomes (between the good and poor outcome groups), and 5 percent died. About two-thirds of patients continue to have considerable weight and food issues and up to 40 percent have symptoms of bulimia. It is also noteworthy that even those who have good outcomes as measured by restoration of weight may have other psychological problems, including depression, social anxiety, obsessive-compulsive disorder, and substance abuse.

In a study of the long-term course of anorexia patients six years after treatment, 34.7 percent had good outcomes, 38.6 percent had intermediate outcomes, 20.8 percent had poor outcomes, and 6 percent had died (Fichter & Quadflieg, 1999). This study of 103 individuals treated for anorexia shows that the half of people treated for anorexia do not meet the criteria for an eating disorder, but about 25 percent still have anorexia and 10 percent have bulimia, and 2 percent have an eating disorder not otherwise specified. An interesting pattern of recovery was noted; during therapy, patients generally improved, but experienced declines in the one or two years after therapy ended. In years three through six after treatment, recovery stabilized. Another study of the outcome of treatment of anorexia indicated that 50 percent of patients did not improve until six years after inpatient treatment (Herzog, Schellberg, & Deter, 1997). In this study, patients with the restricting type of anorexia had earlier recoveries than the binge-eating/purging type.

In another study, twenty-three individuals treated for anorexia were contacted six years after they were diagnosed (Smith, Feldman, Nasserbakht, & Steiner, 1993). One of the major findings was the current status of those individuals; that is, how many still had an eating disorder or other psychological problem? Of the 23, 43 percent still fit the criteria for an eating disorder (9 percent anorexia, 17 percent bulimia, 22 percent eating disorder not otherwise specified). Additionally, 40 percent had an anxiety disorder and 30 percent had an affective disorder (such as depression). About 35 percent no longer had anorexia or any other eating or psychiatric disorder (Smith et al., 1993).

The most recently published study of this sort also has the longest follow-up of twenty-one years posttreatment (Lowe, Zipfel, Buchholz, Dupont, Reas, & Herzog, 2001). This study indicates that of 84 females treated for anorexia nervosa, 17 percent had died (most due to reasons associated with their eating disorder, such as dehydration and electrolyte imbalance, malnutrition, and suicide). Of the 63 living people, 8 met criteria for anorexia (7 of the binge-eating/purging type), and 3 met criteria for eating disorders not otherwise specified. The remaining 52 did not have any eating disorder. These 63 people were assessed for depression, anxiety problems, and other psychological issues as well; results indicate that 17 percent met the criteria for depression, 16 percent met criteria for anxiety disorders, and substance abuse disorders were found in 11 percent of the group. The individuals with poorer outcomes in their eating disorder status also had higher rates of other psychological problems. In summary, this study shows a 50 percent rate of full recovery from anorexia nervosa, but a 17 percent mortality rate.

Taken together, these statistics suggest that, although recovery is possible, many patients with anorexia struggle with weight-related issues throughout their lives. These data suggest that there is a large variability in response to treatment. Poorer prognosis for recovery is associated with lower initial weight, presence of vomiting as a method of purging, previous failures in treatment, and disturbed family relationships (APA, 2000b). Prevention of anorexia seems critical since recovery can be quite difficult for many who develop the disorder.

Before finishing this section, it is valuable to consider the cases of individuals who are considered recovered from anorexia nervosa (Hsu, Crisp, & Callender, 1992). These authors interviewed six women more than twenty years after their anorexia began. Each of these women described their history, along with what they believed helped them recover. Certain factors, such as personality strength, self-confidence, being ready, and being understood were associated with recovery (Hsu et al., 1992). One client reported that "she made a conscious decision to get well and was proud that indeed she had not experienced a relapse of her anorexia nervosa" (p. 344). Another indicated that her marriage provided a great amount of emotional support, which allowed her to recover. One woman, while pregnant, felt that she was just fed up with being sick and decided not to binge or vomit anymore. These women and the others described in the article demonstrate that it is possible to recover from anorexia nervosa.

PHYSICAL HEALTH ISSUES ASSOCIATED WITH ANOREXIA NERVOSA

Many of the physical symptoms of anorexia nervosa are associated with starvation, though it is worth remembering that some individuals do engage in binge eating, and in those individuals, the medical issues may be associated with binge eating, vomiting, and laxative or diuretic abuse. One interesting thing about patients with anorexia is that they do not present with physical complaints, despite their emaciated state. The medical problems may not be obvious until there is a detailed medical examination. Individuals with anorexia may be able to maintain regular physical activity. They minimize the physical consequences of their situation.

The health considerations of anorexia nervosa include issues that affect the whole body of the person. The central nervous system, cardiovascular, skeletal, muscular, reproductive, endocrine, hematological (blood), gastrointestinal, and integument systems (skill, nails, and hair) are all impacted by starvation, malnutrition, and purging method. A detailed description of these effects on these systems appears in chapter 5.

SUMMARY

Anorexia nervosa (AN) is a very serious eating disorder that plagues millions of young women and is becoming more prevalent in males as well. Although AN seems to be more prevalent among the American and European populations, there appears to be an increase in eating disorders even in cultures where eating disorders are considered rare. The drive for thinness, a criterion in the *DSM-IV-TR* (2000), seems to underlie the disorder. People with anorexia nervosa spend their entire day worrying about food, how they are going to lose one more pound, and how fat they look in the mirror. Along with the psychological issues, there is a long list of physical health issues associated with anorexia. Although treatment may be effective, people who develop anorexia nervosa may struggle with food and body image issues for many years.

REFERENCES

Abou-Saleh, M. T., Younis, Y., & Karim, L. (1998). Anorexia nervosa in an Arab culture. *International Journal of Eating Disorders, 23*, 207–212.

American Psychiatric Association. (2000a). *Diagnostic and statistical manual of mental disorders* (4[th]ed-TR). Washington, DC: Author.

American Psychiatric Association. (2000b). Practice guidelines for the treatment of patients with eating disorders (revision). *American Journal of Psychiatry, 157*(1), 1–39.

Andersen, A., Cohn, L., & Holbrook, T. (2000). *Making weight: Men's conflicts with food, weight, shape, and appearance*. Carlsbad, CA: Gurze.

Andersen, A. E., Bowers, W. A., & Watson, T. (2001). A slimming program for Eating Disorders Not Otherwise Specified. *The Psychiatric Clinics of North America, 24* (2), 271–280.

Apostolides, M. (1998). *Inner hunger*. New York: W. W. Norton & Company.

Blinder, B. J., & Chao, K. H. (1994). Eating disorders: A historical perspective. In L. Alexander-Mott & D. B. Lumsden (Eds.), *Understanding eating disorders* (pp. 3–35). Washington, DC: Taylor & Francis.

Bruch, H. (1962). Perceptual and conceptual disturbances in anorexia nervosa. *Psychosomatic Medicine, 24*, 187–194.

Bruch, H. (1973). *Eating disorders: Obesity, anorexia nervosa and the person within.* New York: Basic Books.

Bruch, H. (1979). *The golden cage: The enigma of anorexia nervosa.* New York: Vintage Books.

Crisp, A. H. (1967). The possible significance of some behavioral correlates of weight and carbohydrate intake. *Journal of Psychosomatic Research, 11*, 117–131.

Crisp, A. H. (1980). *Anorexia nervosa: Let me be.* London: Academic Press.

Dorian, B. J., & Garfinkel, P. E. (1999). The contributions of epidemiologic studies to the etiology and treatment of the eating disorders. *Psychiatric Annals, 29*, 187–192.

Fichter, M. M., & Quadflieg, N. (1999). Six-year course of anorexia nervosa. *International Journal of Eating Disorders, 26* (4), 359–385.

Garfinkel, P. E., Lin, E., Goering, P., Spegg, C., Goldbloom, D. S., Kennedy, S., Kaplan, A. S., & Woodside, D. B. (1995). Bulimia nervosa in a Canadian community sample: Prevalence and comparison of subgroups. *American Journal of Psychiatry, 152* (7), 1052–1058.

Garner, D. M. (1991). *Eating disorders inventory-2.* Odessa, FL: Psychological Assessment Resources.

Gottlieb, L. (2000). *Stick figure.* New York: Simon & Schuster.

Hanauer, C. (1997). *My sister's bones.* NY: Dell Publishing.

Hautzig, D. (1981). *Second star to the right.* New York: Greenwillow Books.

Heater, S. H. (1983). *Am I still visible: A woman's triumph over anorexia nervosa.* White Hall, VT: Betterway.

Herzog, D. B., & Delinski, S. S. (2001). Classification of eating disorders. In R. H. Striegel-Moore and L. Smolak (Eds.), *Eating disorders: New directions in research and practice* (pp. 31–50). Washington, DC: American Psychological Association.

Herzog, W., Schellberg, D., & Deter, H. C. (1997). First recovery in anorexia nervosa patients in the long-term course: A discrete time survival analysis. *Journal of Consulting and Clinical Psychology, 65* (1), 169–177.

Holbrook, T. (2000). Walking in the woods. In Anderson, A., Cohn, L., & Holbrook, T. (2000). *Making weight: Men's conflicts with food, weight, shape, and appearance.* Carlsbad, CA: Gurze Books.

Hsu, L. K. G., Crisp, A. H., & Callender, J. S. (1992). Recovery in Anorexia nervosa—the patient's perspective. *International Journal of Eating Disorders, 11* (4), 341–350.

Kalodner, C. R. (1996). Eating disorders from a multicultural perspective. In J. L. DeLucia-Waack (Ed.), *Multicultural counseling competencies: Implications for training and practice* (pp. 197–216). Alexandria, VA: Association for Counselor Education and Supervision.

Kashubeck-West, S., Mintz, L. B., & Saunders, K. J. (2001). Assessment of eating disorders in women. *The Counseling Psychologist, 29,* 662–694.

Lask, B. (2000). Eating disorders in childhood and adolescence. *Current Pediatrics, 10,* 254–258.

Lask, B., & Bryant-Waugh, R. (1997). Prepubertal eating disorders. In D. M. Garner & P. E. Garfinkel (Eds.), *Handbook of treatment for eating disorders* (2nd ed., pp. 476–483). New York: Guilford Press.

Lawrence, B. K. (1999). *Bitter ice.* New York: William Morrow.

Lee, S., Ho, T. P., & Hsu, L. K. G. (1993). Fat phobic and non-fat phobic anorexia nervosa: A comparative study of 70 patients in Hong Kong. *Psychological Medicine, 23,* 999–1017.

Levenkron, S. (1979). *The best little girl in the world.* New York: Warner.

Levenkron, S. (2001). *Anatomy of anorexia.* New York: W. W. Norton.

Lowe, B., Zipfel, S., Buchholz, C., Dupont, Y., Reas, D. L., & Herzog, W. (2001). Long-term outcome of anorexia nervosa in a prospective 21-year follow-up study. *Psychological Medicine, 31,* 881–890.

Marce, L.-V. (1860). On a form of hypochondriacal delirium occurring consecutive to dyspepsia, and characterized by refusal of food. *Journal of Psychological Medicine and Mental Pathology, 13,* 264–266.

Mermelstein, H. T., & Basu, R. (2001). Case reports: Can you ever be too old to be too thin? Anorexia nervosa in a 92-year-old woman. *International Journal of Eating Disorders, 30,* 123–127.

Miller, M. N., & Pumariega, A. J. (2001). Culture and eating disorders: A historical and cross-cultural review. *Psychiatry, 62,* 93–110.

Nasser, M. (1988). Culture and weight consciousness. *Journal of Psychosomatic Research, 32* (6), 573–577.

Nasser, M. (1997). *Culture and weight consciousness.* London: Routledge.

Nielsen, S. (2001). Epidemiology and mortality of eating disorders. *The Psychiatric Clinics of North America, 24,* 210–214.

Norcross, J. C., Santrock, J. W., Campbell, L. F., Smith, T. P., Sommer, R., & Zuckerman, E. L. (2000). *Authoritative guide to self-help resources in mental health.* New York: Guilford.

O'Neill, C. B. (1982). *Starving for attention.* New York: Continuum.

Pawluch, D. E., & Gorey, K. M. (1998). Secular trends in the incidence of anorexia nervosa: Integrative review of population-based studies. *International Journal of Eating Disorders, 23,* 347–352.

Pope, H. G. Jr., Phillips, K. A., & Olivardia, R. (2000). *The Adonis complex.* New York: Free Press.

Reiff, K. L. (1993). Perseverance overcomes. In L. Hall (Ed.), *Full lives: Women who have freed themselves from food and weight obsession* (pp. 197–214), Carlsbad, CA; Gurze Books.

Rubel, J. (1993). Are you finding what you need? In L. Hall (Ed.), *Full lives: Women who have freed themselves from food and weight obsession* (pp. 32–51), Carlsbad, CA: Gurze Books.

Russell, G. F. M. (1970). Anorexia nervosa: Its identity as an illness and its treatment. In J. H. Price (Ed.), *Modern trends in psychological medicine* (Vol. 2, pp. 131–164). London: Butterworths.

Shandler, S. (1999). *Ophelia speaks*. New York: HarperPerennial.

Silverman, J. A. (1992). The seminal contributions of Samuel Fenwick (1821–1902) to our understanding of Anorexia nervosa: A historical essay. *International Journal of Eating Disorders, 12* (4), 453–456.

Silverman, J. A. (1997). Anorexia Nervosa: Historical perspectives on treatment. In D. M. Garner & P. E. Garfinkel (Eds.), *Handbook of treatment for eating disorders* (2nd ed., pp. 3–10). New York: Guilford Press.

Smith, C., Feldman, S. S., Nasserbakht, A., & Steiner, H. (1993). Psychological characteristics and DSM-III-R diagnoses at 6-year follow-up of adolescent anorexia nervosa. *Journal of American Academic Child and Adolescent Psychiatry, 32*(6), 1237–1245.

Smolak, L. & Striegel-Moore, R. H. (2001). Challenging the myth of the golden girl: Ethnicity and eating disorders. In R. H. Striegel-Moore and L. Smolak (Eds.), *Eating disorders: Innovative directions in research and practice* (pp. 111–132). Washington, DC: APA.

Way, K. (1993). *Anorexia nervosa and recovery: A hunger for meaning*. New York: Harrington Park Press.

4

Bulimia Nervosa

My relationship with food changed dramatically. I no longer had to clean
my plate. I ate if my body was hungry and not to please anyone else or fit to
a work/family schedule. I could choose to eat one or two cookies and stop.
If I wanted, I ate breakfast foods at night and dinner foods in the morning.
I stopped halfway through a meal if I got full and ate the rest later or threw
it away. This was freedom.

(Radcliffe, 1993, p. 139)

I was learning to reclaim myself and my body, and have some control over
my life. It had nothing to do with weight, I learned. It had to do with hon-
esty—self-honesty and the courage to be honest with others. The end result
was that I lost the desire to binge-eat because I was taking care of my emotions and taking care of myself.

(Virtue, 1993, p. 174)

The word "bulimia" is derived from the Greek word *limos* (hunger) with
the prefix bou denoting bull or ox. According to scholars, bulimia means
"hunger as great as that of an ox" or "hunger sufficient to consume an
entire ox" (Crichton, 1996). Some people have used the word bulimia
alone (without "nervosa") as a shortcut for the full name of the disorder.

Bulimia nervosa is an eating disorder known for binge eating. The *Diagnostic and Statistical Manual of Mental Disorders- IV-TR* (APA, 2000a) provides the criteria for defining bulimia nervosa. There are five criteria used
to define bulimia nervosa. The first concerns the definition of a binge. In

an eating binge, a person eats a great deal of food in a short time period. During the binge, the individual with bulimia feels out of control. It is as if it is impossible to stop eating. An example of the food eaten in a binge could be six or more donuts, and a pint of ice cream, along with a box of cookies and several glasses of milk. The technical definition is "eating, in a discrete period of time (e.g., within any 2-hour period), an amount of food that is definitely larger than most people would eat during a similar period of time and under similar circumstances" (APA, 2000a, p. 594).

Diagnostic Criteria for Bulimia Nervosa

A. Recurrent episodes of binge eating. An episode of binge eating is character-
    ized by both of the following:

    (1) eating, in a discrete period of time (e.g., within any 2-hour period), an
        amount of food that is definitely larger than most people would eat during a
        similar period of time and under similar circumstances

    (2) a sense of lack of control over eating during the episode (e.g., a feeling that
        one cannot stop eating or control what or how much one is eating)

B. Recurrent inappropriate compensatory behavior in order to prevent weight
    gain, such as self-induced vomiting; misuse of laxatives, diuretics, enemas, or
    other medications; fasting; or excessive exercise.

C. The binge eating and inappropriate compensatory behaviors both occur, on
    average, at least twice a week for 3 months.

D. Self-evaluation is unduly influenced by body shape and weight.

E. The disturbance does not occur exclusively during episodes of Anorexia
    Nervosa.

Purging Type: during the current episode of Bulimia Nervosa, the person has regularly engaged in self-induced vomiting or the misuse of laxatives, diuretics, or enemas.

Nonpurging type: during the current episode of Bulimia Nervosa, the person has used other inappropriate compensatory behaviors, such as fasting or excessive exercise, but has not regularly engaged in self-induced vomiting or the misuse of laxatives, diuretics, or enemas. (APA, 2000a, p. 594 Reprinted with permission from the *Diagnostic and Statistical Manual of Mental Disorders, Fourth Edition, Text Revision*. Copyright 2000 American Psychiatric Association.)

Although people with bulimia binge eat, they are afraid to gain weight because they do not want to get fat (see criterion D). They know that eating great amounts of calories will probably cause them to gain weight, so they control weight gain by getting rid of calories consumed in binges. They may do this by vomiting, or they may use laxatives, diuretics, or other medications. In the *Diagnostic and Statistical Manual of Mental Disorders-IV-*

TR (2000) criteria for bulimia, this is referred to as "recurrent inappropriate behavior." A laxative is an over-the-counter medication (brand names such as Ex-Lax and Correctol) used by people when they have problems with bowel movements. Laxatives produce a watery diarrhea; a person with bulimia believes this will prevent weight gain. (Actually, this is not true since by the time food reaches the large intestine most of the caloric value of the food has been absorbed by the small bowel.) A diuretic can be an over-the-counter or prescription medication that people may take to rid the body of fluids. Although people who take diuretics will lose weight, it is weight lost by dehydration and is loss of water, rather than a loss of fat. Another drug used by people with bulimia is Syrup of Ipecac. This is actually a poison that the body rejects, which leads to vomiting. It is an especially dangerous drug since it builds up in the body and is associated with heart abnormalities. Other ways of keeping from gaining weight include excessive exercising or fasting. Like those with anorexia, people with bulimia who excessively exercise may be active for hours a day, including running, swimming, or using exercise machines. Fasting means that a person does not eat any food at all for a certain period of time.

Technically, there are two different types of bulimia, which are distinguished by the methods used to compensate for the calories consumed in binge eating episodes. These are called the purging and nonpurging methods. These types are defined in the *Diagnostic and Statistical Manual of Mental Disorders-IV-TR* (APA, 2000a). The purging methods include vomiting or the misuse of laxatives, diuretics, or enemas. The nonpurging types include fasting or excessive exercise.

The purging type of bulimia is more common, and is the one depicted in popular movies about bulimia. People with the purging type of bulimia may have more depression and more concern about body weight and shape. These individuals are more likely to have fluid and electrolyte imbalances caused directly by the purging. Electrolytes are elements in the body that carry electrical charges and are essential for normal functioning of nerves and muscle cells. When individuals vomit, they lose potassium, chloride, and sodium. The loss of these electrolytes leads to an imbalance in electrolytes available in the body. These electrolyte imbalances cause tiredness, weakness, constipation and depression. The more serious consequence of electrolyte imbalances is cardiac arrhythmias (irregular heartbeats), which can lead to sudden death. However, it is important to remember that a person can have bulimia without vomiting and without using laxatives or diuretics. In the nonpurging type, individuals may fast for days between binge eating episodes or may exercise for hours to burn calories consumed in a binge.

An important part of bulimia is the negative feelings that individuals have about themselves (see criterion D). This is because they view themselves as fat even when they are not, and this seems like the most important thing in life. A client with bulimia might say that she would rather be thin even if it means that she has an eating disorder than be fat without an eating problem. The connection between body size and shape and negative feelings about self-image can be seen in this quote from one of the authors in *Full Lives*, who wrote, " I began to blame my body for all my problems. If I weren't so ugly, so big, so soft and flabby, I would be happy and popular. I was convinced that a cute, tiny body would fix everything" (Rubel, 1993, p. 36).

As you look at the criteria that define bulimia, you will see that the criteria concern binge eating, the ways in which individuals compensate for binge eating, and the negative feelings associated with body image. Additionally, the criteria indicate that binge eating and weight control behaviors have to occur at least twice a week for three months (criterion C). People who do not meet the criteria for bulimia may have an eating disorder not otherwise specified or an eating disturbance. A person cannot be diagnosed with bulimia if she meets the criteria for anorexia nervosa. See the chapter on anorexia for the defining characteristics of anorexia.

CASE EXAMPLES OF BULIMIA NERVOSA

Following are two short descriptions of people who have been diagnosed with bulimia nervosa. The cases provide information about each individual, and they highlight the fact that there are two types of bulimia.

Shae is a first year college student who reported to the counseling center in response to an advertisement for an eating disorders group. She had been binge eating and purging since her senior year in high school, but was doing it daily now and was afraid that she could not stop. She described her binges as something that just seems to happen most nights after she eats a normal dinner and has been studying for a short time. She drives to a fast food restaurant and orders several sandwiches, fries, and two milkshakes and begins eating on her way home. Eating seems out of her control and once she starts she cannot stop until all the food is finished, and then she immediately vomits in the hall bathroom. This description fits with the criteria for bulimia nervosa, purging type.

Devin is a high school senior who described herself as "popular and perky" before she developed bulimia. She was a cheerleader, involved in student government, and had a part-time job at the local bakery. She began to diet after overhearing one of the other cheerleaders say "Devin's thighs are getting chunky." She tried to limit herself to salads without dressing, nonfat yogurt, and some fruit and vegetables. She found this restricting diet to be very difficult, and she began to crave food. After a few weeks of dieting, she began to binge eat. She described a sense of complete loss of control, saying that she would eat leftovers in the refrigerator, discarded stale rolls from the bakery, and lots of chocolate, which she hoarded under her bed. She hated the idea of throwing up, and had heard that you could die from using laxatives, so she decided to exercise her binge calories away. She got in the habit of waking up at 5 A.M. to run, went to cheerleading practice at 6 A.M., and after school she went to the gym to take an aerobics class. In total, she exercised three hours a day. Devin fits the criteria for bulimia nervosa, nonpurging type.

HOW A CLIENT DESCRIBES WEIGHT CONTROL, BINGE EATING, AND PURGING

This is a word for word transcript of a first counseling session with an individual with bulimia nervosa (Chiodo, 1987). You will see how the client describes her attempt to control her eating and weight gain, the binge eating that results from her restrictive diet, and the way she describes her vomiting.

Therapist (Th): Describe the eating problem which brought you to our clinic.
Client (Ct): I get up, and usually have something to drink. Sometimes I'll be hungry, but I won't eat. Then I go to school and get a break around 10:00, so I usually drink something like a diet soda. Occasionally I'll have something from the snack machines. But I never have anything fattening. Then at lunch on my long days, I'll just have something to drink again. Unless someone says "Come eat with us," then I might go 'cause they usually go for pizza. And when I get home, I try not to eat.
Th: What about dinner?
Ct: I try not to eat. But if I've had pizza, it's over for the day.
Th: What do you mean?
Ct: If I ate that much, I might as well go ahead and eat more. Usually it ends up in a binge.
Th: You say "that much." When you're eating pizza with your classmates, how much do you eat?
Ct: I watch what they eat, and that's how much I eat. For a while there, I just didn't eat pizza, because it's too fattening. But now I never pass up the opportunity.
Th: And what do you do for lunch on your short days?
Ct: If I decide to eat that day, then I'll save lunch for 2:00 when I watch my favorite soap opera. I try to eat nice and balanced meals. But sometimes, though, I'm just so hungry that a whole bunch of things sound good. It's real hard for me to decide what I'm going to have, so I decide to have everything.

Then I do a lot of store hopping because I don't want people to know and say "Look what she bought."

Th: What are you concerned about that other people in the store might know or think about you?

Ct: That I eat a lot of food…that I'm a pig…that I shouldn't be eating because I am so fat. That's why I won't eat in restaurants, where everybody is looking at you eating. Sometimes I've gone into a grocery store and bought a whole bag of cookies and eaten them in the car. Like once, I've gone for donuts, then ice cream, and then I got two cheeseburgers, a large order of fries, and then decided that chocolate chip cookies sounded good. So I got some of those. And then I got hungry for a candy bar, but I couldn't decide which kind, so I got both. Sometimes I'll get real full, and sometimes I'll just be a bottomless pit.

Th: Can you tell us why you sometimes get full, and sometimes you feel like a bottomless pit?

Ct: Usually if I haven't eaten for a long time, like two days, then I get fuller faster. But if I binged the day before, then I can eat more and it will take a lot longer to make me feel really stuffed and sick.

Th: What happens when you feel stuffed and sick?

Ct: I don't like food to stay in my stomach…because I get very scared …because it's very uncomfortable and it feels like it's pressing on my heart. So then I go throw up immediately, as much as I can. And I'll keep doing that as long as I can see what's coming up in reverse order.

Th: Is that how you tell when to stop vomiting—by the reverse order of food—or are there other means?

Ct: I've always wondered how I would know if I emptied my stomach because a friend went to a psychologist who said that you can't possibly get everything out of your stomach. And I say that there's got to be a way.…

Later in the session:

Th: When did the eating problem begin?

Ct: Well, I never really had a problem until I came here to college. I was around food all the time because I got assigned work-study in the cafeteria. When I left for college, my mom said, "You're probably going to gain weight and be fat when you come back." And I had to prove my mom wrong. You see, when one of our neighbors went away to college and came back, she had gained some weight. Everyone noticed it. So when my mom told me that, I was determined not to gain any weight while I was away. I became really weight conscious. I knew she would tease me if I was fat when I came back home.

Later…

Th: Where and how did you get the idea to induce vomiting?

Ct: I had read it in some magazines, and I learned some things in my physiology class. I read that if you vomit, then the body breaks down fat cells, because it has nothing in it and it starts to use it for energy. So I thought "Hmmm...sounds like the way to go." I didn't think I could make myself do that. But it got easier. Then I thought that I better quit doing it because it will become a habit. Then I tried not to do it, but that didn't last (Chiodo, 1987).

This client has described her attempts to avoid eating and how she loses control in her binge eating. This example is a typical description of how fear of weight gain, binge eating, and purging are related in a person who has bulimia.

WHAT IS A BINGE?

In order to understand bulimia, one must understand a binge. However, it is not as simple as it seems. For example, Cohn wrote, "I had quite a few binges myself. Some of my fondest memories from childhood are of my grandmother's candy bowl and the cookie jar my mom kept filled. I won the water melon eating contest at my high school class picnic; and, I had a reputation among my friends for how many donuts I could eat" (Hall & Cohn, 1986). However, this is NOT what is meant by a binge. (Cohn became an expert on eating disorders and cowrote the best-selling book *Bulimia: A Guide to Recovery* [1999], which is now in its fifth edition). There is a major difference between overeating and binge eating; it concerns control. Most often, when people overeat, they are aware of their behavior and can stop. However, a person who is in the middle of a binge feels entirely out of control and is not able to stop eating until no more food is available.

Research on the choice of binge foods has led to interesting findings. Foods most often chosen for binges are ice cream, cookies, cake, chocolate, and other sweet desserts (Drewnowski, Bellisle, Aimez, & Remy, 1987; Rosen, Leitenberg, Fisher, & Khazam, 1986). Rosen et al. (1986) reported that 1,500 calories were consumed in an average binge; although this is a large amount of calories eaten at one time, binges did not appear to be the kind of fantastic proportions that have been popularized by the lay press (p. 264). Some individuals binge on nonsweet but high fat foods such as cheese, yogurt, and other dairy products. It seems as though there is a relationship between the foods that are selected for binge eating and those that are normally consumed by someone with bulimia. Forbidden or restricted foods are those that are most often consumed during a binge. If someone never allows herself to have sweet foods, then she is much more likely to select these sweet foods to be binge foods. Binge eating may be an uncontrollable craving for sweet taste (Drewnowski, Bellisle, Aimez, & Remy, 1987).

A STUDY OF BINGE EATING

This section of the chapter describes binge episodes in considerable detail. In one study based on the reports of thirty-two female patients with bulimia, we can see a detailed picture of binge eating, including the actual binge (what they ate, where, how long it took), the things that led up to the binge (called precipitants), and what followed when the binge was over (Abraham & Beumont, 1982). Although this descriptive material was published in 1982, it remains the best description of binge eating in the literature. There are many interesting, but alarming, findings of this description.

Precipitants to Binge Eating

All thirty-two patients indicated that their bulimia began after a period of intense dieting, reinforcing the point that dieting is a risk factor for the development of eating disorders (Ghaderi, 2001). Binges were preceded by feelings of tension, being alone, going home (from school or work, or to the parent's home after living away), feeling bored or lonely. There were also food-related cues to binge eating that included eating, thinking about food, craving food, and eating out. Hunger was not mentioned as a precursor to binge eating as often as might be expected; 66 percent of the time, binges had little to do with feeling hungry.

All thirty-two individuals had attempted to resist the urge to binge. There are lots of things that people have tried to resist the urge to binge eat; for example, they chew food and spit it out, avoid social events where food is served, avoid family meals, lock themselves in the bathroom, and keep no money with them. Other attempts to avoid the binge include distraction like calling a friend or knitting, trying not to be alone, going on long walks, and driving home on a route that avoided food stores.

The Binge

Binge eating is a solitary activity; all patients binged alone. Most were extremely secretive about their binge eating and more secretive about their purging. The most frequent place to binge is at home. Some patients reported that they binged more often at certain times of the day, but others said that it could happen at any time. When asked how long the binge was, some patients reported that it was as short as fifteen minutes while others reported that it lasted three weeks. No single binge could last three weeks, of course, but the patient is describing an ongoing reaction to food in which she binge eats and purges so often during a three-week period that it is as if nothing else is happening in her life.

Binge eating is sometimes planned. Planning might include hoarding or saving food, and even preparing large quantities of food. When binge eating, patients report that they eat fast. The rate of eating slowed as the binge progressed. Some individuals reported that they made a mess opening containers and getting to the food as quickly as possible. Others however, said that they were very neat so that they could avoid calling attention to their eating. Some individuals reported that if they knew they would be uninterrupted, they ate more slowly.

What did they eat? Patients ate until all the food available was consumed, or sometimes they would go out and buy more food. They usually ate "bad" or binge food, such as cake, ice cream, and other forbidden, high-calorie foods. Often, food that the patient did not allow herself to eat during other times became binge food. Patients refer to binge food as junk food or fattening food. Some individuals would just eat what was available in the cupboards and refrigerator. In at least one case, the parents of a patient locked the kitchen cabinets to keep the individual from eating the foods inside. The amount, type, and nutritional value of food eaten might depend on what was available in the home at the time of the binge. Some patients would eat anything, including baby food, frozen food, and scraps of leftovers.

Sometimes a binge would end only when interrupted by other people. Others vomited and did not want to binge any more. After a binge, patients described swollen hands and feet, abdominal fullness and pain, fatigue, headache, and nausea. At the end of every binge, patients promised themselves that they would not do this again. Often they went to sleep.

Thoughts of suicide following binges are common; about 70 percent reported thinking about killing themselves. Seven individuals reported that they made suicide attempts following a binge. However, in spite of the negative feelings following a binge, all individuals described pleasure in eating, especially early in the binge.

Patients indicated that they increased the number and severity of forms of behavior aimed at weight loss as their eating disorder continued. They tried to avoid family meals, concealed the amount of food eaten, used slimming tablets and commercial weight control pills; some even took thyroid medicine, went to health spas, wore plastic suits to induce sweating, and exercised excessively.

No one smoked during a binge; 66 percent of the patients were smokers, but none ever smoked during a binge. Also, only one of the thirty-two used alcohol as part of her binge.

After the Binge

Some patients took purgatives like Ipecac immediately following the binge, but some patients did not like to use them, or they were aware of the negative health consequences of using them. Five were able to vomit easily by contracting abdominal muscles and others used fingers or spoons to induce vomiting. Five people found it difficult to vomit. In this study, those who had a hard time inducing vomiting asked doctors, nurses, and other staff how to do it! The vomiting could either end the binge, or allow the individual to continue to eat more so that she could vomit again.

The vomiting experience was described in detail by patients. They often used markers in their binge so that when they vomited, they could be sure that all food was removed. Some kept drinking and vomiting until the vomit was clear liquid with no food residue. To avoid detection, patients reported that they vomited into plastic bags, buckets, or saucepans.

From the thirty-two patients, these common findings arise

- Binge eating and bulimia nervosa are different from overeating.
- In all binges, the amount of food eaten was excessive when judged against nutritional requirements or social expectations.
- All patients tried to avoid the urge to binge.
- Bulimia was invariably associated with forms of behaviors directed at weight loss.
- All patients were secretive about their behavior, at least initially.
- Depressed mood was often relieved after the binge. (Abraham & Beumont, 1982, p. 633)

Other descriptions of binge eating have revealed similar findings (Stickney, Miltenberger, & Wolff, 1999). In this work, sixteen undergraduate students who engaged in repeated binge eating (but were not described in the article as having bulimia) completed a study that included keeping detailed records of their thoughts, feelings and behaviors before, during, and after binge eating. This is called real time assessment. Thus, the data collected in this study were not retrospective; the data did not rely on the memory of the participants but was based on data recorded at the time of the binge eating episodes. The sixteen subjects reported that there were ninety-four binge episodes in the four weeks of data collection, an average of 1.5 episodes a week per person. They experienced the lack of control that is part of the binge-eating experience (5.25 on a 7-point scale). Most of the binge episodes occurred in the evening, and tended to happen in their dorm room or car. Almost all bingers ate alone, but there were five participants who reported that they binge ate with others.

The data describing thoughts and feelings before, during, and after binge eating are interesting. Individuals reported a decrease in all negative states during binge eating; this means that during the binge they were less anxious, bored, angry at self or others, worried, lonely, frustrated, and sad than they were before the binge started. However, the "after binge" ratings increased. In many cases, the "after binge" ratings were higher than the "before binge" ratings, indicating that the relief experienced during the binge was very short in duration. The most frequent function of binge eating was relief from negative thoughts and feelings (suggesting that a form of therapy that addresses these might be helpful in treatment; see cognitive-behavioral therapy in chapter 9).

The previous studies have focused on the binge aspect of bulimia. One study provides some interesting data on the way that people learned about vomiting as a weight control practice (Chiodo & Latimer, 1983). The participants in this study were twenty-seven people with bulimia who were seeking treatment for their eating disorder. They were asked about how they developed the idea that vomiting could be used as a way to control weight. Twenty-four of the twenty-seven were able to clearly recall how they got this idea. The most common way (ten people) was through a friend or acquaintance, who admitted that she vomited or knew someone who did. Next, and quite disturbing, is that five patients said that they learned to vomit through reading a popular magazine article on bulimia that described vomiting; and the patient learned that this is a way to control weight. Another five patients were told by family members or friends that if they ate something that did not agree with them that they could make themselves throw up and they would feel better. In this case, the family member or friend did not know that the person had binge ate or had an eating problem. However, this is a warning about telling people that they can force themselves to throw up and then feel better. The remaining patients had a variety of recollections, which included reading about how horse jockeys control their weight, reading a chapter on anorexia nervosa, and vomiting after drinking too much. This article is important since it challenges those who educate about eating disorders to be careful about how they describe eating disordered behaviors. The author hopes that those reading his book will be doing it to understand eating disorders so as to avoid developing one.

HISTORICAL CASES OF BULIMIA NERVOSA

The term bulimia nervosa was not actually coined until 1979, so there is not a long history to describe. There is, of course, a history of binge eating, purging, and body image problems that includes cases that might be considered bulimia by the definition of bulimia used today. Two Roman emperors, Claudius and Vitellius, both engaged in binge eating and purging (Crichton, 1996). These emperors may be the first well-documented cases of individuals who regularly binged and purged. Claudius ate very heavily and never left the dining room until he was bloated and stuffed with food. When he was fast asleep after a large amount of food was eaten, his servants would insert a feather into his throat to induce vomiting. Vitellius regularly ate four large meals daily. He liked to serve extravagant feasts to guests but also was known to eat altar meats and sacrificial cakes and even half-eaten scraps. Vitellius may have been sensitive about his obese body and feared becoming fatter, which may have motivated his use of vomiting to attempt to control his weight. It is difficult to know if Claudius and Vitellius would meet the criteria for bulimia nervosa. It is clear that they both engaged in binge eating and vomiting, but we do not know how regularly they did this. There are hints of the "loss of control" aspect of binge eating in Vitellius's eating. It is possible that Vitellius evaluated his body and placed emphasis on body shape and weight. Neither would meet the diagnostic criteria for anorexia nervosa.

Although the cases of the two Roman emperors are interesting from a historical perspective, the first true case of bulimia described in the literature is the work of Janet in France in 1903 (cited in Russell, 1997). Janet wrote about a patient named Nadia. Part of Nadia's story is included here to provide a historical example of bulimia. From Janet's case notes, we learn that Nadia felt shame about her body and this shame began at a very early age. For example, when she was 4 years old, she thought she was too tall. At age 8, she thought that her hands were long and ridiculous. By age 11, she thought everyone looked at her legs. She was ashamed of her feet, hips, and muscular arms. When she reached puberty, she removed her pubic hair, and when her breasts began to grow, she refused to eat. She tried to hide the fact that she was becoming a woman. At this point, it might appear that the appropriate diagnosis is anorexia nervosa. However, although she ate very small amounts of food (soup, egg yolk, vinegar, tea) and was extremely thin, she sometimes felt very hungry and ate everything she could. Sometimes she ate biscuits in secret. She feared becoming fat and resisted temptations to eat. The case of Nadia may be the first true case of bulimia nervosa. The term bulimia nervosa did not yet exist, but Janet recognized that Nadia did not appear to meet the diagnosis of anorexia nervosa because of the extreme hunger and feelings for food that she described.

A more contemporary case was described in 1958 (Binswanger). This case is a detailed description of Ellen's life until her death at age 33. Her eating problem was first noted when she was 20, when she gained some weight and was teased for being overweight. (Teasing is now known to be a risk factor for the development of eating problems; Cattarin & Thompson, 1994.) She developed a fear of becoming fat and began to avoid food. Her varied moods were associated with her eating problems. By age 24, she was eating little, taking long hikes, and was taking up to 48 thyroid tablets a day. (Thyroid medication is used to regulate metabolism. In this case, Ellen was abusing thyroid medication to speed up her metabolism. This is a dangerous and potentially deadly practice.) Although she had a few years of fewer complications, at age 30 she was extremely ill and stopped eating meat, took great quantities of laxatives, and vomited daily. She deteriorated and weighed only 92 pounds. At this time, she was known to put food in her handbag rather than eating it, and held weights when being weighed so no one would know how little she weighed. During this time, she refused most foods, but did eat tomatoes and oranges only (several pounds of tomatoes and twenty oranges a day!). She became depressed, made several suicide attempts, and was admitted to a psychiatric hospital. At the hospital, she was described as devouring food like a wild animal. She continued to take laxatives and vomited regularly. Her mood was depressed and she described a feeling of emptiness and a desire to die. She was released from the hospital based on her request to return home. On her third day home, she ate, went for a walk, and then took a fatal dose of poison. She was 33 when she died.

One important historical milestone in the development of the criteria used to define bulimia occurred in 1975 in Berlin (Vandereycken, 1994). In a conference of clinicians and researchers from Great Britain, Germany, and the United States, overeating and vomiting were discussed. The group agreed that "one group of subjects with chronic anorexia nervosa exemplify many aspects of addition; they habitually/constantly ingest and vomit food in large quantities. They frequently do this covertly. They are usually restless, preoccupied with food and its ingestion, and with an associated disgust at the thought and experience of weight gain.... This behavior, in less severe form, can characterize subjects of more normal weight and who retain menstrual function (Garrow, 1976, pp. 407–408).

Gerald Russell was one of the participants in this international conference. We can see that the topics discussed became part of the criteria for bulimia nervosa that Russell played a role in developing. As indicated earlier, the cases of bulimia presented above predate the official definition and recognition of this eating disorder. In 1979, Gerald Russell actually coined the term bulimia nervosa. He wrote about this in 1979 in an article entitled "Bulimia Nervosa: An Ominous Variant of Anorexia Nervosa." (In the section of this chapter on males, there is an article called "Machismo Nervosa: An Ominous Variant of Bulimia Nervosa" [Connan, 1998] which refers to the issues that are present in males who develop eating problems.) In 1980, bulimia nervosa was first included as a diagnostic category used by psychiatrists and psychologists (APA, 1980). The criteria for bulimia have been revised several times since 1980. The most recent revision was published in 2000 (APA, 2000a).

Before moving on to the prevalence of bulimia, it is worth mentioning that there have been other terms used to describe bulimia. Other words used to what we now call bulimia nervosa include binge eating syndrome and dietary chaos syndrome (Vandereycken, 1994). One especially noteworthy term is bulimarexia (Boskind-White & White, 1987). Bulimarexia was defined as a habitual behavior of gorging (binge eating) and purging. It also included the psychological issues of perfectionism, obsessive concerns with food and body proportions, isolationism, low self-esteem and a strong commitment to please others. Although this term is not used in the current literature, it is interesting since it includes both the behavior of binge eating and purging, along with some of the psychological problems that individuals with anorexia often face. In the third edition of the book, Boskind-White and White (2000) discontinued the use of the word bulimarexia and follow the DSM-IV-TR terminology of bulimia and anorexia.

PREVALENCE OF BULIMIA NERVOSA

Studies have found quite different prevalence estimates of bulimia, probably due to the way the data were collected and who the subjects were. It can be difficult to know for sure how many people actually do have bulimia. The American Psychiatric Association estimated that approximately 1 percent to 3 percent of adolescent and young adult females meet full criteria for bulimia (APA, 2000a). This means that, out of 100 teenage girls, 1 to 3 of them may have bulimia. The rate of occurrence in males is one-tenth of that in females. For every one male with bulimia, there are 10 females with bulimia (APA, 2000a). Nielson (2001) reports that the lifetime prevalence of bulimia is approximately 1 percent in women and .01 percent in men. However, like anorexia, bulimia may be underdiagnosed in males.

Like for anorexia, there is controversy over the answer to the question "is there an increase in the prevalence rates for bulimia?" For bulimia, there seems to be a cohort effect, which means that there is increased frequency of bulimia in people born after 1960 (Dorian & Garfinkel, 1999). It is possible that the increased social pressure to be thin combined with individual predispositions may explain the greater prevalence of eating disorders in women born after 1960. Nielsen's review of the data (2001) indicates that there is support for an increase in incidence rates for bulimia.

Bulimia usually begins in late adolescence or early adulthood. Most cases of bulimia have been identified in females who are below the age of 40, with the majority of incidences occurring among young women who are 13 to 20 years of age. Most adult females report that eating problems began in adolescence. Bulimia is very rare in children prior to puberty (Lask, 2000). A study of early onset bulimia (under age 15) found that in all cases, the adolescent had begun to menstruate prior to the onset of bulimia (Lask & Bryant-Waugh, 1997).

CULTURAL ISSUES AND BULIMIA NERVOSA

According to APA (2000a), bulimia occurs with similar frequencies on most industrialized countries, including the United States, Canada, Europe, Australia, Japan, New Zealand, and South Africa. Miller and Pumariega's (2001) review of articles published from 1968–2000 concluded that Western-oriented countries have comparable rates of eating disorders to the United States. There are fewer published studies about the prevalence of bulimia in other cultures, such as the Middle East, Africa, and South America. Those who are interested in reading more about the prevalence of bulimia and other eating problems in other countries can see the review of articles by Miller and Pumariega (2001).

Some studies have focused on populations of students outside of the United States and have found similar prevalence rates; for example, a study of freshman medical students in China yielded a prevalence rate of 1.1 percent for female students (Chun et al., 1992). Interestingly, in this study of Chinese students, none met the criteria for anorexia, but there were high numbers of students who reported binge-eating episodes (40 percent of females and 27 percent of males).

A study of the prevalence of bulimia and bulimic behaviors among a large sample (over 8,000 people) of Canadian residents also yielded a prevalence rate of 1.1 percent (Garfinkel et al., 1995). However, like many other studies, researchers found that a higher proportion have symptoms of bulimia but did not meet all the criteria required for a diagnosis of bulimia. In this group, 8.2 percent of females and 7.8 percent of males reported that they had engaged in binge eating.

Interestingly, people who immigrate to the United States may be at risk for developing eating disorders. Several case reports of students who came to the United States for school indicates that the culture clash may be a factor that contributes to the development of an eating disorder (Bulik, 1987; Van Den Broucke & Vandereycken, 1986). Adolescents who are separated from their family and adjusting to new social roles may face challenges that make them vulnerable to eating disorders (Miller & Pumariega, 2001). Both bulimia and anorexia may occur in immigrants; Bulik's case reports include descriptions of two young adult women who immigrated from the Soviet Union, one of who developed anorexia, while the other developed bulimia. The woman who developed bulimia noted that she learned about the culture through watching television. She gained weight as a result of her access to different kinds of foods and began a diet when her American boyfriend suggested that she should. This began a cycle of weight loss, binge eating, and purging and led her to seek treatment for bulimia.

More research should focus on a variety of racial and ethnic groups in and outside the United States, because the number of cases of bulimia among different racial and cultural groups may be increasing (see Kalodner, 1996). As suggested earlier in this book, although whites may be at greater risk than nonwhites, no racial group has been identified as immune to eating disorders, including bulimia (Miller & Pumariega, 2001; Smolak & Striegel-Moore, 2001). Older research suggested that there was lower rates of bulimia among ethnic minority groups in the United States, but newer reviews conclude that there is a trend toward increasing prevalence in all minority groups (Miller & Pumariega, 2001; Smolak & Striegel-Moore, 2001). As cultural norms change as members of minority groups become acculturated to the Western societal norms, rates of eating disorders increase.

BULIMIA NERVOSA IN MALES

Although there may be an increase in the number of males who are concerned about their weight and appearance, bulimia is still uncommon among males. In 1990, Fairburn and Beglin wrote that "it seems reasonable to conclude that the comparatively small number of men who present for the treatment of bulimia nervosa reflects a genuine difference in the prevalence of the disorder between the two sexes rather than being an artifact attributable to factors such as differential case detection and referral" (p. 404). At that time, these researchers believed that the number of males with eating disorders was really different than the number of females with eating disorders and that this was not solely because men were not accurately diagnosed with bulimia or that they were referred for treatment. They simply noted that bulimia was much more common in females.

The fact that bulimia exists much less frequently in males is still true. However, in Andersen, Cohn, and Holbrook's (2000) book on male eating problems, they point out that men are more *shape* concerned than *weight* concerned. Teenage boys and adult men describe that they want to "be tall, show off well-chiseled pectorals, have prominent biceps, display outstanding deltoids, and increasingly, demonstrate well-defined abdominals" (p. 56). The set of prominent muscles in the abdominal area commonly referred to as a "six-pack" is desired by many males. This may be related to a disorder called body dysmorphic disorder (APA, 2000a) which is defined by a preoccupation with "an imagined defect in appearance" (p. 510) when the "preoccupation causes significant distress or impairment in social, occupational, or other important areas of functioning" (p. 510). Pope has used the phrase "muscle dysmorphia" to describe this phenomenon (Pope, Gruber, Choi, Olivardia, & Philips, 1997) and suggested that it is placed in the category of dysmorphic disorders in the *Diagnostic and Statistical Manual of Mental Disorders* (APA, 2000a). Males may have higher rates of body dysmorphic disorder than females (Smolak & Murnen, 2001).

Connan (1998) proposed a new term "machismo nervosa" to describe a male variant of bulimia nervosa, and believes that this disorder should be classified as an eating disorder rather than a dysmorphic disorder. Machismo nervosa is defined as a disorder characterized by undue influence of body shape and weight on self-evaluation with behaviors such as excessive weight training, abnormal eating habits (binge eating, dieting, preoccupation with food and fluid restriction), along with thoughts about body image like those found in bulimia nervosa. Connan notes that males are driven to achieve a body image that is the mesomorphic type (lean and muscular), or hypermesomorphic like Arnold Schwartzeneger. Males, then, are driven to gain lean muscle bulk through weight training and abnormal eating habits. Bodybuilders are an example of those who engage

in extreme weight training and strict dietary regimens and often experience several large weight loss and gain cycles during a year. Some males
who are attempting to achieve a mesomorphic body may use anabolic
steroids, which are dangerous for physical morbidity and possibly increased
mortality.

Although there are not many cases of males with bulimia published,
one article includes descriptions of nine cases of males with bulimia
(Robinson & Holden, 1986). The nine males ranged in age from 17–28
and began dieting between the ages of 15 and 19. Of the nine, three were
homosexual (an issue discussed below). Two of the cases are reported here
to provide examples of how bulimia may present in males.

Case six (of the nine in the article) was 17 years old when he presented
for treatment. He reported that he first became preoccupied about his
weight when he was 15 years of age and weighed 147 pounds. He began to
diet strictly, and by his sixteenth birthday, he weighed 112 pounds. He
was depressed, admitted to feeling hungry most of the time, and began to
suffer from the symptoms of bulimia. He would fast all day and then at
night eat everything in a "well-stocked refrigerator" and then vomit. He
felt guilty and depressed. He attempted suicide on several occasions. His
eating disorder improved during a family vacation but worsened again
when his brother and sister-in law separated and his parents had severe
issues in their marriage. When he left the home of his parents to live with
his sister, things improved. He gained some weight (136 pounds) and
stopped binge eating. However, then he moved into an apartment with
college friends, he adopted a "punk" style of dress and began to lose weight
again. At the last point of information about him, he weighed 125
pounds, which he thought was excessively heavy. He reported that he was
drinking at least half a bottle of hard alcohol a day for several months.

Case 5 was 18 years old when he presented for treatment. He was overweight from age 13, weighing 147 pounds. He increased in weight to 203
pounds when he was 16. When he started to diet at age 17, he began to be
preoccupied with thoughts of food and weight and had episodes of binge eating during which he would eat large amounts of toast with butter and cereal
with milk. The binges made him feel depressed, which led to his purging. On
days that he binge ate, he dieted strictly and began to run many miles each
day to compensate for calories that he consumed. He participated in individual therapy and seemed to recover quite well. Interestingly, he reported
that he had begun to date a woman who was also diagnosed with bulimia.

Gay males may be a group that is at higher risk for developing eating
disorders. Andersen (1999) reported that 20 percent of males with eating
disorders have a gay sexual orientation. According to Williamson (1999),

studies of male clients with eating problems reliably show higher frequencies of eating disturbances and disorders in gay males. He believes that some gay males may develop problematic eating because while they struggle to work through issues of their homosexuality, they may have less support and fewer effective adaptive strategies for coping with feelings of self-hatred. This makes them vulnerable to developing eating disorders and other behaviors that are harmful. Andersen (1999) believes that the most likely reason why males with eating disorders have an increased probability of being gay is due to the higher value of thinness in the gay male community. Some gay men may develop an exaggerated sense of the focus on youthfulness, slimness, and attractiveness that does exist in some gay cultures. When a gay man is not able to meet the ideal of being slim and attractive, he may become vulnerable to body dissatisfaction and eating problems (note that this is very similar to the sociocultural model that is such a powerful issue for females as well).

BULIMIA NERVOSA IN FICTION

There are a number of novels that describe the development of bulimia and the process of recovery and treatment. The Gurze Web site is an excellent place to find out more about these and other books on bulimia (www.gurze.com).

Perk! The Story of a Teenager with Bulimia (Hall, 1997) is about a typical high school student who develops bulimia, purging type. The novel highlights the problems in her relationship with her mother (who is described as gorgeous and classy and who never gains a pound) and also includes a focus on Perk's relationships with her friends, pet mouse, and a dedicated art teacher. At one point in the story, Perk goes to the library to find out about bulimia and some of her scary symptoms (like blood in her vomit). A very dangerous incident involving Perk's baby sister led to a trip to the hospital where Perk's bulimia was identified by a nurse. This was the beginning of her recovery. The book provides a focus on Perk's thoughts and feelings about growing up, her relationships, and her body image. Although it does not follow her progress in treatment, it does provide an epilogue.

Picture Perfect (Byrd, 2000) is about two adolescents who sign up for modeling school, where they expect to learn about clothes and makeup. At the end of the modeling school, there is a photo session and a chance to be selected as a model. The story does not focus on eating problems per se but does have a focus on the importance of "looking perfect." Both girls in the story react to the pressure to look perfect on the photo session day with anxiety and a tremendous amount of dissatisfaction about their appearance. When the mother of one of the girls has a baby born with a birthmark on her face, the girls think more about what is really important, and this seems to reduce attention to the need to look perfect. Note that there is a heavy emphasis on talk with God in this story.

In *Life in the Fat Lane*, a popular sixteen-year-old cheerleader develops a fictitious disorder that causes her to gain weight rapidly (Bennett, 1998). As she weighs 218 pounds, she experiences the discrimination that people who are fat are faced with on a daily basis. The heroine in this story does not appear to meet the criteria for bulimia nervosa, but the thoughts and feelings that she expresses are similar to those expressed by people with bulimia.

AUTOBIOGRAPHIES

Inner Hunger by Marianne Apostolides (1998) is an exceptionally well-written book about a young woman who begins her eating disorder with anorexia but develops bulimia. This pattern of beginning with anorexia and progressing to the development of bulimia is common. She chronicles her life through high school, college, and in the years beyond college and describes the role that her eating disorder played in her view of herself and how the eating issues impacted her relationships with her family, friends, boyfriends, and her lover. Her story addresses how diets lead to weight cycling, a sense of failure, and binge eating. The book also contains three chapters with advice to "Communities and Institutions" (such as schools, health care providers, the media, and community members), "Parents, Siblings, Partners, Friends, and Mentors," and "Girls and Women Experiencing an Eating Disorder."

Marya Hornbacher's (1998) book *Wasted* is a strikingly powerful story of her long struggle with anorexia, bulimia, and eating disorders not otherwise specified. The book provides disturbing detail about her feelings associated with her eating problems, sometimes using obscenities and very strong language. She was hospitalized repeatedly and describes permanent health damage in her reproductive and immune systems. Although the book has no real ending, it does provide a sense of the ongoing struggle Marya faces. The book is quite powerful and is recommended only for those who are ready to face the dramatic story of her life.

RECOVERING FROM BULIMIA NERVOSA

There is a large body of research that provides information about recovery from bulimia nervosa. How do you know when someone has recovered from bulimia? Is it the absence or reduction of binge eating? Or the absence of methods of purging? What about the importance of body shape? Or a more accurate view of one's own body? Most of the research has focused on the reduction of binge eating and purging but a few have provided information on the patient's self-perception.

Once one develops bulimia, symptoms tend to continue anywhere from six months to more than twenty years, with an average duration of approximately six and a half years (APA, 2000b). Although bulimia can be treated, recovery depends on several factors (e.g., Is the person in treatment? Do they have family support? Do they have another psychological or physical disorder?). Recovery from bulimia may involve lengthy treatment. Many women report significant struggles in reversing their bingeing and purging behaviors, especially when they make these attempts on their own. Recovery can be difficult because individuals have to relearn eating patterns and change their expectations about their body size and shape.

What does research suggest about the outcome of treatment for bulimia? In a document that summarizes the tremendous number of research articles on the outcome of treatment, the American Psychiatric Association reports that the overall success rate for clients who received a psychosocial treatment for bulimia is between 50 percent and 70 percent (APA, 2000b). Bulimia is associated with high relapse rates of 30 percent to 50 percent, which suggest that long-term treatment might be necessary for some individuals. In a large meta-study (a summary of eighty-eight studies of the outcome of bulimia), 50 percent fully recovered from their disorder, while 20 percent still met the full criteria for bulimia nervosa. The remaining 30 percent relapsed into some bulimic symptoms (Keel & Mitchell, 1997). This is consistent with the results of another study, which indicated that 60 percent had good outcomes, 29 percent had intermediate outcomes, 10 percent had poor outcomes, and 1 percent had died (Fichter & Quadflieg, 1997). These studies show that the majority of people treated for bulimia recover although many still struggle with eating disorders and disturbances. An interesting pattern of recovery was noted: during therapy, patients generally improved but experienced declines in the one or two years after therapy ended. In years three through six after treatment, recovery continued and stabilized.

Keel and her colleagues have conducted several analyses of the long-term follow-up of people treated for bulimia (Keel, Mitchell, Davis, Fieselman, & Crow, 2000; Keel, Mitchell, Miller, Davis, & Crow, 2000a; Keel, Mitchell, Miller, Davis, & Crow, 2000b). Keel and colleagues (2000) reported that part of the difficulty in describing the outcome of treatment of bulimia is the varied ways in which the outcome is defined and measured. For example, studies have had wide variations in the definitions of full recovery, partial recovery, and poor outcomes. Full recovery has been defined as "no binge eating or purging for 6 months," "not binge eating or purging at all or less than once a month," "no symptoms for twelve months," "no eating disorder," and "did not meet criteria for anorexia, bulimia, or eating disorder not otherwise specified." A rating scale used to rate the outcome of bulimia, called the Psychiatric Status Rating scale for bulimia (Herzog et al., 1993) was used in several of the studies, but they varied in their determination of outcome on the scale as well; one indicated a score of less than 3 determined a good outcome, while another one indicated a score of 1 or 2 was the criteria for a good outcome. These variations in definitions of a good outcome make it very difficult to compare studies and to know the true outcome of treatment of bulimia.

Keel and colleagues (2000a) described the social adjustment of women diagnosed with bulimia over a decade earlier. There were 177 women interviewed for this study. Women in the study reported improved social adjustment, including better social functioning at work, in social activities and with family members. The longer a woman had been free of the symptoms of eating disorder symptoms, the more likely she would report better functioning at work and better overall social adjustment. The same 177 women were described by Keel et al. (2000b) in terms of their eating behavior. Ten years after receiving treatment for bulimia, 19 percent met the criteria for bulimia, only one (1.6 percent) met criteria for anorexia, and 18.5 percent had an eating disorder not otherwise specified. The women were also assessed for current psychiatric diagnoses, and it was found that mood disorders (depression; 21 percent), anxiety disorders (11 percent), and substance use disorder (15 percent) were prominent. The authors suggest that women who continue to struggle with an eating disorder were more likely to have depression, anxiety, and substance use problems.

These data suggest that there is a large variability in response to treatment. Some people did recover from their eating problems, some improved but still had some eating problems, and some did not improve much at all. It is possible that some of the differences in response to treatment are due to the level of eating problems prior to treatment. Indeed, those who had the worst outcomes of treatment were those who had more severe eating problems before treatment began. As a group, they binged more frequently and purged more often than those who had better treatment outcomes. Interestingly, they did not differ in weight, but they did experience more weight fluctuations, meaning that the group who recovered was those who had the most stable weights.

Bulimia nervosa is not a simple, short-term problem that goes away easily. It can be a chronic, ongoing problem. Even after successful treatment, some individuals have periods during which they slip into bulimic eating patterns and may need help to regain control. Some people believe that recovery from an eating disorder is like recovery from alcohol or drug abuse. This means that individuals must continue to struggle with eating and body image issues long after formal treatment is over. This is especially difficult since people *have* to eat, although they do not have to drink alcohol or take drugs.

PHYSICAL HEALTH ISSUES ASSOCIATED WITH BULIMIA NERVOSA

Many of the physical symptoms of bulimia are associated with the method of purging used. The health considerations may affect the whole body of the person, including the metabolic, gastrointestinal, reproductive, cardiovascular, and integument (skin, hair, and nails) systems. Detailed descriptions of the effects of behaviors associated with bulimia on these systems appears in chapter 5.

One physical health consideration relates to caffeine abuse by individuals with bulimia. Although people with eating disorders may abuse laxatives, diuretics, and appetite suppressants, the use of caffeine as a weight control strategy also occurs. The caffeine use of three individuals with bulimia was described. They took pills with caffeine, and drank coffee, tea, or Diet Coke in very large quantities. For example, one patient took up to 20 tablets of caffeine and drank 5 or 6 Cokes and 5 or 6 cups of coffee a day. Caffeine in these amounts made the patients feel anxious, restless, nauseated, and lead to headaches and difficulties sleeping. People may consume this quantity of caffeine to provide them with the energy that they do not have due to poor nutritional habits. In addition, people who are struggling with eating problems may believe that the caffeine can help them to lose weight, but the diuretic effects are not useful in leading to meaningful weight loss (Fahy & Treasure, 1991).

SUMMARY

Bulimia nervosa, a serious eating disorder known for binge eating, is more prevalent than anorexia nervosa. The binge is the defining characteristic of bulimia; during a binge, a person eats a large quantity of food in a short period of time. Furthermore, a person with bulimia feels out of control during the binge; he or she can not stop even if they want to. A person with bulimia has a fear of gaining weight because they do not want to get fat. Since this fear and the binge conflict, a person with bulimia is faced with various ways to compensate for the binge, such as self-induced vomiting, or the use of laxative, diuretics, enemas, excessive exercise, or fasting. Medical and health complications arise from the abuse of these methods of compensation. Treatment for bulimia may be effective for many people, though it can be a long-term process and recovery may be marked with periods of recurrences.

REFERENCES

Abraham, S.U., & Beumont, P.J.V. (1982). How patients describe bulimia or binge eating. *Psychological Medicine, 12*, 625–635.

American Psychiatric Association (APA). (1980). *Diagnostic and statistical manual of mental disorders* (3rd ed.). Washington, DC: Author.

American Psychiatric Association (APA). (2000a). *Diagnostic and statistical manual of mental disorders* (4th ed.-TR.). Washington, DC: Author.

American Psychiatric Association (2000b). *Practice guidelines for the treatment of patients with eating disorders* (2nd ed.). Washington, DC: Author.

Andersen, A., Cohn, L., & Holbrook, T. (2000). *Making weight: Men's conflicts with food, weight, shape, and appearance*. Carlsbad, CA: Gurze Books.

Andersen, A.E. (1999). Eating disorders in gay males. *Psychiatric Annals, 29*, 206–212.

Apostolides, M. (1998). *Inner hunger*. New York: W. W. Norton.

Bennett, C. (1998). *Life in the fat lane*. New York: Bantam Doubleday.

Binswanger, L. (1958). The case of Ellen West: An anthropological-clinical study (W.M. Mendel & J. Lyons, Trans.). In R. May, E. Angel, & H.F. Ellenberger (Eds.), *Existence: A new dimension in psychiatry and psychology* (pp. 237–364). New York: Basic Books.

Boskind-White, M., & White, W.C. (1987). *Bulimiarexia: The binge/purge cycle*. New York: W.W. Norton & Company.

Boskind-White, M., & White, W.C. (2000). *Bulimia/anorexia: The binge/purge cycle and self starvation*. New York: W.W. Norton.

Bulik, C.M. (1987). Eating disorders in immigrants: Two case reports. *International Journal of Eating Disorders, 6*, 133–141.

Byrd, S. (2000). *Picture perfect*. Colorado Springs, CO: Waterbrook Press.

Cattarin, J., & Thompson, J.K. (1994). A three-year longitudinal study of body image and eating disturbance in adolescent females. *Eating Disorders: The Journal of Prevention and Treatment, 2*, 114–125.

Chiodo, J. (1987). Invited case transcript: Bulimia: An individual behavioral analysis. *Journal of Behavior Therapy and Experimental Psychiatry, 18* (1), 41–49.

Chiodo, J. & Latimer, P.R. (1983). Vomiting as a learned weight control technique in bulimia. *Journal of Behavior Therapy and Experimental Psychiatry*, *14* (2), 131–135.

Chun, Z.F., Mitchell, J.E., Li, K., Yu, W.M., Lan, Y.D., Jun, Z., Rong, Z.Y., Huan, Z.Z., Filice, G.A., Pomeroy, C., & Pyle, R.L. (1992). The prevalence of anorexia nervosa and bulimia nervosa among freshman medical college students in China. *International Journal of Eating Disorders*, *12* (2), 209–214.

Connan, F. (1998). Machismo nervosa: An ominous variant of bulimia nervosa? *European Eating Disorders Review*, *6*, 154–159.

Crichton, P. (1996). Were the roman emperors Claudius and Vitellius bulimic? *International Journal of Eating Disorders*, *19* (2), 203–207.

Dorian, B.J., & Garfinkel, P.E. (1999). The contributions of epidemiologic studies to the etiology and treatment of the eating disorders. *Psychiatric Annals*, *29*, 187–192.

Drewnowski, A., Bellisle, F., Aimez, P., & Remy, B. (1987). Taste and bulimia. *Physiology & Behavior*, *41*, 621–626.

Fahy, T.A., & Treasure, J. (1991). Caffeine abuse in bulimia nervosa. *International Journal of Eating Disorders*, *10* (3), 373–377.

Fairburn, C.G., & Beglin, S.J. (1990). Studies of the epidemiology of bulimia nervosa. *The American Journal of Psychiatry*, *147*, 401–408.

Fichter, M.M., & Quadflieg, N. (1997). Six-year course of bulimia nervosa. *International Journal of Eating Disorders*, *22* (4), 361–384.

Garfinkel, P.E., Lin, E., Goering, P., Spegg, C., Goldbloom, D.D., Kennedy, S., Kaplan, A.S., & Woodside, D.B. (1995). Bulimia nervosa in a Canadian community sample: Prevalence and comparison of subgroups. *The American Journal of Psychiatry*, *152* (7), 1052–1058.

Garrow, J.S. (1976). Pathology of eating group report. In T. Silverstone (Ed.), *Appetite and food intake* (pp. 405–416). Berlin: Abakon (Life Sciences Research Report 2).

Ghaderi, A. (2001). Review of risk factors for eating disorders: Implications for primary prevention and cognitive behavioural therapy. *Scandinavian Journal of Behaviour Therapy*, *30*, 57–74.

Hall, L.F. (1997). *Perk! The story of a teenager with bulimia*. Carlsbad, CA: Gurze Books.

Hall, L., & Cohn, L. (1986). *Bulimia: A guide to recovery*. Santa Barbara, CA: Gurze Books.

Hall, L., & Cohn, L. (1999). *Bulimia: A guide to recovery* (5th ed.). Calsbad, CA: Gurze Books.

Herzog, D.B., Sachs, N.R., Keller, M.B., Lavori, P.W., von Ranson, K.B., & Gray, H.M. (1993). Patterns and predictors of recovery in anorexia nervosa and bulimia nervosa. *Journal of the American Academy of Child and Adolescent Psychiatry*, *32*, 835–842.

Hornbacher, M. (1998). *Wasted: A memoir of anorexia and bulimia*. New York: Harper Collins.

Kalodner, C. R. (1996). Eating disorders from a multicultural perspective. In J. L. DeLucia-Waack (Ed.), *Multicultural counseling competencies: Implications for training and practice* (pp. 197–216). Alexandria, VA: Association for Counselor Education and Supervision.

Keel, P. K., & Mitchell, J. E. (1997). Outcome in bulimia nervosa. *American Journal of Psychiatry, 154*, 313–321.

Keel, P. K., Mitchell, J. E., Davis, T. L., Fieselman, S., & Crow, S. J. (2000). Impact of definitions of the description and prediction of bulimia nervosa outcome. *International Journal of Eating Disorders, 28*, 377–386.

Keel, P. K., Mitchell, J. E., Miller, K. B., Davis, T. L., & Crow, S. J. (2000a). Social adjustment over 10 years following diagnosis of bulimia nervosa. *International Journal of Eating Disorders, 27*, 21–28.

Keel, P. K., Mitchell, J. E., Miller, K. B., Davis, T. L., & Crow, S. J. (2000b). Predictive validity of bulimia nervosa as a diagnostic category. *American Journal of Psychiatry, 157*, 136–138.

Lask, B. (2000). Eating disorders in childhood and adolescence. *Current Pediatrics, 10*, 254–258

Lask, B., & Bryant-Waugh, R. (1997). Prepubertal eating disorders. In D. M. Garner & P. E. Garfinkel (Eds.), *Handbook of treatment for eating disorders* (2nd ed., pp. 476–483). New York: Guilford Press.

Miller, M. N., & Pumariega, A. J. (2001). Culture and eating disorders: A historical and cross-cultural review. *Psychiatry, 62*, 93–110.

Nielsen, S. (2001). Epidemiology and mortality of eating disorders. *The Psychiatric Clinics of North America, 24*, 210–214.

Pope, H. G., Gruber, A. J., Choi, P., Olivardia, R., & Philips, K. A. (1997). Muscle dysmorphia: An under recognised form of body dysmorphic disorder. *Psychosomatics, 38*, 548–557.

Radcliffe, R. R. (1993). Hunger for more. In L. Hall (Ed.), *Full loves: Women who have freed themselves from food and weight obsession* (pp. 132–143), Carlsbad, CA: Gurze Books.

Robinson, P. H., & Holden, N. L. (1986). Bulimia nervosa in the male: A report of nine cases. *Psychological Medicine, 16*, 795–803.

Rosen, J. C., Leitenberg, H., Fisher, C., & Khazam, C. (1986). Binge-eating episodes in bulimia nervosa: The amount and type of food consumed. *International Journal of Eating Disorders, 5*, 255–267.

Rubel, J. (1993). Are you finding what you need? In L. Hall (Ed.), *Full loves: Women who have freed themselves from food and weight obsession* (pp. 32–51), Carlsbad, CA: Gurze Books.

Russell, G. F. M. (1979). Bulimia nervosa: An ominous variant of anorexia nervosa. *Psychological Medicine, 9*, 429–448.

Russell, G. F. M. (1997). The history of bulimia nervosa. In D. M. Garner & P. E. Garfinkel (Eds.), *Handbook of treatment for eating disorders* (2nd ed). pp. 11–24). New York: Guilford Press.

Smolak, L., & Murnen, S.K. (2001). Gender and eating problems. In R.H. Striegel-Moore & L. Smolak (Eds.), *Eating disorders: Innovative directions in research and practice* (pp. 91–110). Washington, DC: APA.

Smolak, L., & Striegel-Moore, R.H. (2001). Challenging the myth of the golden girl: Ethnicity and eating disorders. In R.H. Striegel-Moore & L. Smolak (Eds.), *Eating disorders: Innovative directions in research and practice* (pp. 111–132). Washington, DC: APA.

Stickney, M.I., Miltenberger, R.G., & Wolff, G. (1999). A descriptive analysis of factors contributing to binge eating. *Journal of Behavior Therapy and Experimental Psychiatry, 30,* 177–189.

Van Den Broucke, S., & Vandeneycken, W. (1986). Risk factors for the development of eating disorders in adolescent exchange students: An exploratory study. *Journal of Adolescence, 9,* 145–150.

Vandereycken, W. (1994). Emergence of bulimia nervosa as a separate diagnostic entity: Review of the literature from 1960 to 1979. *International Journal of Eating Disorders, 16* (2), 105–116.

Virtue, D.L. (1993). Whose body is it, anyway? In L. Hall (Ed.), *Full lives: Women who have freed themselves from food and weight obsession* (pp. 161–175), Carlsbad, CA; Gurze Books.

Williamson, I. (1999). Why are gay men a high risk group for eating disturbance? *European Eating Disorders Review, 7* (1), 1–4.

5

⊷∞⊶

Medical Care and Physical Health Issues Associated with Eating Disorders

I had a complete physical, but as far as my physician could tell me, there was nothing wrong with me. "Just bad luck—a lot of bugs going around," he concluded after all the test results came back. But I continued to get sick, again and again.

(Kano, 1993, p. 123)

Eating disorders are associated with a variety of physical health problems and medical complications due to starvation, vomiting, and use of laxatives, diuretics, or other medications. These complications may be mild, moderate, or life threatening. In eating disorders not otherwise specified, the medical issues depend on the type of eating problem, the presence or absence of purging, and the type of purging used. In anorexia, the health issues that arise are often the result of starvation and malnutrition. In anorexia of the binge eating/purging type, there may be physical complications similar to those experienced by those with bulimia. In the purging type of bulimia, health issues usually develop as a consequence of the methods of purging used. Vomiting, laxative, or diuretic abuse can cause different physical effects in the body. Individuals with eating disturbances may also experience some of the health issues described here.

Many of these health issues are relevant to all types of eating disorders and may require medical attention. However, it is interesting to note that people with bulimia seem to have more physical complaints than patients with anorexia nervosa despite the fact that the physical condition of patients with bulimia is not generally as seriously impacted as in anorexia

(Mitchell, Pomeroy, & Adson, 1997). People with bulimia generally look healthy on physical examination (Walsh, Wheat, & Freund, 2000). Patients with anorexia may not describe present physical complaints, despite their emaciated state (Mitchell et al., 1997). They may minimize the physical consequences of their situation and their medical problems may not be obvious until there is a detailed medical examination. Often, individuals with anorexia are able to maintain regular physical activity.

The medical management of anorexia is more complicated than bulimia. This is largely due to the medical issues that arise from starvation. Although patients with both anorexia and bulimia require routine medical screening, ongoing medical issues are more often associated with anorexia than bulimia. Medical assessment of individuals with eating disorders includes detailed questions about eating, fasting, starvation, vomiting, use of laxatives, diuretics, or diet pills, and any use of ipecac. It is important to look for other medical issues that may complicate the treatment of an eating disorder. Diabetes is an example of such a medical problem (Peveler, 2000). A physical examination includes accurate assessment of height and weight, hydration (the amount of water in the body), and blood pressure. The physical exam may also include examination of the teeth to assess for signs of damage due to vomiting. Laboratory analysis of blood and urine is necessary to look for electrolyte levels, liver function tests, and tests of thyroid functioning (among many other things). Other tests such as an electrocardiogram (EKG) of the heart might be ordered. Some of these laboratory analyses may not be sensitive to detecting eating disorders in early stages.

Medical consultation with a physician knowledgeable about eating disorders is necessary to assess the health of individuals with eating disorders. A curriculum used to educate pediatricians, obstetricians, internists, and nurses about eating disorders includes training in the diagnosis, medical assessment, and treatment of eating disorders (Gurney & Halmi, 2001). However, this presentation was limited to only one hour, and eating disorders may receive "cursory attention in medical schools" (Gurney & Halmi, 2001), thus it is wise to seek out a physician with special expertise in eating disorders. (This article also contains detailed information regarding the training of social workers, which is much more comprehensive.) Medical doctors who specialize in working with individuals who have eating disorders are trained to look for abdominal pain/bloating, constipation, irregular menses, swollen cheeks or glands, dental complaints, and overall weakness as symptoms of eating disorders. They are also advised to ask about eating behavior, vomiting, use of laxatives and diuretics, attitudes about body weight and shape, physical exercise, mood disturbances, menstrual patterns, and perfectionistic attitudes and behaviors (Noordenbos, 1998). Asking about these eating and body image issues may give the person with an eating disorder an invitation to talk about some of the problems that he or she may be experiencing.

DIFFICULTIES IDENTIFYING A PERSON WITH AN EATING DISORDER

Even before a physician can assist in the treatment of a patient with an eating disorder, the patient must be identified as a person with an eating problem. There are several problems in the interaction between the person with an eating disorder and physicians; patient delay, doctor delay, difficulties in doctor-patient communication, including negative attitudes of some general practitioners toward patients with eating disorders, and gender differences between the patients and doctors might explain some of the problems in the interaction between people who have an eating problem and physicians (Noordenbos, 1998).

Patient Delay

Patient delay refers to the time that it takes for someone with an eating disorder to tell a physician that she has an eating problem. Research in the Netherlands (cited in Noordenbos, 1998) shows that nearly 90 percent of patients with anorexia and bulimia went to their general practitioner with complaints related to their eating disorder. However, there was a four-year delay between the start of an eating disorder and the first visit to the physician. This delay might be due to the fact that in the beginning many people with eating disorders do not think that they have a problem, thus they are not seeking treatment. As time goes one, this denial often increases before help is sought. People with an eating disorder may not think that the eating disorder is a problem because they are losing weight and they feel well.

Doctor Delay

Eventually people with eating disorders may have a physical complaint and seek medical care. When a person with an eating disorder goes to the doctor, she may be reluctant to say, "I think that I have an eating disorder," and rather she may complain about menstrual irregularities, loss of hair, fatigue, weakness, constipation. Sometimes people even ask the doctor for ways to lose more weight. A patient may complain about constipation or repeated stomachaches and ask for a special diet or medication. If a special diet is prescribed, he or she may use the diet prescribed by the doctor as a way to legitimate restricted eating behavior to family members (Noordenbos, 1998).

Of course, when people go to the doctor and describe secondary problems (from the primary problem of the eating disorder), the doctor needs to ask more questions about eating problems in general. A short tool that can be used to quickly assess for eating problems (the SCOFF; Morgan, Reid, & Lacey, 1999) includes questions such as Do you make yourself sick because you feel uncomfortably full? and Do you believe yourself to be fat when others say you are too thin? Questions such as these can help physicians to identify patients who have eating problems so that appropriate referral to an expert can be made.

Patients do not usually present with the chief complaint of an eating disorder (Walsh, Wheat, & Freund, 2000). Some patients with eating disorders want their doctors to ask more questions about eating issues. Noordenbos (1998) tells of a patient who didn't tell the family physician about her eating disorder, but went to the doctor to find out whether her health was in danger. It is not clear if this patient met the criteria for anorexia or bulimia, but she was quite thin and she wondered if the doctor would notice her thinness. But instead of asking direct questions, she told him that she was concerned about having a tumor in her breast. She figured that when he asked about how thin she was, he would ask about her eating. If he did not notice, she would be assured that she was not too thin. And, in this case, the physician did not ask about how thin she was, and the client assumed that she was not too thin and continued to diet.

Doctor delay is the failure of physicians or dentists to make the diagnosis of an eating disorder in an early stage (Noordenbos, 1998). Many physicians and dentists do not know the early signs of eating disorder, but this knowledge is essential in identifying eating disorders and making the appropriate referral to an eating disorders specialist. In the era of managed care, a person with an eating disorder may need to see a primary care doctor first to be referred to a person who can treat the eating disorder (Walsh, Wheat, & Freund, 2000).

Research suggests that dentists and hygienists do not routinely assess dental patients for eating disorders. For example, a survey of fifteen dental practices, including both dentists and dental hygienists in North Carolina and Georgia, indicated that they are aware of some of the health problems associated with eating disorders, but more than 20 percent of the dentists and hygienists did not know that eating disorders are related to the development of periodontal (gum) disease (DiGioacchino, Keenan, & Sargent, 2000). All dentists and hygienists knew that eating disorders can cause erosion of the enamel of the teeth, and almost all knew that dental caries (cavities) can be caused by eating disorders; however, there was some very specific dental information that the majority of the group did not know (i.e., the location of the greatest damage caused by vomiting). Overall, the authors reported that there were gaps in the knowledge of these dental professionals. Further, while 72 percent of dentists and 68 percent of hygienists suspected that their patients might have a kind of disordered eating, only 44 percent of dentists and 21 percent of hygienists referred the patient for treatment.

Physicians may miss the early signs, especially when patients do not meet all the criteria for anorexia or bulimia. It may be especially likely in the case of males for both anorexia and bulimia (Andersen, Cohn, & Holbrook, 2000). Many health care professionals are not well informed about eating disorders in males, and clinicians who have less experience with males who have eating disorders are likely to miss the symptoms (Andersen, 1999). It may be easier to identify anorexia by observing weight loss, amenorrhea, cold hands, and a great deal of obsessiveness about weight and shape. Those with bulimia may be more difficult to identify because they are of normal weight (although they may have weight fluctuations). Some of the signs and symptoms of eating disorders appear in chapter 1 of this book. These signs and symptoms can be helpful in identifying a person who may have an eating problem or eating disorder.

Difficulties in Doctor-Patient Communication

Shortcomings in the doctor-patient relationship may also contribute to difficulties in identifying those who have an eating disorder and referring to an appropriate treatment (Noordenbos, 1998). Doctors may have negative attitudes about patients with eating disorders. "Anorexics often evoke frustration and outrage in doctors who regard them as imposters because they do not have a 'genuine illness' deliberately harm themselves, and refuse to co-operate in treatment, just like self-poisoners and addicts do" (Vandereycken, 1993, p. 13). More recently, Kaplan and Garfinkel (1999) indicated that people with anorexia or bulimia evoke feelings of anger, hostility, stress, and a sense of hopelessness in their therapists and other people who provide care. A battle over control between the patient and doctor may occur since the patient may continue to try to lose weight while the doctor may feel a sense of challenge to authority; this dynamic may create a less than ideal working relationship.

Gender differences between patients and doctors can also cause difficulty in the interaction. When the doctor is male, female patients may have difficulty revealing their eating behavior. Likewise, male patients may be reluctant to tell their doctors that they have an eating disorder since eating disorders are "a girl's disease" (Noordenbos, 1998).

When a physician correctly identifies a person with an eating disorder, it is most appropriate for the physician to refer the patient to a person who specializes in the treatment of eating disorders. A main goal for the general practitioner might be to help the patients realize the seriousness of their disorder and to motivate them for treatment. As general practitioners become more familiar with eating disorders, they prescribe less medication and refer more often to a dietician, a psychologist, a psychiatrist, or an outpatient clinic for eating disorders.

MORTALITY

Mortality associated with anorexia has been reported to be between 4 and 13 percent (Neumarker, 2000). This means that as many as 1 in 6 people who develop anorexia may die from it. This is the highest mortality rate of any psychiatric disorder (Agras, 2001). Although treatment has improved in the last decade, more people die from anorexia than bulimia or any other eating problem. The two most common causes of death are starvation and suicide (Neumarker, 2000). Starvation, which leads to collapse of the metabolic (physical and chemical processes by which food is transformed into energy and tissues are broken down into waste products) and cardiovascular (includes the heart, arteries, and veins) systems, along with nutritional complications, such as electrolyte imbalance and dehydration, often explains death in those with anorexia. Sometimes, patients with anorexia commit suicide. Other possible causes of death include potassium deficiency, stroke, pulmonary edema, chronic inflammation of various parts of the body (e.g., myocarditis, which is inflammation of the heart) and accidents (Neumarker, 2000). For about 20 percent of the deaths, no cause is identified (Neumarker, 2000).

Bulimia nervosa is also a serious disorder, although it is has a much lower mortality rate than anorexia. There have been fewer studies to document the mortality rate associated with bulimia (Agras, 2001). Keel and Mitchell (1997) report a rate of .3 percent in a study of people with bulimia (7 of 2,194 subjects). The risk of mortality is also increased in people with binge eating disorder, since it is associated with obesity that has health consequences (Agras, 2001).

In one study that followed 246 women with eating disorders for eleven years, 5 percent of those diagnosed with anorexia died (Herzog, Greenwood, Dorer, Flores, Ekeblad, Richards, Blais, & Keller, 2000). Among the seven individuals who died from the disorder, they struggled with anorexia for an average of twenty years. Detailed analysis of the behaviors of those who died indicates that three committed suicide. The remaining four died from alcohol intoxication, cardio-respiratory failure, hepatic failure, and cirrhosis, pneumonia, cardiac arrhythmia and seizure disorder. The authors indicated that fatal outcome is associated with a longer duration of anorexia, binge eating and purging, use of alcohol and drugs, and affective disorders (such as depression).

HEALTH ISSUES

The physical consequences of eating disorders affect the entire body. Starting from the mouth and working through the body, we will see the impact of eating disorders on the body and some of the systems within it. Most of the information that follows comes from a special issue of *The European Eating Disorders Review* called "Physical Complications of Eating Disorders: A Clinical Review." Published in March 2000, this journal reviews the most current research available on physical issues associated with eating disorders. Other resources for medical information include Mitchell, Pomeroy, and Adson (1997), as well as a number of Internet resources. Although some technical language is used in this chapter, definitions have been provided to facilitate an understanding of some complex information.

Medical issues include

- Electrolyte disturbances (electrolytes are chemical substances that can transmit electrical impulses when dissolved in fluids. Sodium, potassium, magnesium, and chloride are electrolytes. Disturbance of these chemicals in the human body can lead to severe physical complications)

- Cardiac irregularities with arrhythmias (cardiac refers to the heart and arrhythmias are abnormal rates or rhythms of the heartbeat)

- Kidney dysfunction (the kidneys are a pair of organs located in the right and left side of the abdomen which clear "poisons" from the blood, control the level of some chemicals in the blood such as hydrogen, sodium, potassium, and phosphate, regulate acid concentration and maintain water balance in the body by excreting urine)

- Cerebral atrophy (cerebral refers to the major hemispherical components of the brain, which serve higher mental functions. Atrophy is the wasting of tissue or an organ)

- Neurological abnormalities (refers to problems in the central nervous system. The nervous system is the body tissue that records and distributes information in the body using electrical and chemical transmission. It has two parts. The "central" nervous system is comprised of the brain and spinal cord. The "peripheral" nervous system is the nerve tissue that transmits sensation and motor information back and forth from the body to the central nervous system)

- Gastrointestinal (GI) disturbances (The GI tract is the part of the body responsible for making energy and nutrients available for use in the body. The gastrointestinal tract consists of mouth, esophagus, stomach, duodenum, small and large intestines, rectum, and anus. Hunger and satiety are controlled, in part, in the GI tract)

- Dental deterioration (refers to the breakdown of the enamel of the teeth)

- Edema (swelling of body tissues due to excessive fluid)

- Dehydration (a lack of an adequate amount of fluid in the body; may be accompanied by dry mouth, thirst, constipation, concentrated urine, or fever. Dehydration occurs when a person's body water content has decreased to a dangerously low level. Water accounts for 60 percent of a man's weight and 50 percent of a woman's weight)

- Menstrual and reproductive functioning (In women, this refers to the organs that are directly involved in producing eggs and in conceiving and carrying babies. Infertility is an issue that affects women with eating disorders.)

- Abnormalities in the skeletal system (composed of bones and is the framework of the body)

ORAL COMPLICATIONS

Beginning at the mouth, an oral complication present in individuals who vomit is erosion of the enamel of the teeth (called perimylolsis). This is caused when the teeth are exposed to acid of the stomach during vomiting. When vomiting occurs on a regular basis, the teeth begin to show damage. A dentist may notice some of this damage after vomiting has occurred for less than six months. However, many of the signs of tooth damage that are noticeable to the person who has an eating disorder may only be noticeable when the tooth erosion has become severe. Serious dental erosion occurs in patients who vomit three times a week or more for four years (Newton & Travess, 2000). As the enamel erodes, individuals may complain about sensitivity to hot or cold foods, notice discoloration in teeth, or feel changes in fillings in teeth. Teeth may turn brown or gray, cavities may form and periodontal disease may develop. Although tooth erosion does not happen with the first vomit, the long-standing difficulty with stopping the binge-purge may mean that many individuals who vomit have significant dental problems. Other oral trauma may result when individuals cut their mouths or throats with objects intended to induce vomiting.

Swollen salivary glands can occur in individuals who vomit repeatedly. Swollen glands often signal that a person may have an eating disorder, but not all people who have an eating disorder will have swollen glands. In addition, swollen glands may be caused by infections and appear in people who do not have any eating problem. The swelling is painless and not a medical problem, though it may be upsetting to individuals with eating disorders who are already sensitive to their body appearance. The swelling usually disappears when vomiting is stopped.

THE GASTROINTESTINAL TRACT

Individuals with eating disorders may do a great deal of damage to the GI tract over the course of many years, thus this system is the site of many serious and chronic medical complications of eating disorders (Robinson, 2000). Many patients with eating disorders complain about abdominal pain, which may be caused by the repeated damage done to the gastrointestinal system. Some of the problems could have serious consequences; for example, a tear in the esophagus or gastric walls may require immediate surgery.

Vomiting is the cause of a great deal of damage to the GI tract. Sometimes, people who vomit often develop a "spontaneous regurgitation" of food. This may be due to the loss of the gag reflex. When it becomes easier to vomit, or people vomit even when they do not intend to, this can add to the difficulty in recovering from an eating disorder. The acidic gastric juices may damage the esophagus and pharynx, neither of which is protected from these acidic substances. This may result in sore throats or heartburn. An uncommon occurrence of vomiting is aspiration (during vomiting some of the substance from the stomach enters the lungs). Aspiration can result in a lung infection, pneumonia, or death.

Individuals with eating disorders also frequently use laxatives as a way to control weight. As indicated in the chapter on psycho-education, this is not an effective strategy since the majority of calories are removed before laxatives can have an effect. When someone uses large doses of laxatives, the effects are constipation or diarrhea, abdominal cramping or pain, nausea and vomiting, and bloating. Dependence on laxatives can happen when people have become adjusted to using them for long periods of time. This can cause serious damage to the GI system. Laxative abuse may lead to difficulty passing bowels without the use of laxatives. This is called cathatic colon and is serious because the colon may be damaged so severely that it ceases to function normally. In this event, the patient may experience constant constipation, requiring surgery and removal of the colon. Since abrupt cessation of laxatives may have unpleasant effects on the body, some physicians recommend tapering the use of laxatives slowly (Robinson, 2000).

CARDIOVASCULAR EFFECTS

The cardiovascular effects of eating disorders are profound and important. Although some of the cardiac complications may not be life threatening, others are extremely lethal. Some complications associated with heart functioning include bradycardia (very slow heart rate of less than 60 beats per minute), tachycardia (rapid heartbeat), and hypotension (low blood pressure). Others, such as ventricular arrhythmias (irregular rhythm in the ventricular chambers of the heart) and cardiac failure, are quite serious. Starvation and electrolyte disturbances lead to these heart problems. Winston and Stafford (2000) reviewed the data available on heart irregularities in people with eating disorders. One researcher found that 31 percent of patients hospitalized with bulimia and 40 percent of those with anorexia had significant cardiac disease (Hall, Hoffman, Beresford, Wooley, Hall, & Kubasak, 1989).

When a person dies as a result of an eating disorder, it is often due to cardiac problems (Winston & Stafford, 2000). Cardiovascular collapse may be the major cause of sudden death in people with anorexia. While the technical nature of heart rhythms is not discussed here, an example of a cardiac problem that is associated with anorexia is called "prolongation of the QT interval." With this heart rhythm, the impulses controlling the heart to contract and relax do not operate and the person dies within several minutes. When the QT interval is prolonged, ventricular arrhythmias may develop, and these arrhythmias are associated with sudden death. Another serious cardiac problem may be caused by the abuse of ipecac, which may be used to induce vomiting. Ipecac accumulates in the body and may lead to cardiac arrest.

Cardiac issues may be caused by electrolyte imbalances, which result from decreased liquid and potassium lost because of vomiting, laxative abuse or diuretic abuse (Winston & Stafford, 2000). Electrolytes are elements in the body that carry electrical charges and are essential for normal functioning of nerves and muscle cells. When individuals vomit, they lose potassium (hypokalemic alkalosis), chloride (hypochloremic alkalosis), and sodium (hypoatremic alkalosis). The loss of these electrolytes leads to an imbalance in electrolytes available in the body. Hypokalemia (loss of potassium) is the most urgent metabolic complication. These electrolyte imbalances cause tiredness, weakness, constipation, and depression. The more serious consequence of electrolyte imbalances is cardiac arrhythmias (irregular heartbeats) which can lead to sudden death. Electrolyte disturbances are prevalent in people with eating disorders (Winston & Stafford, 2000).

NEUROLOGICAL ISSUES

Malnutrition, electrolyte imbalances, and vitamin deficiencies are linked to neurological abnormalities. Neurology refers to brain structure and function, both of which may be influenced by the effects of eating disorders. Brain scans of patients with anorexia and bulimia show deterioration of brain tissue. With renourishment, some of these brain effects are reversible. For example, adolescent patients with anorexia show a reduction in gray and white matter in the brain. After weight regain, the white matter returned to normal levels, but the gray matter did not (Chowdhury & Lask, 2000). Along with brain deterioration, electrolyte disturbances may cause seizures, which were found to occur in individuals with bulimia nervosa.

OSTEOPOROSIS AND OSTEOPENIA

Osteoporosis refers to reduced skeletal bone mineral density. This loss of bone mass makes individuals susceptible to fractures and breaks in the spine and hips. Osteopenia is low bone mass but is not as severe as in osteoporosis. Research indicates that up to 45 percent of people with anorexia have low bone mineral density (Zipfel, Herzog, Beumont, & Russell, 2000). These individuals have a higher than expected risk (based on age) of fracturing the vertebrae in the back, wrist, hip, humerus (upper arm bone, connecting the shoulder to the elbow), and tibia (the shin bone, connecting the knee to the ankle). The research on low bone mineral density in bulimia is not clear; some studies report problems similar to those found among individuals with anorexia, while others do not find this to be the case (Zipfel et al., 2000). Although we usually think of osteoporosis as a disease of older women, it is a treatment issue of importance in anorexia.

Symptoms of osteoporosis and osteopenia include pain in the back, which may be caused by the deterioration of the lower vertebrae. Patients may report deep pain when they move suddenly. Osteoporosis and osteopenia may be caused, in part by the failure to reach a peak bone mass in development when the eating disorder begins at an early age. Low levels of estrogen are related to the development of reduced density in bones.

Other risk factors associated with osteoporosis and osteopenia include a family history, low body weight, low calcium intake, smoking, alcoholism, and lack of or excessive exercise (Zipfel et al., 2000). Males with anorexia show comparable levels of osteopenia (Andersen, 1990) probably due to low weight and changes in the hormone levels. Individuals with long-term anorexia who are at very low weight may benefit from hormone replacement therapy (Zipfel et al., 2000).

REPRODUCTIVE SYSTEM DIFFICULTIES

The reproductive system is influenced in people who have eating disorders because of low body weight (Key, Mason, & Bolton, 2000). Amenorrhea (loss of regular menstrual periods) is part of the diagnosis of anorexia in females. Pregnancy in women with eating disorders may be complicated and result in low birth weight infants. Miscarriage is twice as common in patients with anorexia than in those with no eating disorder. Additionally, women with anorexia have more cesarean deliveries, premature babies, and low birth weight babies than women without an eating disorder. Women with bulimia also have a much higher than normal rate of miscarriage (Key et al., 2000).

In the opinion of Key et al. (2000), women with eating disorders should be told about the complications that can arise in pregnancy and should be encouraged to delay having children until recovery is complete. In *Full Lives*, Reiff (1993) wrote about this issue, saying, "I think that it would have been very difficult for me to have been pregnant while I had my eating disorder. I know that I would not have been able to stop my behaviors completely, despite my best intentions. The ensuing guilt, fear, and anxiety about what effects, if any, my actions would have had on the growing child within me would have overshadowed, if not eclipsed, the joy of pregnancy" (p. 209).

There are also reproductive issues in males with eating disorders (Andersen, 1990). Men with anorexia have lower levels of several hormones, including luteinizing hormone, follicle stimulating hormone, and testosterone, which may return to normal after weight regain. Perhaps due to the rare occurrence of anorexia in males, these physical changes in males have not been well studied.

DERMATOLOGICAL COMPLICATIONS

Changes in the skin may occur in individuals with eating disorders (Gupta & Gupta, 2000). Sometimes these changes are a sign that an eating disorder is present. One example of such a sign is excessive hair growth, called lanugo, which appears on the back, arms, legs, and face. The development of lanugo usually occurs at the time when weight is lost. Lanugo is associated with loss of menstruation, one of the major criteria for diagnosis of anorexia. Dry and itchy skin is associated with eating disorders. Acne may also occur due to changes in the endocrine system.

KIDNEY DYSFUNCTION

The kidneys are responsible for regulating water and electrolyte balance, and the excretion of waste from the body in the form of urine. Edema and dehydration may result from dieting, vomiting, laxative or diuretic abuse. Edema may occur initially when an individual stops vomiting and using laxatives or diuretics. Once the body readjusts without the use of laxatives or diuretics, the edema reduces and weight stabilizes. Tests of the functioning of the kidneys involve levels of urea and creatinine (Connan, Lightman, & Treasure, 2000). When levels of urea and creatinine are high, it is indicative of poor renal functioning and is associated with severe purging.

A MEDICAL ISSUE OF NOTE

Diabetes is an example of a disorder that has special implications for people with eating disorders (Peveler, 2000). The co-occurrence of diabetes and eating disorders is not uncommon; the case of a sixteen-year old girl with diabetes and anorexia is described in Levenkron's (2001) book. This patient was changing the amount of insulin that she was using so that she would lose weight. However, medically, this practice was causing her to damage her kidneys. In diabetes, it is important to maintain control of blood sugar levels. When someone who has diabetes binge eats, the person risks hyperglycemia (high blood sugar), which can be severe enough to cause serious health problems. On the other hand, the person who restricts food intake may develop hypoglycemia (low blood sugar) which is also a health hazard. Even some people who have diabetes and do not have an eating disorder manipulate their insulin levels as a method of weight control.

SUMMARY

It is important for those with eating disorders to see a physician who has the specialized skills necessary to assess the health problems associated with eating disorders. Physicians and health professionals should look for signs of eating disorders in their patients since patients may be reluctant to present their eating disorder as their primary concern. It is clear that the health of patients may be affected by eating disorders of various types. The physical complications are associated with vomiting, and laxative and diuretic abuse. Vomiting is responsible for dental erosion, pharyngeal/esophageal inflammation and esophageal and gastric tears. Chronic laxative use may lead to dependence on laxatives to stimulate colon functioning. Diuretic use is associated with dehydration that can lead to loss of kidney function. Vomiting, laxative abuse and diuretic abuse may cause metabolic complications, which can cause serious cardiac problems and death. The whole body and its subsystems are impacted by the purging techniques used. Malnutrition and starvation also cause serious medical problems, which can result in death. It is vitally important that the individual with an eating disorder receive proper medical attention.

REFERENCES

Agras, W. S. (2001). The consequences and costs of the eating disorders. *The Psychiatric Clinics of North America, 24* (2), 371–379.

Andersen, A. E. (1990). *Males with eating disorders.* New York: Brunner/Mazel.

Andersen, A. E. (1999). Eating disorders in gay males. *Psychiatric Annals, 29,* 206–212.

Andersen, A., Cohn, L., & Holbrook, T. (2000). *Making weight: Men's conflicts with food, weight, shape, and appearance.* Carlsbad, CA: Gurze Books.

Chowdhury, U., & Lask, B. (2000). Neurological correlates of eating disorders. *European Eating Disorders Review, 8* (2), 126–133.

Connan, F., Lightman, S., & Treasure, J. (2000). Biochemical and endocrine complications. *European Eating Disorders Review, 8* (2), 144–157.

DiGioacchino, R. F., Keenan, M. F., & Sargent, R. (2000). Assessment of dental practitioners in the secondary and tertiary prevention of eating disorders. *Eating Behaviors, 1* (1), 79–91.

Gupta, M. A., & Gupta, A. K. (2000). Dermatological complications. *European Eating Disorders Review, 8* (2), 134–143.

Gurney, V. W., & Halmi, K. A. (2001). Developing an eating disorder curriculum for primary care providers. *Eating Disorders: The Journal of Treatment and Prevention, 9* (2), 97–107.

Hall, R. C. W., Hoffman, R. S., Beresford, T. P., Wolley, B., Hall., A. K., & Kubasak, L. (1989). Physical illness encountered in patients with eating disorders. *Psychosomatics, 30,* 174–191.

Herzog, D. B., Greenwood, D. N., Dorer, D. J., Flores, A. T., Ekeblad, E. R., Richards, A., Blais, M. A., & Keller, M. B. (2000). Mortality in eating disorders: A descriptive study. *International Journal of Eating Disorders, 28* (1), 20–26.

Kano, S. (1993). Leap of faith. In L. Hall (Ed.), *Full lives: Women who have freed themselves from food and weight obsession* (pp. 110–127), Carlsbad, CA: Gurze Books.

Kaplan, A. S., & Garfinkel, P. E. (1999). Difficulties in treating patients with eating disorders: A review of patient and clinical variables. *Canadian Journal of Psychiatry, 44,* 665–670.

Keel, P. K., & Mitchell, J. E. (1997). Outcome in bulimia nervosa. *American Journal of Psychiatry, 154,* 313–321.

Key, A., Mason, H., & Bolton, J. (2000). Reproduction and eating disorders: A fruitless union. *European Eating Disorders Review, 8*(2), 98–107.

Levenkron, S. (2001). *Anatomy of anorexia.* New York: W. W. Norton.

Mitchell, J. E., Pomeroy, C., & Adson, D. E. (1997). Managing medical complications. In D. M. Garner & P. E. Garfinkel (Eds.), *Handbook of treatment for eating disorders* (2nd ed., pp. 383–393). New York: Guilford Press.

Morgan, J. F., Reid, F., & Lacey, J. H. (1999). The SCOFF questionnaire: Assessment of a new screening tool for eating disorders. *British Medical Journal, 319,* 1467–1468.

Neumarker, K. J. (2000). Mortality rates and causes of death. *European Eating Disorders Review, 8* (2), 181–187.

Newton, J. T., & Travess, H. C. (2000). Oral complications. *European Eating Disorders Review, 8* (2), 83–87.

Noordenbos, G. (1998). Eating disorders in primary care: Early identification and intervention by general practitioners. In W. Vandereycken & G. Noordenbos (Eds.), *The prevention of eating disorders* (pp. 214–229). New York: New York University Press.

Peveler, R. (2000). Eating disorders and insulin-dependent diabetes. *European Eating Disorders Review, 8* (2), 164–169.

Reiff, K. L. (1993). Perseverance overcomes. In L. Hall (Ed.), *Full loves: Women who have freed themselves from food and weight obsession* (pp. 197–214), Carlsbad, CA; Gurze Books.

Robinson, P. H. (2000). The gastrointestinal tract in eating disorders. *European Eating Disorders Review, 8* (2), 88–97.

Vandereycken, W. (1993). Naughty girls and angry doctors: Eating disorder patients and their therapists. *International Review of Psychiatry, 5,* 13–18.

Walsh, J. M. E., Wheat, M. E., & Freund, K. (2000). Detection, evaluation, and treatment of eating disorders. *Journal of General Internal Medicine, 15,* 577–590.

Winston, A. P., & Stafford, P. J. (2000). Cardiovascular effects of anorexia nervosa. *European Eating Disorders Review, 8* (2), 117–125.

Zipfel, S., Herzog, W., Beumont, P. J., & Russell, J. (2000). Osteoporosis. *European Eating Disorders Review, 8* (2), 108–116.

6

Psycho-Education—Information about Eating Disorders and Disturbances

Just as set-point theory predicted, the physical symptoms of being underweight went away over time. In less than a year, I stopped feeling insatiably hungry and I stopped craving large quantities of sweets. My body reachieved a balance and my appetite and weight became self-regulating again. For the first time in five years, I could eat a meal and feel truly satisfied with no desire to eat more.

(Kano, 1993, p. 117)

Psycho-education is designed to provide information to individuals or groups with the goal of changing attitudes and behaviors in those who are exposed to the material. It is not counseling or therapy, more like a classroom in which there is a teacher who talks about a topic and provides information that will keep the listeners healthy or alert them to the need to seek help from a trained expert. This type of information can be written in a book, taught in a classroom, or presented on a computer. In all of these cases, the reason for psycho-education is to provide information in a way that helps the person learn more about eating disorders so that they may be less likely to develop these problems. In this sense, it is a kind of prevention program. Psycho-education can also be helpful for the family and friends of those who are struggling with an eating disorder.

Psycho-education may also be used as an adjunct to traditional counseling or psychotherapy for people with eating disorders. Psychoeducational programs are a part of many treatment programs; cognitive-behavioral programs include psycho-educational components as part of treatment (Stein, Saelens, Dounchis, Lewczyk, Swenson, & Wilfley, 2001). When used with people who have an eating disorder, psycho-education may be helpful to correct misconceptions about eating disorders. It is assumed that if people have an understanding of the scientific evidence for issues related to eating disorders (such as the effects of various methods of purging on the body), then they will be more motivated to make healthy changes.

The purpose of this chapter is to provide psycho-education on eating disorders. It provides important information that can be used to prevent a person from developing an eating problem, to assist someone who does have a problem (though professional help is required to recover from an eating disorder), and to teach about the issues related to eating problems and disorders. Research on the effectiveness of psycho-education and psycho-education as an adjunct to treatment is covered in chapter 9.

A beginning point for psycho-education about eating disorders might be the definition of eating disorders. It should be noted that the following studies of knowledge about eating disorders are all more than ten years old and there are no new studies on this topic available in the literature. None of the studies included binge eating disorder or other eating disorders not otherwise specified, which did not exist as diagnoses at the time. It is quite possible that different findings would emerge if the studies were conducted again. With the increase of media attention to eating disorders, it could be that many more people would have more complete knowledge about eating disorders. This is an area for research opportunities.

Some research tells us that people may not be accurate in their knowledge of what anorexia and bulimia really are. In three different studies, many people could not answer accurately questions about bulimia nervosa, even simple ones such as, "What is Bulimia?" (Huon, Brown, & Morris, 1988; Murray, Touyz, & Beumont, 1990; Smith, Pruitt, Mann, & Thelen, 1986). Authors of one study rated the definitions written by college students of anorexia nervosa and bulimia nervosa and found that only 44 percent of the students could accurately define bulimia nervosa, but 71 percent could define anorexia nervosa (Smith et al., 1986). This difference in knowledge between anorexia nervosa and bulimia nervosa may be the result of greater media attention to anorexia nervosa. It is somewhat ironic though, because bulimia nervosa is a more common eating problem.

In studies of high school, college students and adults, almost everyone had heard of anorexia nervosa (Huon et al., 1988; Murray et al., 1990; Smith et al., 1986). When asked to describe what they knew about anorexia nervosa and bulimia nervosa, people indicated that anorexia nervosa was associated with excessive dieting, refusal to eat, deliberately undereating, extreme thinness, and body image problems, such as "cannot see her body properly" and "thinks she's too fat when really she's thin." Bulimia nervosa was defined as overeating, or binge eating and vomiting. As we see in the chapter on bulimia nervosa, this information is only partially accurate, because a person can have bulimia nervosa and not vomit. Interestingly, when asked about what causes anorexia nervosa and bulimia nervosa, 38 percent of individuals indicated that anorexia nervosa could be caused by social pressure for slimness and 25 percent indicated that poor self-image may cause anorexia nervosa, while 51 percent did not know what caused bulimia nervosa (Huon et al., 1988). Of those who did try to list a cause, the most common answer was social pressure for thinness (21 percent). In another study, causes of bulimia nervosa included emotional problems, influence of friends or family, and pressure from males or females, physical problems, or influence of movies and TV (Smith et al., 1986). The causes of anorexia nervosa were thought to be similar to those of bulimia nervosa. These are not the actual causes of eating disorders, but are the perceptions of the participants in the studies.

One alarming finding is that individuals did not know that anorexia nervosa or bulimia nervosa have serious medical consequences (Huon et al., 1988; Murray et al., 1990; Smith et al., 1986). Because there are serious medical problems associated with eating disorders, they are an important topic for psycho-education (see chapter 5). Females knew a lot more about both anorexia nervosa and bulimia nervosa than did males (Huon et al., 1988; Murray et al., 1990; Smith et al., 1986). Males had less exposure to information about eating disorders in the books and magazines than did females. This makes sense because magazines for girls and women have much greater coverage of eating issues than do magazines for men (Andersen & DiDominico, 1992). Fewer males reported that they knew someone with an eating problem (Huon et al., 1988; Murray et al., 1990; Smith et al., 1986).

People with eating disorders, along with their family and friends, express a great deal of interest in learning about eating disorders. In a study of eighty-four patients treated for an eating disorder and their family and friends, an "Index of Interest" was calculated for each item on a list of topics that are typically found in psycho-educational materials on eating disorders. Some of these items include strategies for solving problems related to the eating disorder, early warning signs of the disorder and returning signs, how an eating disorder diagnosis is made, and psychiatric medication. The researchers were interested in finding out if people with anorexia nervosa, bulimia nervosa or their family members would express different interest in the psycho-educational items. The index of interest combined for all the items on this list of the patients and their family/friends was quite high, with the relative/friend group expressing slightly more interest than the patients. The researchers also wanted to know if there were differences between the interest levels of the patients with different types of eating disorders on these psycho-educational topics. In this study, only minor differences were found, with those patients with bulimia nervosa having slightly more interest in the symptoms of the eating disorders, how to set limits on behavior related to the eating disorder, and how common eating disorders are. It appears that there is not a need to develop different psycho-educational programs for patients with anorexia nervosa or bulimia nervosa (Surgenor, Rau, Snell, & Fear, 2000).

This information highlights the need for accurate information about anorexia nervosa, bulimia nervosa, and other eating problems (Garner, 1997). This chapter provides detailed information about eating disorders. This is the type of information that may be provided to clients as a part of their treatment for an eating disorder. Although there are many references to the use of psycho-educational materials as part of a prevention or treatment program, there are few manuals available. Garner's (1997) chapter provides the best information about the breadth of issues that should be included in a psycho-educational intervention. An older manual (Davis, Dearing, Faulkner, Jasper, Olmsted, Rice, & Rocket , 1989) includes much of the same information structured for a psycho-educational group. No newer manual of this type is available. Nine major topic areas are included here (Garner, 1997, p. 146):

- Multiple causes of eating disorders
- The cultural context for eating disorders
- Set-point theory and the physiological regulation of weight
- The effects of starvation on behavior
- Restoring regular eating patterns
- Vomiting, laxatives, and diuretics in controlling weight
- Determining a healthy body weight
- Physical complications
- Relapse prevention techniques

ISSUE 1, MULTIPLE CAUSES

Eating Disorders are multidetermined; cultural, individual, and family factors contribute to their development in different ways for different individuals.

(Garner, 1997, p. 146)

Eating disorders are complicated because they are multifactorial (meaning caused by many different factors); there is not a single answer about what causes someone to have an eating disorder (Striegel-Moore & Steiner-Adair, 1998). Risk factors are those that increase the likelihood that someone will develop an eating disorder. Some of these risk factors include the world in which we live (cultural), individual issues (such as gender, race or ethnicity, or socioeconomic status), and family influence. In addition, there are some specific risk factors (which mean that these factors are uniquely associated with the development of eating disorders) and general risk factors that are associated with the development of a variety of psychological problems. Risk factors may be critical in setting the stage for the development of eating problems and other psychological concerns (Striegel-Moore & Steiner-Adair, 1998).

Cultural factors include media influence and the general sociocultural climate that emphasizes thinness, especially for women. Television and magazines are examples of media that inundate people with messages about the importance of being thin. The media bombards us with thin and attractive actors and models. A link develops between thinness and attractiveness and success and power, intelligence, and an active social life. (See chapter 7 on sociocultural aspects of eating disorders for more information.)

Individual factors are those factors that are unique to an individual. Those at risk of developing an eating disorder are often described as "young white females from middle or upper class backgrounds" (Connors, 1996, p. 286). Taking each of these characteristics one at a time, young is important because almost all cases of eating disorders begin in adolescence. Eating disorders often extend into adulthood, but the starting point is most often during late adolescence or early adulthood for anorexia and bulimia nervosa (APA, 2000). White refers to the fact that the majority of cases of eating disorders occur in individuals who are white, rather than African American, Hispanic, or Asian. However, it is worth noting that this stereotype may be changing, as there is an increase in prevalence of eating disorder among these minority groups (Smolak & Striegel-Moore, 2001). Female is a very important descriptor, because over 90 percent of all cases of eating disorder are in females (APA, 2000; Smolak & Murnen, 2001). The issue of socioeconomic status (SES; in this case, middle or upper class) is included because the literature reports that as SES goes up, so does the prevalence of eating disorder (Drewnowski, Kurth, & Krahn, 1994). Again, this may be changing too, as more cases of eating disorders occur in people of all SES levels. Another individual factor is body weight. A higher body weight, especially associated with more weight in the hips and thighs, is a risk factor for developing an eating disorder (Connors, 1996). (These issues are discussed in greater detail in chapter 8.)

In a review of the literature on the factors that may predict the development of an eating disorder, Stice (2001) found that there is support for the relationship between sociocultural pressures, internalization of the thin body ideal and body dissatisfaction, and the development of eating disorders. However, he notes that despite assumptions to the contrary, there is limited research to support relationships between self-esteem, childhood sexual abuse, the role of control issues (in family dynamics), awareness of internal experiences and feelings of ineffectiveness, and development of eating disorders. The search for risk factors continues to receive a great deal of attention in the literature on the development of eating disorders.

Family factors may contribute to the risk factors for eating disorders. For example, daughters of mothers with histories of eating disorders may be at higher risk of eating disorders (Waugh & Bulik, 1999). A comparison of ten mothers with a history of an eating disorder and ten health control women indicated that children born to mothers with a history of eating disorders were smaller at birth. These mothers had more difficulty maintaining breast-feeding during the first year of life of the babies. Further, the early feeding patterns indicate differences between the two groups of mothers. Control group mothers made more positive comments while the child was eating and ate with their children more often than did the mother with a history of an eating disorder. (Other material about the role of early feeding and relationships to the development of eating disorders is discussed in chapter 8.)

There have also been some interesting studies of twins who have eating disorders; twin studies have been used to study the genetic and environmental influences of the development of psychological problems. After analysis of twin and family studies, Bulik, Sullivan, Wade, and Kendler (2000) concluded that bulimia nervosa is familial, which means that genetic components play a role in the development of this disorder. The data are not clear for anorexia because anorexia appears in low numbers, and there are not enough data to clearly indicate a clear role of genetics at this time. Bulik et al. (2000) points out that work in this area may identify susceptibility genes, which would enable us to understand why only a small percentage of people develop eating disorders when all are exposed to the same sociocultural climate. It seems likely that those who have little genetic risk may be able to engage in weight control behaviors without developing an eating disorder, while those with a greater genetic risk may find that they develop an eating disorder after the first attempt to control weight.

Risk factors may predispose an individual person to develop an eating problem. But not everyone with risk factors develops an eating disorder (Smolak & Levine, 1996). It may be that there needs to be a trigger, or special event that begins the eating disorder. A trigger could be something as seemingly innocent as teasing (Ghaderi, 2001) or more traumatic, such as rape or incest. Transitions (e.g., between high school and college) may be times that an eating disorder may develop, perhaps due to the new challenges imposed on people who already are unsure of their ability to meet expectations (Smolak & Levine, 1996). These transitions may include starting a new school, beginning a new job, death, divorce, marriage, family problems, or graduation from school. (Chapter 8 contains more information about these transitions and risk factors.)

In summary, we do not know the exact cause of eating disorders. These are complicated disorders caused by a variety of factors that can be different in each individual. Risk factors make a person vulnerable to developing an eating disorder, but not everyone who has risk factors develops an eating disorder. An interesting twist to this concerns protective factors, such as high self-esteem and peers who do not accept society's messages about thinness, which may keep someone from developing an eating disorder in spite of risk factors (Crago, Shisslak, & Ruble, 2001). Less research is available on these protective factors, but this is a promising research opportunity for the future.

ISSUE 2, CULTURAL CONTEXT FOR EATING DISORDERS

> For several decades, the fashion, entertainment, and publishing industries have bombarded women with role models for physical attractiveness who are so gaunt as to represent virtually no woman in the actual population; this has resulted in restrictive dieting and increased vulnerability to eating disorders.
> (Garner, 1997, p. 146. Reprinted with permission of Guilford Press.)

Eating disorders are based on an intense feeling of concern about fatness, body shape and desire to be thin. This is part of the diagnosis of anorexia nervosa, bulimia nervosa and eating disorders not otherwise specified. Women, and increasingly men, are faced with tremendous pressure at a societal level to have a certain kind of body. The body of a woman is supposed to be thin and fit, while men's bodies are supposed to be muscular. This is linked to pressure from the media that tells women and men to diet and exercise if they want to be attractive. As pressure to diet increases, eating problems also increase.

Models who appear on television and magazines are very thin. Many of these models meet the weight criteria for anorexia nervosa. Because it is difficult (or impossible) for most women to look like these models, these images set a goal that is not achievable for almost everyone. However, many people try. A media advocacy group called About-Face (www. about-face.org) has focused attention on the very thin models and high-lights how these images are harmful to women and girls. About-Face shows how the media makes a "harmful impact, through negative or distorted images, on the physical, mental, and emotional well-being of women" (Sanders, 2001, p. 59).

Playboy centerfolds were studied up until 1987 in a study that continues to be cited as a way to document the shape of female models (Garner, Garfinkel, Schwartz, & Thompson, 1980). Almost 75 percent of the models were 15 percent or more below their expected weight based on height; thus they met the weight criteria for anorexia. The authors indicated that while models continued to get thinner, the average American woman was getting heavier, creating a larger disparity between the real weights of women and models. Other research of this kind is presented in chapter 7.

The cultural expectations for males to have a muscular build, as studied through analysis of the centerfolds in *Playgirl* magazine, have been documented by Leit, Pope, and Gay (2000). Following the procedures used by Garner, Garfinkel, Schwartz, and Thompson (1980) on *Playboy* center-folds, Leit et al. used the height and weight as published in the magazine along with a rater's estimates of body fat to look at how the male bodies changed from 1973 through 1997. They found that male bodies became more muscular; the most muscular models (who likely attained their body shape through the use of steroids) were from the most recent years.

One of the keys to overcoming an eating disorder is to avoid strict dieting. It is difficult to combat the societal norms, and acceptance of those norms is clearly a problem. Recovery requires giving up the idea that people will look like the ideal female or male fashion model because so few people do. For more information on this see chapter 7, which addresses the sociocultural influence on eating and body image issues.

ISSUE 3, SET-POINT THEORY

Generally speaking, body weight resists change. Weight appears to be phys-iologically regulated around a "set-point," or a weight that one's body tries to "defend." Significant deviations from this weight result in a myriad of physiological compensations aimed at returning the organism to this set-point.

> (Garner, 1997, p. 149. Reprinted with permission of Guilford Press.)

This information about weight set-point is important because it indicates that for most people there is a predetermined weight range. Set-point is the idea that individuals have a preset weight range determined by genetics that the body will reach and maintain; Keesey wrote about this theory in 1986, and research in the 1980s and 1990s supported the notion of set-point. According to this theory and the data that support it, a person's body will defend any changes in eating or exercising to maintain this weight. Much of the research on set-point comes from animal studies, in which rats were put on a diet and then refed to see what their weight would be. Studies involving people also demonstrated that when people increased their food intake in a study of weight gain, they did gain weight, but they lost the weight when they returned to normal eating. This research collectively demonstrates that there is a kind of weight range that seems to be predetermined.

Set-point theory can be explained by thinking about how the air temperature is controlled by a thermostat. The set-point is the number set on the thermostat. When the house gets too cold, the thermostat tells the heat to go on. When the house gets too hot, the thermostat tells the air conditioning to go on. Data suggest that our bodies work the same way; our weight is ranged around a set-point and when we try to lose weight, our body slows down metabolism so that it can maintain the set weight range. Likewise, if we eat more than usual, our body defends against gaining weight.

ISSUE 4, STARVATION

> One of the most important advancements in the understanding of eating disorders is the recognition that severe and prolonged dietary restriction can lead to serious physical and psychological complications. Many of the symptoms once thought to be primary features of anorexia nervosa are actually symptoms of starvation.
>
> (Garner, 1997, p. 153. Reprinted with permission of Guilford Press.)

This is a fascinating issue. It is extremely interesting to learn that starvation itself will lead to symptoms like those of anorexia nervosa. This is particularly important for understanding anorexia nervosa, but it also has implications for anyone who is dieting or restricting food intake. A landmark study conducted in the 1940s is the basis for this material (Keys,

Brozek, Henschel, Mickelsen, & Taylor, 1950). This study was not conducted to understand eating disorders per se, but the results are important for the role of starvation in eating disorders. In this research, thirty-six young, healthy, psychologically normal men were studied while their calorie level was severely restricted and they were observed for changes in their attitudes and behaviors related to food and eating. The study concerns the reactions of these men and provides data that indicate that starvation is associated with many symptoms of anorexia nervosa. (This kind of research would no longer be possible to implement because it would not be approved by Human Subjects Review Boards.) Thus, anorexia nervosa is a disease of starvation. This highlights the importance of regaining weight as a necessary part of treatment, to reduce the symptoms of starvation.

In the baseline first phase of the study, the men ate normally and were monitored to study their behavior, personality, and eating patterns. There was no plan during this phase to change the men, rather to collect data before any change was made. After three months of normal eating, the calorie restriction phase began. Over the next six months, the men were restricted to half of their normal food intake. As a result, the men lost about 25 percent of their former weight. For example, a man who weighed 160 pounds at the start of the project might have lost 40 pounds during this phase and weighed 120 pounds. This level of food intake was designed to be semistarvation. (Interestingly, this caloric level is comparable to many weight loss programs undertaken by individuals to lose weight.) After the six months of weight loss, there were three months of rehabilitation during which the men were gradually refed their normal food intake. Some men were followed for a longer period of time to assess the long-term changes.

One of the things that changed as the men were in the semistarvation phase is that the men began to focus on food and become preoccupied with it. They reported that they thought about food all of the time, and there was an increase in the amount of time that the men talked about food. Some men became interested in cookbooks and menus. They reported that they had dreams about food and enjoyed watching others eat, and some men began to smuggle food from the common eating area and ate this food in a ritualized way in their rooms. Men began to collect food-related appliances (hot plates and kitchen utensils). They even hoarded nonfood items, something that some people with anorexia nervosa also do. After the study was over, three men became chefs.

Food became a major topic of each man's attention. They planned when they would eat and worked out ways to prolong eating. The men were unusually quiet in the common eating room, and devoted their attention to eating. Some men would dawdle over a meal for two hours; this same meal during the baseline they would have eaten in a few minutes. The men made unusual concoctions by mixing foods together. They increased use of salt and spices. They also increased consumption of coffee and teas so much that the experimenters set a limit of nine cups a day. This is a very large amount of caffeine, which may be associated with a variety of symptoms, including anxiety, restlessness, nausea, headaches, and difficulty sleeping (see Fahy & Treasure, 1991, which focused on caffeine use by those with bulimia nervosa. Patients also reported that they felt anxious, restless, nauseated, and had headaches and difficulties sleeping.). Some of the men began to chew gum; some up to forty packs a day, which lead to sore muscles in the mouth and jaw. These abnormal behaviors and attitudes continued when the men were allowed free access to food again.

During the semistarvation phase, there were several reports of men finding opportunities to steal food and binge eat. One man ate cookies, popcorn, and bananas, and then vomited, saying that he was disgusted by his behavior. During the refeeding phase, many men ate continuously and reported feeling continuously hungry. This overeating was extremely common. Men ate between 8,000 and 10,000 calories per day. Some continued to binge eat for months after the study was over. The majority of men regained normal eating patterns about five months after the refeeding phase began.

In the social and sexual areas, the men became withdrawn and isolated. Their use of humor decreased. Their friendship patterns changed. When they had the opportunity to interact with women, many chose not to. They reported a large decrease in sexual activities. These social and sexual changes were slow to return to normal. At three months after refeeding, the men continued to show lessened interest in social and sexual activities. These patterns returned to normal by eight months after the study ended.

The physical consequences of the semistarvation phase includes gastrointestinal discomfort, decreased need for sleep, dizziness, headaches, hypersensitivity to noise and light, reduced strength, poor motor control, edema (an excess of fluid causing swelling), hair loss, decreased tolerance for cold temperatures (cold hands and feet), visual disturbances (i.e., inability to focus, eye aches, "spots" in visual fields), auditory disturbances (i.e., ringing noise in the ears), and parathesias (i.e., abnormal tingling or prickling sensations, especially in the hands or feet) (Garner, 1997, p. 159). Thus, it is clear that starvation may cause all kinds of physical problems.

In the areas of emotions and personality, it is important to remember that these men were selected for this study if they were psychologically healthy. No one had any psychological issues or problems prior to this study. However, as the semistarvation part of the study progressed, many developed significant emotional problems (depression, irritability, and anxiety). Two men had to be excluded from continuing in the study and were released to a psychiatric ward of a hospital after they were caught stealing small items from a store. During refeeding, these symptoms lessened but very slowly. Some had an increase in depression at the beginning of the refeeding, which slowly reduced.

This starvation study is very important because it shows that many of the symptoms of anorexia nervosa and bulimia nervosa may really be the result of starvation. The changes in the men were profound, and some of them lasted quite a while after the starvation was over. This means that when someone is restricting their food intake, weight loss and other behaviors may be due to starvation effects. The implications for treatment of eating disorders lies in the need to return food intake and weight to normal so that people with eating disorders can participate fully in counseling to recover from their eating disorder.

ISSUE 5, RESTORING REGULAR EATING PATTERNS

> Restoring regular eating involves meal planning and the following components: (1) mechanical eating, (2) spacing meals, (3) specifying the quantity of foodstuffs, and (4) specifying the quality of foodstuffs.
> (Garner, 1997, p. 161. Reprinted with permission of Guilford Press.)

For recovery, attention to planning meals is key. Individuals need to plan the structure and content of meals, including the time and place and the quantity of food as determined. This allows individuals to reduce some of their own rigid rules about food, and it assures them that they will not go too far in over- or undereating (neither of which facilitates recovery). Mechanical eating means that people eat at specified times and according to a predetermined plan. At this phase of recovery, food may be thought of as medication that needs to be taken regularly to inoculate the person against food cravings and binge eating. Taking the decision-making factor away is especially important early in treatment when people with eating disorders are likely to be anxious and concerned about eating. These new rules about eating should be used until eating is under the control of natural internal signals to eat when hungry and stop when full. The structured rules can be removed when the person demonstrates that they can eat without the associated anxiety.

Mechanical eating requires three meals a day and two snacks. It does not allow patients to save calories for later in the day or to avoid eating. Growing hunger during the day is a risk for binge eating later in the day. Mechanical eating will help to lessen food cravings and reduce urges to overeat or undereat. They assist in maintaining control. People recovering from an eating disorder cannot rely on internal sensations as guides until healthy eating patterns are established and under control.

What people eat when recovering is also important. Because people with eating disorders divide food into categories of good and bad, it is necessary to reeducate them about the nutritional value of food. In the end, it is best if individuals can become relaxed about eating a wide range of foods. Weekly meal plans can be negotiated, which include small amounts of food previously considered forbidden. Foods that patients enjoyed before the onset of the eating disorder are a good choice. Binge foods eaten in small quantities can be thought of an inoculant against future binges on that food. This reduces psychological cravings. Sometimes, it may be helpful to develop a hierarchy of feared foods and move slowly through it. Feared foods should be incorporated into meals.

Garner (1997) advises that those who have selected a vegetarian diet should be encouraged to give up this preference during recovery. This recommendation is consistent with some research that was recently published. This new research compared vegetarians to nonvegetarians on tests of eating attitudes and behaviors associated with eating disorders (Lindeman, Stark, & Latvala, 2000). Vegetarians had higher scores on measures of behaviors and attitudes related to bulimia nervosa, body dissatisfaction, and drive for thinness. Vegetarians also had higher scores on measures associated with some of the psychological aspects of eating disorders, such as ineffectiveness, interpersonal distrust, and maturity fears. These psychological variables are associated with the psychopathology of anorexia nervosa. Twenty percent of the vegetarians scored above a cutoff score used to identify those who may have serious eating disorders. The authors of the study suggest that vegetarianism and eating disorders may be intertwined food issues and that some people with eating disorders may turn to vegetarian eating as part of their disorder. It seems possible that some people with eating disorders are hiding their eating problems behind a socially acceptable vegetarian eating preference. Other research has also documented a relationship between vegetarian eating styles and eating disordered behaviors such as frequent dieting, binge eating, self-induced vomiting, and laxative abuse (Neumark-Sztainer, Story, Resnick, &

Blum, 1997). It should not be assumed that just because a person chooses to be a vegetarian that he or she has an eating disorder. Of course, many people select a vegetarian eating style for religious reasons or due to animal rights beliefs. These individuals would probably not show elevated scores on measures of eating problems.

Self-monitoring is a useful adjunct to establishing a routine and is helpful in gaining control over eating. Self-monitoring consists of writing down all food eaten and the circumstances surrounding it. For example, the type of food eaten is listed along with noting if binge eating or vomiting occurred and the thoughts and feelings associated with eating. This is an excellent way to gain control of the eating disorder symptoms. A patient's reluctance to self-monitor should be discussed in treatment because it may be indicative of low motivation to change and may put the patient at risk for worsening of symptoms. In addition, the client and therapist should review the importance of providing accurate information on these food records. When clients do not report binges or purges, the therapist is missing information that is necessary to develop effective treatment plans.

ISSUE 6, VOMITING, LAXATIVES, AND DIURETICS IN CONTROLLING WEIGHT

> Vomiting is not entirely effective in removing food from the stomach and it usually makes binge eating worse by perpetuating food cravings. Laxatives and diuretics are ineffective methods of weight control because they do not cause malabsorption; they just cause temporary water loss. All of these symptoms have serious health consequences.
> (Garner, 1997, p. 163. Reprinted with permission of Guilford Press.)

Most people with eating disorders begin to vomit or use laxatives and diuretics because these measures are assumed to be solutions to weight control associated with binges. Once someone begins to use vomiting or these other ways to counteract binges, it is likely that they will increase the number of times they binge, and, subsequently, their use of vomiting, laxatives, and diuretics will increase. Once vomiting establishes itself as a habit, it serves as a kind of permission to binge, and the cycle of binge eating and vomiting continues and worsens. This cycle is a dangerous one, because increases in the number of episodes of vomiting and the increased use of laxatives and diuretics can have serious health consequences, which were described in chapter 5.

The Web site for Anorexia nervosa and Related Eating Disorders, Inc. (ANRED) contains the following information about the problems associated with continuing to use laxatives and enemas. (http://www.anred.com/lax.html). This kind of information is helpful to explain the effects of laxative and enemas and may prevent people from starting to use these unhealthful strategies. In addition, information about what laxatives and enemas do to the body may assist someone to stop using them.

- You can upset your electrolyte balance. Electrolytes are minerals like sodium and potassium that are dissolved in the blood and other body fluids. They must be present in very specific amounts for proper functioning of nerves and muscles, including the heart muscle.
- Laxatives and enemas (and also vomiting) remove needed fluid from the body. The resulting dehydration can lead to tremors, weakness, blurry vision, fainting spells, kidney damage, and, in some cases, death. Severe dehydration requires medical treatment. Drinking fluids may not hydrate cells and tissues quickly enough to prevent organ damage or death.
- Laxatives irritate intestinal nerve endings, which in turn stimulate muscle contractions that move the irritant through the gut and out of the body. After a while the nerve endings no longer respond to stimulation. The person must now take greater and greater amounts of laxatives to produce bowel movements. S/he has become laxative dependent and without them may not have any bowel movements at all.
- Laxative abusers seem to have more trouble with the following problems than do nonusers: irritable bowel syndrome (rectal pain, gas, and episodes of constipation and diarrhea) and bowel tumors (both benign and cancerous).

ISSUE 7, HEALTHY WEIGHT

Weight tables should not be used to determine the desirable weight of an individual; "healthy body weights" naturally vary in the population and must be determined on the basis of each person's weight history and likely genetic background.
(Garner, 1997, p. 165. Reprinted with permission of Guilford Press.)

Using weight charts to determine a goal weight is a common practice. Many people have seen the height and weight charts in magazines. Even physicians may have used weight charts to educate individuals about goal weight and to select a weight goal for a person. However, especially for individuals with an eating problem, weight charts should not be used in this fashion. (Actually, weight charts are not designed for this purpose and shouldn't be used to establish a weight goal for people without eating problems either.) Body weights for individuals vary based on a variety of issues, such as genetics and weight history. Selecting a goal weight from a weight table like this is as wrong as it would be to select a height from a height chart. Height varies between individuals; some are taller and some are shorter, and most people would never think about attempting to adjust height to be taller or shorter. Of course, the difference is that people have more control over their weight than their height, but perhaps we do not have as much control over our body weight as we might think.

The best way to determine a weight that is healthy for an individual is to have the person stop restrictive dieting and binge eating and participate in a regular moderate exercise program. Then the body will find its own natural weight. The body weight that is right for a person is the weight at which a person is healthy, strong, and energetic. The body feels good at this weight. It can be very hard for someone with an eating disorder to believe that she can stop dieting and let the body find a healthy weight. Part of the eating disorder is fear of becoming fat. However, when people with bulimia nervosa stop binge eating and purging, they rarely gain weight; in most cases treatment has little or no effect on weight during or after treatment (Fairburn, Marcus, & Wilson, 1993). People with bulimia nervosa are advised that they can eat much more than they think without gaining weight.

Some research suggests that setting a goal of 90 percent of the highest weight pounds that a person weighed before an eating disorder developed might be realistic. For example, if a person with anorexia nervosa weighed 120 pounds before developing anorexia nervosa, a goal weight might be about 108. However, because weight varies throughout the day, a range of acceptable weights is preferable to a single number. In this case, a range of 105–111 would be used.

Overall, the following has been recommended for establishing a normal body weight goal: (Garner, 1997, p. 166. Reprinted with permission of Guilford Press.)

1. It is preferable for a person to avoid choosing a specific goal weight; rather, the person should simply concentrate on establishing appropriate eating patterns and discontinuing binge eating and purging.
2. Weight often varies because of daily fluctuations in water balance and the contents of the digestive tract; thus, the aim is a five-pound weight range rather than an exact weight.
3. A goal weight range should take personal and family weight history into consideration.
4. A good estimate of a healthy body weight is 10 percent below one's highest weight prior to the onset of eating problems.
5. As long as body weight is a matter of medical concern, it should be monitored once a week, preferably by a trusted therapist.

ISSUE 8, PHYSICAL COMPLICATIONS

> Physical complications are common with eating disorders, and they can be life-threatening. Complications result primarily from starvation; vomiting; and abuse of laxatives, diuretics, and other medications. Risks can be reduced by understanding the complications and correcting eating disorder symptoms.
>
> (Garner, 1997, p. 166. Reprinted with permission of Guilford Press.)

It is important to know that there are major medical complications of eating disorders. A list of medical issues include electrolyte imbalances, cardiac irregularities, kidney dysfunction, cerebral atrophy, neurological abnormalities, swollen salivary glands, gastrointestinal disturbances, dental deterioration, edema and dehydration, menstrual and reproductive functioning, and bone abnormalities. This daunting list of medical issues associated with eating disorders can be used to educate people struggling with an eating disorder about the very real medical problems that their eating disorder can cause. This can provide motivation to stop the binge eating, vomiting, and abuse of laxatives, diuretics, and other drugs. See chapter 5 for detailed information about the physical consequences of the behaviors associated with eating disorders.

ISSUE 9, RELAPSE PREVENTION

> When relapses occur, rather than becoming discouraged, patients should follow the "four R's" in reframing relapses: (1) reframing the episode as a "slip" rather than as a "blown recovery"; (2) renewing the commitment to long-term recovery; (3) returning to the regular eating plan without engaging in compensatory behaviors; and (4) reinstituting behavioral controls to interrupt future episodes.
>
> (Garner, 1997, p. 170. Reprinted with permission of Guilford Press.)

Eating disorders rarely go away without relapses into old behavior. Recovery consists of moving ahead, with steps backward at times. For this reason, individuals should be prepared for the times when they will binge or purge or restart a behavior that they had stopped. Using a binge as an example, when a person binges, he or she should work hard to understand that this is a normal part of recovery from an eating disorder and use the binge as a reminder to work hard to avoid situations in which he or she might be tempted to binge. Although it is very tempting to compensate for the binge by vomiting, it is very important to instruct the person with bulimia nervosa to avoid this behavior.

Preparing for relapses includes understanding what might trigger either a binge or purge episode. These triggers might include hunger, use of alcohol or other drugs, feeling lonely or angry or depressed, or a variety of individual issues. In one of the first books available on recovery from bulimia nervosa, Hall and Cohn (1999) include a chapter entitled, "Things to Do Instead of Bingeing." This chapter contains some excellent strategies that can be used by a person who feels the urge to binge but is working to avoid food binges. Some of the ideas in the chapter include pampering yourself with a facial, massage, or hot bath; writing in a journal about the feelings and circumstances that are influencing you to binge; and making lists about your life, things you like and dislike, your goals, and your needs, which can serve as a reminder of possible distractions to a binge.

SUMMARY AND ADDITIONAL RESOURCES

Information about eating disorders may be an important part of preventing the development of eating disorders and a valuable part of the treatment process. It is important to know what resources are available. In several national studies of psychologists who work with individuals who have eating disorders and eating disturbances, the following materials were rated as helpful to clients (Norcross, Santrock, Campbell, Smith, Sommer, & Zuckerman, 2000). This material is available in the book entitled *Authoritative Guide to Self-help Resources in Mental Health* (Norcross et al., 2000). (Books are listed in chapter 9 and will not be repeated here.)

A Selection of Internet Resources

www.nationaleatingdisorders.org—This Web site of the National Eating Disorders Association was developed in 2001, when several major eating disorders associations (Eating Disorders Awareness and Prevention, American Anorexia Bulimia Organization, the National Eating Disorders Organization, and Anorexia Nervosa and Related Disorders) merged to create a centralized prevention and advocacy organization. The Web site is comprehensive and well organized; it is a highly recommended place to look for information about eating disorders on the internet. Links on this Web site provide additional places to look for information about eating disorders on the Internet.

In addition, this organization operates a nationwide toll-free Information and Referral Program at 1-800-931-2237. Callers can receive referrals for physicians, nutritionists, and counselors in the United States and Canada and information about eating disorders.

www.anad.org—The National Association of Anorexia Nervosa and Associated Disorders maintains a Web site with information, a referral list for finding therapists, has support groups across the country, and participates in research and advocacy efforts.

www.nedic.ca—The National Eating Disorder Information Centre is a Canadian organization that maintains a Web site that provides a newsletter, an eating disorder glossary, and links to other information about eating disorders.

www.eating-disorders.com—This Web site is part of the Center for Eating Disorders, which is a treatment program in Towson, Maryland. The Web site operates a moderated online support group.

www.aedweb.org—The Academy for Eating Disorders is a professional organization that has information for the public as well.

www.nimh.nih.gov/publicat/eatingdisorder.cfm—The National Institute of Mental Health of the U.S. government has a Web site that provides scientifically written documents about anorexia, bulimia, and binge eating disorders and provides information about treatment and research.

www.gurze.com—This is the Web site of a bookstore that has books and videos on eating disorders.

www.something-fishy.org—This is another Web site that provides comprehensive coverage of eating disorders. It is maintained by a person who is recovering from an eating disorder.

REFERENCES

American Psychiatric Association (APA). (2000). *Diagnostic and statistical manual of mental disorders (4th ed.-TR.)*. Washington, DC: Author.

Andersen, A. E., & DiDomenico, L. (1992). Diet vs. shape content of popular male and female magazines: A dose-response relationship to the incidence of eating disorders? *International Journal of Eating Disorders, 11*, 283–287.

Bulik, C. M., Sullivan, P. F., Wade, T. D., & Kendler, K. S. (2000). Twin studies of eating disorders: A review. *International Journal of Eating Disorders, 27*, 1–20.

Connors, M. E. (1996). Developmental vulnerabilities for eating disorders. In L. Smolak, M. R. Levine, & R. Striegel-Moore (Eds.), *The developmental psychopathology of eating disorders* (pp. 285–310). Mahwah, NJ: Lawrence Erlbaum Associates Press.

Crago, M., Shisslak, C. M., & Ruble, A. (2001). Protective factors in the development of eating disorders. In R. H. Striegel-Moore & L. Smolak (Eds.), *Eating disorders: Innovative directions in research and practice* (pp. 75–89). Washington, DC: American Psychological Association.

Davis, R., Dearing, S., Faulkner, J., Jasper, K., Olmsted, M. P., Rice, C., & Rocket, W. (1989). The road to recovery: A manual for participants in the psychoeducational group for bulimia nervosa. In H. Harper-Giuffre & K.R. MacKenzie (Eds.), *Group psychotherapy for eating disorders* (pp. 279–340). Washington, DC: American Psychiatric Association Press.

Drewnowski, A., Kurth, C.L. & Krahn, D.D. (1994). Body weight and dieting in adolescence: Impact of socioeconomic status. *International Journal of Eating Disorders, 16* (1), 61–65.

Fahy, T. A., & Treasure, J. (1991). Caffeine abuse in bulimia nervosa. *International Journal of Eating Disorders, 10* (3), 373–377.

Fairburn, C.G., Marcus, M.D., & Wilson, G.T. (1993). Cognitive-behavioral therapy for binge eating and bulimia nervosa: A comprehensive treatment manual. In C.G. Fairburn & G.T. Wilson (Eds.), *Binge eating: Nature, assessment, and treatment* (pp. 361–404). New York: Guilford Press.

Garner, D.M. (1997). Psychoeducational principles in treatment. In D. M. Garner & P. E. Garfinkel (Eds.), *Handbook of treatment for eating disorders* (2nd ed., pp. 145–177). New York: Guilford Press.

Garner, D. M., Garfinkel, P. E., Schwartz, D., & Thompson, M. (1980). Cultural expectations of thinness in women. *Psychological Reports, 47,* 483–491.

Ghaderi, A. (2001). Review of risk factors for eating disorders: Implications for primary prevention and cognitive behavioural therapy. *Scandinavian Journal of Behaviour Therapy, 30,* 57–74.

Hall, L., & Cohn, L. (1999). *Bulimia: A guide to recovery* (5th ed). Calsbad, CA: Gurze Books.

Huon, G. F., Brown, L., & Morris, S. (1988). Lay beliefs about disordered eating. *International Journal of Eating Disorders, 7* (2), 239–252.

Kano, S. (1993). Leap of faith. In L. Hall (Ed.), *Full lives: Women who have freed themselves from food and weight obsession* (pp. 110–127). Carlsbad, CA: Gurze Books.

Keesey, R.E. (1986). A set-point theory of obesity. In K.D. Brownell & J.P. Foreyt (Eds.), *Handbook of eating disorders: Physiology, psychology, and treatment of obesity, anorexia, and bulimia* (pp. 63–87). New York: Basic Books.

Keys, A., Brozek, J., Henschel, A., Mickelsen, O., & Taylor, H.L. (1950). *The biology of human starvation* (2 vols.). Minneapolis: University of Minnesota Press.

Leit, R.A., Pope, Jr., H.G., & Gray, J.J. (2000). Cultural expectations of muscularity in men: The evolution of playgirl centerfolds. *International Journal of Eating Disorders, 29,* 90–93.

Lindeman, M., Stark, K., & Latvala, K. (2000). Vegetarianism and eating-disordered thinking. *Eating Disorders: The Journal of Treatment and Prevention, 8* (2), 157–165.

Murray, S., Touyz, S., & Beumont, P. (1990). Knowledge about eating disorders in the community. *International Journal of Eating Disorders, 9*(1), 87–93.

Neumark-Sztainer, D., Story, M., Resnick, M.D., & Blum, R.W. (1997). Adolescent vegetarians: A behavioral profile of a school-based population in Minnesota. *Archives of Pediatric and Adolescent Medicine, 151* (8), 833–836.

Norcross, J.C., Santrock, J.W., Campbell, L.F., Smith, T.P., Sommer, R., & Zuckerman, E.L. (2000). *Authoritative guide to self-help resources in mental health.* New York : Guilford.

Sanders, P.B. (2001). Art against eating disorders. *Exposure, 34* (1/2), 57–62.

Smith, M.C., Pruitt, J.A., Mann, L.M., & Thelen, M.H. (1986). Attitudes and knowledge regarding bulimia and anorexia nervosa. *International Journal of Eating Disorders, 5* (3), 545–553.

Smolak, L., & Levine, M.P. (1996). Toward an empirical basis for primary prevention of eating problems with elementary school children. *Eating Disorders: The Journal of Treatment and Prevention, 4,* 293–307.

Smolak, L. & Murnen, S.K. (2001). Gender and eating problems. In R.H. Striegel-Moore and L. Smolak (Eds.), *Eating disorders: Innovative directions in research and practice* (pp. 91–110). Washington, DC: APA.

Smolak, L., & Striegel-Moore, R.H. (2001). Challenging the myth of the golden girl: Ethnicity and eating disorders. In R.H. Striegel-Moore & L. Smolak (Eds.), *Eating disorders: Innovative directions in research and practice* (pp. 111–132). Washington, DC: American Psychological Association.

Stein, R.I., Saelens, B.E., Dounchis, J.Z., Lewczyk, C.M., Swenson, A.K., & Wilfley, D.E. (2001). Treatment of eating disorders in women. *The Counseling Psychologist, 29* (5), 695–732.

Stice, E. (2001). Risk factors for eating pathology: Recent advances and future directions. In R.H. Striegel-Moore and L. Smolak (Eds.), *Eating disorders: Innovative directions in research and practice* (pp. 51–73). Washington, DC: APA.

Striegel-Moore, R.H., & Steiner-Adair, C. (1998). Primary prevention of eating disorders: Further considerations from a feminist perspective. In W. Vandereycken & G. Nooredenbos (Eds.), *The Prevention of Eating Disorders* (pp. 1–22). New York: New York University Press.

Surgenor, L.J., Rau, J., Snell, D.L., & Fear, J.L. (2000). Educational needs of eating disorder patients and families. *European Eating Disorders Review, 8,* 59–66.

Waugh, E., & Bulik, C.M. (1999). Offspring of women with eating disorders. *International Journal of Eating Disorders, 25* (2), 123–133.

7

Sociocultural Influences: The Impact of Western Culture on Eating and Body Image Disturbances

> When we talk about the obsession with food, we must also talk about our cultural obsession with the size of women's bodies, and what that obsession does to their minds and hearts. It is almost impossible to be a woman in this culture and feel powerful and gorgeous unless you have no thighs, no belly, no breasts—unless you don't look like a woman.
>
> (Roth, 1993, p. 250)

After reading about the different types of eating disorders, you may be wondering why people develop eating disorders or why females tend to develop eating disorders at much higher rates than males? Cultural factors and societal norms are partly responsible for the high level of preoccupation with weight and desire for thinness in our society. Sociocultural pressures on young women to be thin and attractive are a factor in the development of eating disturbances and disorders (Smolak & Striegel-Moore, 2001). According to the sociocultural explanation, if one lives in a society or culture in which thinness is highly glorified and used as a measurement of beauty and status, one is more likely to engage in extreme behaviors (e.g., dieting, starvation, self-induced vomiting, excessive exercise, use of laxatives and diet pills, fasting) to reach a level of thinness that is culturally desirable. A book, *Exacting Beauty,* by Thompson, Heinberg, Altabe, and Tantleff-Dunn (1999) is an excellent resource on research on the sociocultural model.

Nasser (1988) called eating disorders a "culture-bound syndrome" because eating disorders are "(1) prevalent in Western cultures and reported rare in others, (2) more prevalent in certain subcultures (e.g., ballet dancers), (3) psychopathology is symbolic of notions of thinness, promoted by the culture, (4) blurs and merges with acceptable forms of slimming behavior, (5) emerges in other cultures upon identification with Western cultural norms" (p. 575). Culture-bound does not mean that eating disorders do not exist outside of the dominant Western culture; rather the key point is that there is a relationship between eating disorders and culture such that as Western culture extends influence, there is an increase in the prevalence of eating disorders. For example, in a study of acculturation (measured by number of years in the United States, preference of language spoken and ethnic background of friends), Pumariega (1986) found that indicators of eating disorders increased in a group of Hispanic females along with level of acculturation. In the only study of this sort, Nasser (1986) reported similar findings in a study of Arab females living in Cairo compared to Arab females living in London (those in London had greater acculturation to Western culture and higher levels of eating issues). In Nasser's book on the relationship between culture and weight consciousness (1997), she highlights the sociocultural influences on the pursuit of thinness and eating disorders.

Definitions of words such as culture and Western culture are necessary to provide a common language for this chapter. Culture is a broad term that refers to the way people expect to behave and interact, and how that information is passed on to children. When culture is looked at as a way to study the influences on development and behavior (rather than as a distant, general context), we can learn a great deal about socialization and its relationship to attitudes and behavior (Smolak & Striegel-Moore, 2001). It is difficult to know what is meant by Western culture and to understand why at this point in time, there has been such an idealized view of thinness in the western culture. Garfinkel and Dorian (2001) indicate that Western culture refers to industrialization, modernization, and urbanization of a society. A number of factors contribute to the Western cultural societal view of the importance of thinness, such a desire to emulate the higher social classes, a desire for control over the body, and changing role expectations for women. The desire for thinness is also fueled by health concerns and the value of being young "based on the myth that under the right circumstances that one can remain beautiful and live forever." (Garfinkel & Dorian, p. 18).

A study conducted in Fiji found that there were significant changes in the prevalence of eating disturbances three years after television was brought to the country (Becker, Grinspoon, Klibanski, & Herzog, 1999). Data collected before the introduction of television indicated that 13 percent of adolescent girls had an eating disturbance, but in 1998 (three years after satellites began beaming television signals to Fiji), 29 percent engaged in some kind of disordered eating. Becker, director of research at the Harvard Eating Disorder Center, said that eating disorders have increased fivefold since the introduction of television. This is a particularly good example of the potential clash between biological predispositions to obesity and sociocultural expectations for thinness. The island of Fiji is known for the high percentage of obese individuals; 84 percent of women in one village were obese by Western standards. Thus, if people with a genetic disposition for obesity are exposed to the thin standards, an increase in eating disorders is expected and did occur. The findings also reflect how rapid social change can occur. As young people in Fiji were exposed to Western cultural values regarding body image, their views of body image and their behaviors changed.

Sociocultural pressures are often cited as an important contributor to the development of eating disorders and the media are often blamed for perpetuating and further developing these sociocultural pressures to be thin (Stice, 2001a, 2001b; Thompson et al., 1999). Sociocultural influences include the media, peers, family, and other things or people in our environment that influence us and set standards for that which we consider to be normal. The media is viewed as a major conduit of sociocultural values. It has been hypothesized that individuals develop an attachment to the symbols of culture presented through television and other media. These symbols become a part of the person's worldview and influence private psychological and fantasy life (Garfinkel & Dorian, 2001).

The thin ideal has been documented from research that began in the 1980s and 1990s (Morris, Cooper, & Cooper, 1989; Nemeroff, Stein, Diehl, & Smilack, 1994; Silverstein, Perdue, Peterson, & Kelly, 1986) and continues to the present (Thompson et al., 1999). The media consists of television, movies, billboards, magazines, the Internet, and newspapers. These are pervasive contributors to societal obsession and preoccupation with thinness; therefore, the majority of this chapter focuses on the media and its impact on eating and body image disturbances.

To have a better sense of the sociocultural influences of the media, take a few minutes to complete the following activity.

Turn on a television to a station that is showing a popular television program and commercials and watch for approximately ten minutes. During this ten minutes, pay particular attention to any female figures you see. When ten minutes have passed, turn off the television, get a piece of paper, and write down the characteristics of the females that you have just viewed on television. Try to come up with as many descriptors of these women as you can. If you get stuck, ask yourself, what did these women look like? Did they all have a certain body type, facial features, etc.?

After you have thought for a while and decide that you have a good idea what the female images were like, go find a magazine that is geared toward women or teenage girls. If you do not have one, the next time you are in the grocery store, take a look! Leaf through the magazine and look at approximately twenty different photographs of models.

What words would you use to describe these women? Again, think about these images until you believe you have made a complete list of descriptors.

When this activity was done with groups of female college students (Coughlin, personal communication, October 1, 2001), some of the words they used to describe the female models they saw in a popular female fashion magazine included thin, skinny, flawless complexion, perfect teeth, and full lips. They also noted that many had long hair and were scantly dressed. They reported that some of the models were fit with large breasts, while others were "bony" with very small breasts. None were overweight or of average weight.

Were the characteristics you used to describe female models and media images the same as or similar to the descriptors the college students identified? If they are similar, you are beginning to understand the sociocultural influences. If not, continue paying attention to billboards, characters in television programs and commercials, movie stars, music stars, and magazine models. You will even find that female characters in children's cartoons and animated movies more often than not meet these descriptions!

The majority of research that has been done on the sociocultural influence of eating disorders focuses on girls and women. This is because females are more frequently exposed, and therefore more vulnerable, to pressures concerning body shape and weight. Although males do develop eating disorders and can be concerned or preoccupied with their appearance (Andersen, Cohn & Holbrook, 2000), eating disorders and body image disturbances are much more common among females than males. Generally speaking, for every 1 male that has an eating disorder, 10 females have eating disorders (APA, 2000). Andersen and DiDomenico (1992) found that the 1 to 10 ratio of prevalence of eating disorders among males and females almost precisely matches the ratio of diet articles found in male magazines versus female magazines. More specifically, after analyzing twenty magazines that are frequently viewed by males and females, they found that for every one diet article found in magazines read most often by men, there were ten diet articles in magazines read by females. This study may provide part of the explanation for the higher prevalence of body image disturbances among females. If women are exposed to advertisements that promote weight loss approximately ten times more than men, they understandably are more likely to become pre-occupied with their weight.

PERVASIVENESS OF MEDIA INFLUENCES ON BODY IMAGE

In the United States, the media reaches the majority of the population, although individuals are exposed at different levels. According to Jean Kilbourne (1999), author of *Can't Buy My Love*, a book on the influence of the media on women, the average American is exposed to at least three thousand ads every day and will spend three years of his or her life watching television commercials. This book is full of examples of the role of *spending time watching adds* advertisers in changing the way we think and feel. Kilbourne argues that even if we think that the ads do not influence us, they do. As evidence of this influence, a study that I conducted demonstrated that even very brief exposure to pictures of models made female college students feel self-conscious and anxious (described later in this chapter; Kalodner, 1997).

Generally speaking, the majority of members of industrialized societies are exposed to the media; however, the level to which they are exposed varies. For example, one individual may not read fashion magazines or watch television, one may watch three hours of television per day without ever picking up a magazine, while another may watch television daily and regularly subscribe to fashion magazines. Even if one consciously avoids the media, he or she will be exposed to it, unless completely refusing to engage in the outside world. Jean Kilbourne wrote that almost everyone holds the misguided belief that advertisements do not affect them and don't shape their attitudes. However, we are all influenced by advertising. There is no way to tune out this much information, especially when it is carefully designed to break through the "tuning out" process" (Kilbourne, 1999, p. 27). What this means is that we are all influenced by the media and acknowledging the role of the media in shaping perceptions of beauty is part of the sociocultural model.

The advertising industry is a multibillion dollar business. Many maga-zines consist of more pages of advertisements than editorial content (count the next time you read one). In many magazines for women, there are incompatible messages such as those that emphasize weight loss while providing recipes for foods that are high in fat and calories. Bishop (2001) noted that this is a double bind because they are told that they should be thin, while being offered recipes and ads for unhealthy foods. For example, the cover of a popular magazine for women has these words "Small Changes for Big Weight Loss" near a picture of a "Super-Easy Cherry Chocolate Chip Ice Cream Pie" (June 26, 2001, issue of *Women's Day*). Kilbourne (1999) notes that the junk food industry and the diet industry depend on each other. Likewise, Garfinkel and Dorian (2001) indicate that the influence of the media on eating disorders is mutually influential, that is, the media creates and reflects the thinness values. One wonders what would happen if eating disorder clinics took out as many adds as food companies and diet product makers (Bishop, 2001).

Seventeen magazine, which is targeted to girls age twelve to fifteen, markets itself to those who might consider placing an ad in the magazine. In these ads to advertisers, *Seventeen* magazine describes itself as the "bible" for girls and tells advertisers that their readers are vulnerable to the ads placed in the magazine. Levine and Smolak (1996) found that almost half of adolescent girls read magazines like *Seventeen* or *Vogue* on a regular basis and that there is a correlation between reading magazines like these and negative body image and disordered eating. *Seventeen* says that their readers are the kind that advertisers want because the girls pursue beauty and fashion as part of their lifestyle. In other words, they buy the products advertised. A particularly difficult problem is that magazines like *Seventeen* convey the message that the body ideals presented are possible if the reader will do the right exercise or buy the right product. Repeated exposure to the thin models conveys the message that it is possible to look like them.

Messages in advertisements also imply that smoking may be a way to keep women thin and to control their emotions. Virginia Slims has many ads that make these implications, and data suggest that half of female smokers indicate that one of the reasons that they smoke is to control eating and that women list fear of weight gain as one of the reasons that they don't want to quit smoking (Meyers, Klesges, Winders, Ward, Peterson, & Eck, 1997).

THE THIN BODY IDEAL

The very thin models' images that are seen so often in the media can be referred to as the thin-body ideal. When these individuals who have very thin bodies are selected as models for television and magazine advertisements and for popular shows and movies, viewers idealize this type of body and come to accept these standards of beauty as those they should adopt for themselves. However, only a very small percentage of the population has the genetic makeup to have a body that matches the thin body-ideal (Kilbourne, 1999); less than 5 percent of the population have the body type that we see in the media.

Garner and colleagues (1980) were among the first to note the influence of culture on eating problems, presenting data on the continuing trends of thinness in *Playboy* centerfolds and Miss America Pageant contestants and the content of women's magazines. This study is considered a classic in the field. Garner and colleagues found that there was a significant increase in weight in American females, thus creating a larger discrepancy between the ideal and the actual weight of women. Other researchers replicated and extended this work, including Wiseman and coworkers (1992) who reported that Miss America contestants continued to decrease in body size and *Playboy* centerfolds remained at a low weight. Alarmingly, they found that approximately 60 to 70 percent of these models weighed 15 percent below their expected body weight. Finding that most of our fashion role models meet the weight criteria for anorexia nervosa is particularly alarming. Current research focuses on other aspects of the role of the media; there is no recent analysis of the thin body images in the media. However, these findings suggest that members of Western society are exposed to thinner, sometimes dangerously unhealthy, models and repeatedly receive messages that suggest or encourage weight loss and thinness.

It is clear that the majority of models who appear in television and magazine advertisements and throughout the media have a body type that is quite thin. The majority of models have 10 to 15 percent body fat, while the normal percentage of body fat for healthy women is 22 to 26 percent. Thus, in order to reach the body fat composition of many of the models, one would have to reduce their body fat by almost one-half.

This type of thin body has become a kind of ideal, and it has become influential to many people. Sometimes people who are in treatment for an eating disorder say that they have cut out images from magazines and posted them on the refrigerator as a kind of goal for themselves. Females, especially adolescent girls, may begin to believe that the models that are seen in the magazines and billboards are what they should look like. Because so few people can actually achieve this, the models are an unachievable ideal.

There have been few studies of the relationship between media exposure and maladaptive eating attitudes and behaviors. Most research has addressed the effects of the media on persons already suffering from eating disorders. Irving (1990) studied the impact of the thin standard of attractiveness on women who exhibited aspects of eating-disordered behavior. It was expected that lower self-evaluation would be related to level of bulimic symptoms; however, female college students without eating disorders experienced decreases in self-evaluation after fifteen minutes of exposure to slides of thin models. Women reported that the greatest amount of pressure to be thin was from the media; peers were the second most influential, and peers are under the same influence of the media. Waller, Hamilton, and Shaw (1992) also found that the media photographs (exposure to less than seven minutes of slides of thin models) affected clients in treatment for eating disorders and a control group of college women. In this study, the degree of overestimation of body size was related to the extent of eating-related psychopathology (Waller et al., 1992). It seems that vulnerability to media influences may not be limited to those experiencing eating-disordered behavior.

INTERNALIZATION OF THE THIN-BODY IDEAL

At this point, you may be asking yourself: if everyone is exposed to the media, why are some people highly influenced by the media while others are less influenced? Why do some people develop eating disorders while others do not? Although awareness of the media messages is one part of understanding the impact of the media, internalization is a second process, which seems to be more important. In reference to eating disorders, internalization refers to a personal acceptance of societal standards of thinness. To understand what is meant by internalization, consider the following examples:

Racquel is a fifteen-year-old female who watches popular television programs each evening and subscribes to popular teenage fashion magazines for females. While leafing through a magazine and occasionally checking out the television commercials in the background, she turns to her girlfriend and says, "I am so fat. I wish I looked like this model. I am going on a diet right now."

Amelia is also a fifteen-year-old female who is a big fan of MTV and popular music magazines for teenage to young adult audiences. Regularly, Amelia watches music videos and reads magazines. While looking at an advertisement with several extremely thin models, she says out loud, "Wow. Those girls are really thin. I could try for a million years and I wouldn't have that type of body. They really need to have more models that look like me and my friends!"

Both Racquel and Amelia are exposed to the media and are aware that the thin-body ideal exists. The difference between these two examples is that Racquel has internalized or accepted the media's standards of thinness for herself, while Amelia has rejected the sociocultural standards of thinness. If someone like Racquel bases her personal goals and aspirations related to appearance and body weight on the media's standards, she has internalized these standards. Internalization puts her at greater risk for developing an eating disorder than her peers that have not internalized the thin-body ideal. For example, Amelia is aware of the thin-body ideal but does not accept these standards of thinness as her own; therefore, she is at less risk for engaging in unhealthy dieting behaviors in order to become more like the images that monopolize the media.

Awareness and internalization of the effects of the media can be measured using a short questionnaire called the "Sociocultural Attitudes Toward Appearance Questionnaire" (SATAQ) (Heinberg, Thompson, & Stormer, 1995). Awareness is assessed by statements like "People think that the thinner you are, the better you look in clothes" and "Attractiveness is very important if you want to get ahead in our culture." Internalization is assessed by items like "Women who appear in TV shows and movies project the type of appearance that I see as my goal" and "I tend to compare my body to people in magazines and on TV." As you can see by looking at these examples, the awareness items are about recognizing that there is an emphasis on thinness and attractiveness in society, and internalization is about making society's values about thinness and attractiveness your own values.

Internalization seems to be more important than exposure to media messages. For example, using the SATAQ, the internalization subscale seems to be more important in understanding body image and eating problems. People who score higher on the Internalization subscale were affected more negatively by media messages than people who have lower scores in a study of females exposed to a ten-minute tape of appearance-related advertisements (Heinberg & Thompson, 1995). In another study, 175 college students completed several body image measures, along with the SATAQ, and provided information about the magazines that they read (Cusumano & Thompson, 1997). Although exposure to magazines did not relate to eating problems, body image dissatisfaction was related to the degree of internalization of sociocultural norms. The authors of this research wondered if the lack of significance of the exposure subscales of the SATAQ might be a function of the "constant bombardment of images" (Cusumano & Thompson, 1997, p. 718). In other words, they wondered if people are so overexposed to thin images that people don't even really notice anymore.

Internalization is not limited to individuals with eating disorders. When a group of females with bulimia nervosa, anorexia nervosa, or with no eating disorders were surveyed, their responses suggested that both individuals with and without eating disorders are susceptible to internalization (Murray, Touyz, & Beumont, 1996). More recently, other research has demonstrated that participants with eating disorders internalized messages to a greater extent than those without eating disorders (Griffiths, Beumont, Russell, Schotte, Thornton, Touyz, & Varano, 1999). Thus, individuals with eating disorders were more likely than individuals without eating disorders to internalize the thin-body ideal; however, neither group was uninfluenced by the media. Stice (2001a) reports that the thin-ideal internalization may be a causal risk factor for the development of eating disorders, which means that studies show the direct relationship between internalization and development of eating problems. Likewise, studies have shown that reducing the thin-ideal internalization leads to reduced body dissatisfaction and fewer symptoms of eating disorders (Stice, Mazotti, Weibel, & Agras, 2000). To better understand how internalization is related to eating and body image disturbances, it is helpful to consider body dissatisfaction.

BODY DISSATISFACTION

Internalization of sociocultural standards of thinness may lead to body dissatisfaction (Stice, 2001a, 2001b). As individuals are exposed to the thin-body ideal and accept these standards as their own, they are at an increased risk to become less satisfied with their body because they do not look like the models they see representing the norm in the media. It is logical that body dissatisfaction can lead to eating disorder symptoms. This is one of the most important risk factors for developing eating disturbances and disorders. In fact, body dissatisfaction has been identified as a factor that can be used to both predict and describe eating disorders. As you will recall, a diagnostic criterion for anorexia nervosa is a disturbance in one's experience of his or her body weight. Often, body disturbances include dissatisfaction with one's body weight, even if that individual is at a dangerously low body weight. Likewise, an important part of bulimia nervosa is the negative feelings that individuals have about themselves. Body dissatisfaction is a part of the negative feelings associated with eating disorders.

Not only has body dissatisfaction been identified as an essential component of eating disorders, it puts adolescent girls at greater risk for dieting (Stice, Mazotti, Krebs, & Martin, 1998). In other words, people who diet or engage in unhealthy eating patterns are often doing so because they are dissatisfied with their weight and appearance. Although body dissatisfaction does not always lead to eating disorders and unhealthy dieting practices, it certainly provides a logical explanation of the relationship between the media and unhealthy eating and body image.

In a group of ninety-four high school students from Australia, there were relationships between body dissatisfaction and watching soap operas and movies; the more they watched this type of television, the more dissatisfied they were with their bodies. However, there was the reverse finding for watching sports; those who watched more sports on television had lower body dissatisfaction. Furthermore, the more they watched music videos, the greater their desire was to be thin. The authors also reported that these students reported watching twenty to twenty-five hours of television a week (Tiggemann & Pickering, 1996). In another study, children and adolescents spent more time watching television than in school, and in fact they spent more time watching television than any other activity aside from sleeping (Levine & Smolak, 1996).

Body dissatisfaction is common among females in our society. In fact, it has been suggested that moderate discontent with weight is so common among females that it should be considered normative; this is the "normative discontent" that is now a classic phrase used to describe the pervasiveness of this attitude (Rodin, Silberstein, & Striegel-Moore, 1984). In other words, it is not uncommon for females to have moderate weight-related concerns and body dissatisfaction. This makes it difficult to distinguish between problematic attitudes associated with eating disorders and normative cultural values (Herzog & Delinsky, 2001). Interestingly, many girls and women are unhappy with their body weight, even if they are of average or low-average body weight. This is an outcome of the long term and repeated exposure to these sociocultural messages.

The Dual Pathway Model (Stice, 2001a) brings together these relationships; sociocultural pressure to be thin lead to an internalization of the thin ideal and body dissatisfaction, which follows because there is a difference between one's own body and the thin ideal. Body dissatisfaction lead to dieting and negative feelings, which increases the risk for developing eating disorders.

MEDIA INFLUENCE—A RESEARCH STUDY

The following is some material from a research study entitled "Media Influences on Male and Female Non-Eating-Disordered College Students: A Significant Issue" (Kalodner, 1997). The purpose of the study was to assess the immediate impact of very brief exposure to images taken from media on the self-consciousness and anxiety levels of male and female college students. This study is an example of the type of research that has been done to assess the influence of the media related to body image issues. Few studies have addressed the importance of media influence on persons who do not have an eating disorder; these persons are usually considered a control group. In addition, there is almost no research on the impact of the media on males. Males have been neglected in this type of research, although the incidence of eating disorders in males appears to be rising.

As background to this study, other studies using female college students as subjects, Stice and Shaw (1994) reported that female college students were negatively affected by exposure to media images of thin women. Stice and Shaw reported that a three-minute exposure to twelve photos of models from women's magazines led to increased depression, stress, guilt, shame, insecurity, and body dissatisfaction relative to exposure to average-sized models (taken from a magazine that was marketed for large women) or control pictures. Stice and Shaw concluded that there is a direct relationship between media exposure and eating pathology in female college students not diagnosed with eating disorders.

The participants in my study were 103 college students enrolled in undergraduate psychology courses at a small private college (Kalodner, 1997). There were 43 males and 60 females. The age ranged from 17 to 40 (X = 18.97). The ethnic background of the sample was predominantly white (86.4 percent); there were 4.9 percent African Americans and 8.7 percent other. Subjects were told that they would "look at some pictures that were taken from popular magazines" and fill out some questionnaires. Because the impact of very brief exposure was the focus of this study, subjects glanced at the photos, as they might if they saw them in magazines. Generally, subjects looked at the pictures for less than one minute.

Three sets of pictures were used. Set one contained twelve pictures of thin female models (exercising, in lingerie, in designer clothes) taken from *Vogue*, *Cosmopolitan*, and other magazines marketed for women. Set two contained pictures of attractive men (exercising, in underclothes, in designer clothes). Pictures were taken from *Gentlemen's Quarterly* (*GQ*), *Rolling Stone*, and catalogs of men's clothing. (Of interest is that it was much more difficult to find suitable pictures of male models in magazines most often read by men.) Set three contained pictures of older men and women, infants, and children playing: these control pictures were chosen so as not to encourage comparison between the subject and the models in the pictures. Female subjects were randomly assigned to see either set one or set three; male subjects were randomly assigned to see either set two or set three.

Females who looked at the twelve pictures taken from popular magazines had higher levels of self-consciousness, a greater sense of body competence, and higher anxiety than females who looked at the control pictures. This means that when females looked at pictures of thin models, they became self-conscious and anxious. The increase in body competence is confusing: this data means that these women may feel stronger and better coordinated than the women who looked at the control pictures. Richins (1991) found that in focus group discussions with female college students, exposure to pictures of thin models may lead to optimism and motivation when the characteristics of the model are seen as consistent with the viewer's self-image and/or if the look is considered attainable.

For males in this study, there was no effect of looking at pictures. In other words, there were no differences between the experimental and control groups. This study demonstrates that college aged males may be affected to a lesser degree than females. Murray, Touyz, and Beumont (1996) also reported that males were much less likely than females to try to become like the ideals portrayed in the media. One wonders if males do not compare themselves to the media images of males, or if they make the comparisons without experiencing negative affect. It seems as though the issue of body image in the media is much more influential on women. Further, Smolak, Levine, and Thompson (2001) have extended this finding with middle school aged boys, who also have not absorbed the sociocultural message to the extent that girls have adopted the thinness ideal.

Body image was described as elastic by Myers and Biocca (1992); this means that body image is unstable and can be manipulated by social cues. Research reviewed in this chapter indicates that it is quite easy to influence college women to feel more negatively about their body. However, we do not know if the negative responses experienced by the college-aged women to the magazine pictures are lasting or a momentary response to the stimuli. In addition, the elasticity of the body image may not be limited to negative influence. Might it also be possible to influence women to feel more positively about their body? Can we teach young women to decrease the comparisons they make with images in magazines and on television? Thinking more critically about the ideals promoted by the media may help to lessen the impact of the message (Murray et al., 1996).

In summary, there is a negative impact of media presentations of thin models on college women without eating disorders even though no such impact exists for male college students. The finding that there is a negative impact of the media on females who do not have eating disorders is especially important, because it indicates the need for media literacy for people regardless of their eating disorder status.

CHALLENGING THE MEDIA'S MESSAGES

One of the ways that media viewers can be less influenced by media images and the thin-body ideal is to reject sociocultural standards of thinness. In the earlier example, one of the differences between Racquel and Amelia is that Amelia did not accept the media's standards of beauty and attractiveness as her own. Many researchers who are dedicated to challenging the media and its impact on women believe that this may be one of the keys to preventing and reducing eating disorders and body image disturbances. If media viewers are more critical of the media, they may be less likely to internalize these standards and may resist putting unrealistic expectations on themselves.

In her video, *Slim Hopes: Advertising and the Obsession with Thinness*, Jean Kilbourne provides information about the media's tactics for creating unrealistic standards for women. Not only does she point out the fact that the media uses only one body type (tall, slim, and beautiful) to represent women, she reveals the lack of reality in some of the media images we see in magazines, movies, and television. For example, many times the models we see in magazines are often airbrushed to make them appear more flawless than they are in reality. Sometimes, a computer is used to create facial features and images that do not even exist or that are more pleasing to the eye. Another tactic used by the media is body doubling. In the movie *Pretty Woman*, some of the scenes were shot using another model's body instead of Julia Roberts. Many of the scenes appear as if you are seeing Julia Roberts when, in reality, you are seeing another woman's body. Additionally, sometimes the media combines different body parts of models to create the "perfect image" (body piecing). In other words, they may use one model's arms, another model's legs, and another model's face. The irony in Jean Kilbourne's revelations is that often times women try to emulate the images they see in the media when, in reality, these images are not real people. What we think may be a person may have been altered using a computer, photography techniques, body doubles, or body piecing. In other words, not even the models who represent the thin-body ideal are able to meet the sociocultural standards of thinness and beauty!

One way to reduce the internalization of sociocultural standards of thinness is to understand that "what you see is not always what you get." In other words, just because models and popular television and movie talents appear to be flawless doesn't mean that they are. In fact, they are often altered to create images that society, in turn, accepts as normal or acceptable. Another way to reject the media's representation of women is to become educated about the physiological and biological realties that clash with cultural standards of thinness.

Many times, those who see the media images neglect to acknowledge that there are biological realities that may prevent them from achieving the media's standards of thinness. In other words, if you are born with a heavy body type, you will fail repeatedly if you try to change your body type to one like the models you see in the media. We cannot change our genetics; what we can change is our acceptance of the body type we were born with and our knowledge that it is possible to be healthy and fit, regardless of our genetic composition.

MEDIA LITERACY

Media literacy is a creative way of reducing the internalization that seems to be associated with the development of eating issues (Berel & Irving, 1998; Irving, DuPen, & Berel, 1998). Feminist writers (Kilbourne, 1999) indicate that teaching women about the way in which the media manipulates women is a way to combat this influence. Media literacy programs are specialized intervention programs designed to teach media observers to reduce the perceived realism of appearance-related media, decrease the acceptance of thin standards of beauty, and reduce those positive expectations associated with thinness and eating (Irving et al., 1998). A program designed to teach college students about the technology used by magazines (i.e., airbrushing, computer graphics) and by models themselves (plastic surgery) to produce images was successful in reducing the internalization of the media messages (Stormer & Thompson, 1998).

About-Face is a media literacy organization focused on the impact mass media has on the physical, mental, and emotional well-being of women and girls. Their Web site (www.about-face.org) has focused attention on the very thin models and highlights how these images are harmful to women and girls. The Web site is full of facts about media and the influence of media on women, especially as it relates to body image issues. They write that "through practical and activist methods we challenge our culture's overemphasis on physical appearance. By encouraging critical thinking about the media, and personal empowerment, About-Face works to engender positive body-esteem in girls and women of all ages, sizes, races and backgrounds. About-Face provides a place where all women count, from the tiniest among us to the very largest. We are frustrated with images depicting women as junkies, stick figures, mannequins, bimbos and inanimate objects.... Research supports our belief that there is a powerful connection between exposure to images of an idealized female ideal and the reported incidences of eating disorders, low self-esteem and depression among women and girls." In addition, the founder of About-Face has developed several posters, two of which are shown here, with stop starvation imagery themes.

About-Face lists their goals (this is not a complete list) as

- To encourage a healthy skepticism about media images and the messages of popular culture
- To empower young people to feel confident about their individuality, their abilities, and their bodies
- To educate parents to empower their daughters and enlighten their sons
- To identify companies that show women in unrealistic, distorted, or vulnerable poses and hold them responsible for their negative imagery
- To endorse companies that promote diverse and healthy images

Media literacy can be a powerful force in the prevention and treatment of eating disorders. In a description of a media literacy program for third

"Please don't feed the models" poster. Reprinted with permission, courtesy of the About-Face Web site. www.about-face.org.

"Fashion Plate" poster. Reprinted with permission, courtesy of the About-Face Web site. www.about-face.org.

graders, Purcell (in Steiner-Adair & Purcell, 1996), described media literacy for this age group as the ability to read, critique, reflect and write images. It is designed to give children the tools to understand various media, including television, movies, magazines, and computer images. As part of this interesting program, Purcell presented several pictures of the same model in various poses (red hair flying wildly; dark brown hair with pale makeup; dressed in conservative clothes; well-dressed woman getting out of a car; and more). The children reacted to the pictures with adjectives ranging from "weird hair and tall and skinny," "ugly, naked," "normal, athletic-looking," and "independent, rich." The children thought they were describing different people and were fascinated to find out that it was the same woman. The message is that that there is no way to know

Bulimia Nervosa

She binged in secret.
            She felt out of control.
She threw up in silence.
            She felt shame and guilt.
She abused laxatives.
            She felt worthless.
Her teeth skinned her knuckles.
            Her habit became an addiction.
Her cheeks were swollen.
            She numbed her feelings.
Her eyes were bloodshot.
            She became deceitful.
Her heart would race.
            She obsessed over her body image.
She kept the pounds off.
            She almost died.

Bulimia Nervosa. Kathryn Silva and Robin Lasser from "Eating Disorders in a Disordered Culture" a visual arts display available at www.eating.ucdavis.edu. Reprinted with permission.

Anorexia Nervosa

FEAR OF FAT EATS US ALIVE

She was afraid to eat.
She lost 25% of her body weight.
She strove for perfection.
Her sexual desires disappeared.
She had angry outbursts.
She stopped having her periods.
She felt isolated.
She was always cold.
She desired control.
She felt weak.
She denied her hunger.
Fine hairs grew over her entire body.
She was depressed.
She suffered from insomnia.
She had a distorted body image.
Her heartbeat was irregular.
She craved attention.
She almost died.

Anorexia Nervosa. Kathryn Silva and Robin Lasser from "Eating Disorders in a Disordered Culture" a visual arts display available at www.eating.ucdavis.edu. Reprinted with permission.

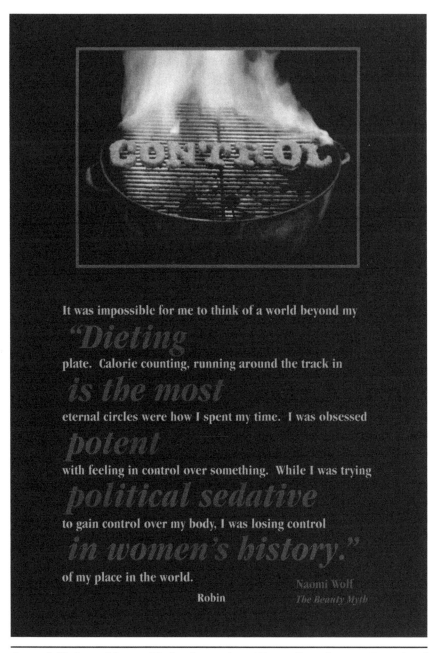

Control. Kathryn Silva and Robin Lasser from "Eating Disorders in a Disordered Culture" a visual arts display available at www.eating.ucdavis.edu. Reprinted with permission.

Fear of Fat Eats Us Alive. Kathryn Silva and Robin Lasser from "Eating Disorders in a Disordered Culture" a visual arts display available at www.eating.ucdavis.edu. Reprinted with permission.

the real person from the media pictures. The media is powerful enough to make us see many different things. (The article goes on to describe a project that the students did to demonstrate the power of the media using themselves as subjects.)

COUNTERMEDIA

Two faculty members—Kathryn Sylva (University of California at Davis) and Robin Lasser (San Jose State University)—have made the media a powerful messenger of antieating disorders messages; this can be viewed at http://www.eating.ucdavis.edu/. Their project, titled "Eating Disorders in a Disordered Culture," is a visual arts display of the cultural dimensions of eating disorders. They present a "visually compelling communication of the individual's personal or subjective experience of living with an eating disorder" (Sylva & Lasser, 2001, p. 4). One advantage of posting their work on the Internet is that it is always available and people can explore the topic in the privacy of their own homes. It is a quite powerful display.

Several images of their work demonstrate the contradiction between the social pressure for thinness and the eating disorders. The Bulimia Nervosa and Anorexia Nervosa photos display lists of the physical and emotional aspects of these eating disorders. Other very powerful images included Control and Fear of Fats Eats Us Alive.

People interested in the relationship between media, art and eating disorders may find the special issue of the journal *Exposure* (volume 34, issues 1 and 2) very informative and provocative.

PEERS AND SOCIAL GROUPS

Peers can promote the thin-body ideal and may encourage weight loss behaviors. When a group of females with bulimia nervosa were asked to identify factors that led to their binge eating and purging behaviors, 45 percent said they engaged in these behaviors after experiencing pressure from a friend to lose weight (Irving, 1990). Suggestions from friends to lose weight are often followed by episodes of dieting. This pressure to lose weight can be compared with the peer pressure that some individuals experience in relation to other unhealthy behaviors such as drinking, doing drugs, and having unprotected sex.

Because social groups are of great value to us, they often serve to define us and to tell us what to think and how to act. Some researchers believe that members of a social group are more likely to engage in certain behaviors if those behaviors are important and meaningful to that group (Van-Lone, 2002). In other words, social groups have social *norms* that define appropriate behaviors and standards for its members. Some examples of social groups include sports teams, cheerleading squads, and sororities. They may also include a group of friends who are particularly close.

If being thin, dieting, and weight loss are important norms within the social group, group members may feel compelled to engage in behaviors that will make them more acceptable. These behavioral patterns are often learned from one's peers. This is often referred to as *modeling*. One example of this was found in a study that looked at college sorority members' binge-eating behaviors. According to the first study of this type, young women whose friends were binge eaters were more likely to be binge eaters themselves (Crandall, 1988). This suggests that peers influence one another's eating behaviors. The more important physical attractiveness and body shape are to the group, the more likely weight loss and dieting are encouraged within the group. Furthermore, the more important the group is to the individual group member, the more likely he or she is to be influenced by the group norms. Recently, VanLone (2002) also found among small friendship groups of college students living in residence halls that there were similarities in eating attitudes and behaviors. This may mean that eating attitudes and behaviors are "contagious" though additional research on this is necessary.

Another way that peers may contribute to the development of eating disorders is through the process of physical appearance comparisons within a social group. Because individuals tend to compare themselves to peers who share similar characteristics (sex, age, or race), their self-evaluations are influenced by their peers. For example, Tina, a high school sophomore, compares herself to other members of her class. Not only does she compare her academic performance to her peers, but she also compares her physical appearance to that of her peers. If Tina believes that being thin is important, she may feel badly about herself when she compares herself to individuals who are thinner than she is. This is called a negative contrast effect. If, however, she compares herself to peers who are heavier than she is, she might feel better about herself. This is called a positive contrast effect.

When individuals experience a negative contrast effect, they may become dissatisfied with their bodies and feel the urge to lose weight. Essentially, they begin to base their thoughts and feelings about themselves based on a comparison they have made with someone else. Because there is almost always someone that is thinner, this comparison may make people feel inadequate and dissatisfied with themselves.

Teasing from peers is another issue that has been studied (Thompson et al., 1999). Peers made up the largest category of teasers in one study (Cash, 1995), and college women reported that they continued to think about times when they were teased, and that 71 percent said that this teasing had a negative effect on their body image. Teasing is clearly associated with body image dissatisfaction.

FAMILIES

Although the media is often identified as the greatest source of pressure to be thin, family also plays a role in the development of eating disorders. As with peers, teasing appears to be a major issue in families. Brothers have been implicated in teasing in several studies. In one such study, 79 percent of college women who were asked about who teased them about their weight indicated that it was brothers. They also reported that the worst teasing was from brothers (Rieves & Cash, 1996). Other studies have also demonstrated that the effects of teasing can be quite powerful; for example, a man in one study reported that "being teased when I was a child made me feel bad about my body for years and years" (Garner, 1997, p. 42). A study of the effect of teasing from parents in African American and Caucasian women resulted in the finding that Caucasian women reported greater teasing, but both groups indicated that they had been teased about their weight and shape (Striegel-Moore, Wilfley, Caldwell, Needham, & Brownell, 1996).

Families may have norms that encourage weight loss. If certain standards of thinness are expected of family members, weight loss behaviors may occur as one attempts to reach these standards. A family relationship that has received particular attention is the mother-daughter relationship. This relationship is of interest because both mothers and daughters are exposed to sociocultural pressures to be thin. Mothers of adolescents who have eating disorders are more likely to think their daughters need to lose weight than mothers of adolescents without eating disorders (Keel, Heatherton, Harnden, & Horning, 1997). Even among elementary school aged children, parental comments about weight and shape are associated with body dissatisfaction and weight loss attempts (Smolak & Murnen, 2001). Unhealthy eating behaviors and a desire to lose weight may develop in response to familial pressure. Consider the child who is encouraged by her parents to lose weight. Or, the teenager who has a mother and an older sister who are on diets. These examples clearly demonstrate the impact that siblings and parents may have on one's desire to lose weight.

Imagine that you are a young girl who, despite being average sized, is being tormented by other children about your weight. When you go home and try to forget about the hurtful things that are being said, you see your mother weighing herself two times a day and skipping meals to lose weight. Furthermore, you are surrounded by television programs and advertisements that show only thin girls and women. What influence do your peers, family, and the media have on your feelings about yourself?

SOCIOCULTURAL INFLUENCE: HOW IT ALL FITS TOGETHER

To bring all of the material on sociocultural influence together, two interview studies are presented here. One is a study of thirty 15-year-old girls who were interviewed individually and asked questions about dieting and about what they discuss with their friends related to weight, weight loss and dieting (Wertheim, Paxton, Schutz, & Muir, 1997). They were asked about pressures related to watching weight from media, peers, and family. The other is a book called *Fat Talk* that tells about adolescent girls with regard to weight and body image issues. This study of 240 girls over several years is described in Nichter's book (2000). Questions such as "Where did you get ideas about how you want to look?" "How has your body changed since last year?" and "Do you think that the way your mother looks affects your ideas about your body? How about the way your dad looks?" were asked of the girls in individual interviews.

The perfect girl was described as 5 feet 7 inches tall and weighing between 100 and 110 pounds. She was blond with long flowing hair. She had a flat stomach, a clear complexion, straight teeth, and good clothes (Nichter, 2000). This description was repeated by many girls. Perfect girls also had perfect bodies, could eat whatever they wanted, and had a perfect life. Because this is a chapter on sociocultural influence, it is interesting to wonder where this image might come from. Although the girls in this study were not asked to explain this, it seems like a strikingly accurate description of Barbie. The girls also knew that not all people can look like this, but many expressed it as a goal. The sense of frustration and self-devaluation that came from recognizing that a girl would not be the "perfect" girl was striking in girls in middle school.

In Wertheim's study (1997), about half of the girls reported that they had dieted. Even those who had not dieted, many indicated that they watched their weight. Of the peer influences, almost all of the girls reported that they could talk openly with their friends about weight and eating concerns. The girls did not feel pressure to be thin from friends. In fact, they often engaged in discussions that sounded like "I'm so fat; no, you're not," in which one girl said she felt fat and her friend said she wasn't fat. It is possible that these conversations are a way for girls to find out what others think about their changing bodies. Social comparison refers to a girl comparing her body to her friends' bodies, other girls at school, models, family members, and others. Some girls said that when their friends diet, they dieted as well because "When my friends talk about eating less that makes me feel like I should be as well…because I am bigger than them" (p. 348). Sometimes girls diet because they want to fit in, or even participate in joint dieting (two or more girls going on a diet together). Popular girls seem to have a great influence in the social climate of the school, and because they set the standards, many girls report that they have to be thin and beautiful to be popular.

Teasing was an issue for some girls. Their friends, boys, popular girls, boyfriends, or a brother teased them. Some girls report that they watch their weight so that they will look good for boys. Although one girl reported that only immature boys focus on body weight and most boys care what is inside a girl more than what is outside (or at least that should be so) (Werthheim et al., p. 349).

Family influences were important too. Fathers were not mentioned by any of the girls spontaneously, and even when asked, it seems that the influence of the fathers in this sample of girls was small. A book called *Father Hunger* addresses the role that fathers play in the development of daughters, especially as related to eating disorders and body image (Maine, 1991). Fifteen of the thirty girls reported that their mothers were dieting, but only two mothers encouraged their daughters to diet. Three daughters reported dieting in a joint diet with their mothers. In one case, a girl in the study found a diet she wanted to try, and she, her mother, and all her sisters dieted together.

The media was a major force in fostering body concerns. They said things like "every time you open a magazine you always see beautiful people...I see all these pretty models, I really wish I could look like one of them." Girls said that some of the fashions available to wear are not suitable for bigger or even medium sized people because most of it is made for slim people.

Interestingly, there were some factors identified that seemed to protect girls from developing an overconcern with weight and body shape. These included self-acceptance, family influences on body acceptance, positive peer influences, and knowledge about the dangers of diets. Girls who said things like "I don't worry about what people think of me, I am just me" seemed to have less problems with body image issues. Family influence can help girls to be protected from the sociocultural messages about thinness. Positive peer messages were also described. One girl reported that two of her friends stopped vomiting when their friends convinced them that it wasn't worth ruining their health over being skinny. Knowing about the negative effects of diets also helped protect some girls from repeatedly dieting.

Nichter's study identified many of the same themes as described above. The issue of "fat talk" seemed so important that Nichter named the book *Fat Talk*, and devoted a whole chapter to explaining it. In this interaction, it appears that girls are looking for support from her peers. She wants her friends to say that she isn't fat at all. Saying "I'm so fat" is a way to check out perceptions with peers. Nichter observed that it is not seen as acceptable for a girl to speak highly of herself, rather she says self-deprecating things about herself and others correct her.

The influence of the media was noted. In a focus group discussion about media with girls in middle school, the cover of magazines with headlines like "How to lose weight, how to look skinnier" was discussed. Girls said that these articles made them wonder if they were fat and needed to lose weight. They also noted that TV was influential because there are so many dieting commercials. One girl noted, "I think it's mostly due to diet-ing commercials, you know like for Dexatrim and stuff, show these very thin people eating the product. So then people who are like me look at that ad and go 'hey, wait a minute, they're thin and they're dieting. I have to diet. I have to be thinner!'" (p. 17).

Dieting was also studied in detail. Nichter (2000) reached some unusual conclusions. She believes that girls talk about dieting, but they do not engage in diet behaviors as much as they say. Food records confirmed that the girls were not often limiting intake in a substantial way. They were not using any formalized diet plans. It seems that "watching what I eat" is a common behavior. This was also reported in Wertheim's study. The girls seem to describe this as a way of eating more healthfully, rather than a way of eating less.

Nicter's (2000) study included a number of questions about the role of family members. Girls were asked if anyone in the family diets, if parents exercise or encourage the girls to exercise, to describe their parents, to won-der if they might get ideas about how they might look from looking at fam-ily members, and more. The notion of a "curse" that is passed on in families was a recurrent theme. Girls said that they saw that their parents, aunts and uncles, or grandparents were fat and feared that is was just a matter of time until they were fat too. Some mentioned that they were going to fight the curse: "Well, my sister and my cousin, we're all like trying to fight off this curse, but it's not easy. We want to try to do something about it" (p. 94). Girls looked toward their parents and wondered if they would look like their parents when they were older. Having an overweight mother seemed to motivate the girls to control their own weight. However, a skinny mom also seemed to pressure girls to be thin, as if in a competition.

Teasing was discussed as a family issue; comments from fathers and brothers occurred more often than from mothers. Although the girls in this study were at a point during which it is age appropriate to gain weight (developmentally), many of the girls reported that their family members teased them about this.

A wealth of additional information is in these interview studies. Clearly they show that the sociocultural model, which asserts that there is a tremendous influence on girls to look a certain way, does explain the experiences of many adolescent girls.

REFERENCES

American Psychiatric Association (APA). (2000). *Diagnostic and statistical man-ual of mental disorders* (4th ed.—TR.). Washington, DC: Author.

Andersen, A., Cohn, L., & Holbrook, T. (2000). *Making weight: Men's conflicts with food, weight, shape, and appearance*. Carlsbad, CA: Gurze Books.

Andersen, A.E., & DiDomenico, L. (1992). Diet vs. shape content of popular male and female magazines: A dose-response relationship to the incidence of eating disorders? *International Journal of Eating Disorders, 11*, 283–287.

Becker, A.E., Grinspoon, S.K., Klibanski, A., & Herzog, D.B. (1999). Eating disorders. *New England Journal of Medicine, 340*, 1092–1098.

Berel, S., & Irving, L.M. (1998). Media and disturbed eating: An analysis of media influence and implications for prevention. *The Journal of Primary Prevention, 18*, 415–430.

Bishop, R. (2001). The pursuit of perfection: A narrative analysis of how women's magazines cover eating disorders. *The Howard Journal of Communication, 12*, 221–240.

Cash, T.F. (1995). Developmental teasing about physical appearance: Retrospective descriptions and relationships with body image. *Social Behavior and Personality, 23*, 123–130.

Crandall, C.S. (1988). Social contagion of binge eating. *Journal of Personality and Social Psychology, 55*, 588–598.

Cusumano, D.L. & Thompson, J.K. (1997). Body image and body shape ideals in magazines: Exposure, awareness, and internalization. *Sex Roles, 37*, 701–721.

Garfinkel, P.E. & Dorian, B.J. (2001). Improving understanding and care for the eating disorders. In R.H. Striegel-Moore & L. Smolak (Eds.), *Eating disorders: Innovative directions in research and practice* (pp. 9–26). Washington, DC: American Psychological Association.

Garner, D.M. (1997). The body image survey. *Psychology Today*, (January/February) 32–84.

Garner, D.M., Garfinkel, P., Schwartz, D., & Thompson, M. (1980). Cultural expectations of thinness in women. *Psychological Reports, 47*, 484–491.

Griffiths, R.A., Beumont, P.J.V., Russell, J., Schotte, D., Thornton, C., Touyz, S., & Varano, P. (1999). Sociocultural attitudes towards appearance in dieting disordered and nondieting disordered subjects. *European Eating Disorders Review, 7*, 193–203.

Heinberg, L.J., & Thompson, J.K. (1995). Body image and televised images of thinness and attractiveness: A controlled laboratory study. *Journal of Social and Personality Psychology, 14*, 1–14.

Heinberg, L.J., Thompson, J.K., & Stormer, S. (1995). Development and validation of the Sociocultural Attitudes Towards Appearance Questionnaire. *International Journal of Eating Disorders, 17*, 81–89.

Herzog, D.B., & Delinsky, S.S. (2001). Classification of eating disorders. In R.H. Striegel-Moore & L. Smolak (Eds.), *Eating disorders: Innovative directions in research and practice* (pp. 31–50). Washington, DC: American Psychological Association.

Irving, L.M. (1990). Mirror images: Effects of the standard of beauty on women's self and body esteem. *Journal of Social and Clinical Psychology, 9*, 230–242.

Irving, L. M., DuPen, J., & Berel, S. (1998). A media literacy program for high school females. *Eating Disorders: The Journal of Treatment and Prevention, 6,* 119–131.

Kalodner, C.R. (1997). Media influences on male and female non-eating-disordered college students: A significant issue. *Eating Disorders: The Journal of Treatment and Prevention, 5* (1), 47–57.

Keel, P. K., Heatherton, T. F., Harnden, J. T., & Hornig, C. D. (1997). Mothers, fathers, and daughters: Dieting and disordered eating. *Eating Disorders: The Journal of Treatment and Prevention, 5* (3), 216–228.

Kilbourne, K. (1999). *Can't buy my love: How advertising changes the way we think and feel.* New York: Simon & Schuster.

Levine, M. P., & Smolak, L. (1996). Media as a context for the development of disorders eating. In L. Smolak and M. P. Levine (Eds.), *The developmental psychopathology of eating disorders: Implications for research, prevention, and treatment* (pp. 235–257). Mahwah, NJ: Erlbaum.

Maine, M. (1991). *Father hunger: Father, daughters and food.* Carlsbad, CA: Gurze Books.

Meyers, A. W., Klesges, R. C., Winders, S. E., Ward, K. D., Peterson, B. A., & Eck, L. H. (1997). Are weight concerns predictive of smoking cessations? A prospective analysis. *Journal of Consulting and Clinical Psychology, 65,* 448–452.

Morris, A., Cooper, T., & Cooper, P.J. (1989). The changing shape of female fashion models. *International Journal of Eating Disorders, 8* (5), 593–596.

Murray, S. H., Touyz, S. W., & Beumont, P. J. V. (1996). Awareness and perceived influence of body ideals in the media: A comparison of eating disorder patients and the general community. *International Journal of Eating Disorders, 4,* 33–47.

Myers, P. N., Jr. & Biocca, F. A. (1992). The elastic body image: The effect of television advertising and programming on body image distortions in young women. *Journal of Communication, 42,* 108–133.

Nasser, M. (1986). Comparative study of the prevalence of abnormal eating attitudes among Arab female students of both London and Cairo universities. *Psychological Medicine, 16,* 621–625.

Nasser, M. (1988). Culture and weight consciousness. *Journal of Psychosomatic Research, 32,* 573–577.

Nasser, M. (1997). *Culture and weight consciousness.* New York: Routledge.

Nemeroff, C. J., Stein, R. I., Diehl, N. S., & Smilack, K. M. (1994). From the Cleavers to the Clintons: Role choices and body orientation as reflected in magazine article content. *International Journal of Eating Disorders, 16* (2), 167–176.

Nichter, M. (2000). *Fat talk.* Cambridge: Harvard University Press.

Pumariega, A. J. (1986). Acculturation and eating attitudes in adolescent girls: A comparative and correlational study. *American Academy of Child Psychiatry, 25,* 276–279.

Richins, M. L. (1991). Social comparison and the idealized images of advertising. *Journal of Consumer Research, 18*, 71–83.

Rieves, L., & Cash, T.F. (1996). Social developmental factors and women's body image attitudes. *Journal of Social Behavior and Personality, 11*, 63–78.

Rodin, J., Silberstein, L., & Striegel-Moore, R. (1984). Women and weight: A normative discontent. *Nebraska Symposium on Motivation, 32*, 267–307.

Roth, G. (1993). Dessert. In L. Hall (Ed.), *Full lives: Women who have freed themselves from food and weight obsession* (pp. 247–254). Carlsbad, CA: Gurze Books.

Silverstein, B., Perdue, L., Peterson, B., & Kelly, E. (1986). The role of the mass media in promoting a thin standard of bodily attractiveness for women. *Sex Roles, 14* (9/10), 519–532.

Smolak, L., Levine, M.P., & Thompson, J.K. (2001). The use of the Sociocultural Attitudes Towards Appearance Questionnaire with middle school boys and girls. *International Journal of Eating Disorders, 29*, 216–223.

Smolak, L., & Murnen, S.K. (2001). Gender and eating problems. In R.H. Striegel-Moore & L. Smolak (Eds.), *Eating disorders: Innovative directions in research and practice* (pp. 91–110). Washington, DC: American Psychological Association.

Smolak, L. & Striegel-Moore, R.H. (2001). Challenging the myth of the golden girl: Ethnicity and eating disorders. In R.H. Striegel-Moore & L. Smolak (Eds.), *Eating disorders: Innovative directions in research and practice* (pp. 111–132). Washington, DC: APA.

Steiner-Adair, C., & Purcell, A. (1996). Approaches to mainstreaming eating disorders prevention. *Eating Disorders: The Journal of Treatment & Prevention, 4* (4), 294–309.

Stice, E. (2001a). A prospective test of the dual pathway model of bulimic pathology: Mediating effects of dieting and negative affect. *Journal of Abnormal Psychology, 110*, 124–135.

Stice, E. (2001b). Risk factors for eating pathology: Recent advances and future directions. In R.H. Striegel-Moore & L. Smolak (Eds.), *Eating disorders: Innovative directions in research and practice* (pp. 51–74). Washington, DC: American Psychological Association.

Stice, E., Mazotti, L., Krebs, M., & Martin, S. (1998). Predictors of adolescent dieting behaviors: A longitudinal study. *Psychology of Addictive Behaviors, 12*, 195–205.

Stice, E., Mazotti, L., Weibel, D., & Agras, W.S. (2000). Dissonance prevention program decreases thin-ideal internalization, body dissatisfaction, dieting, negative affect, and bulimic symptoms: A preliminary experiment. *International Journal of Eating Disorders, 27*, 206–217.

Shaw, H.E. (1994). Adverse effects of the media-portrayed thin ideal and linkages to bulimic symptomatology. *Journal of Social and logy, 13*, 288–308.

Striegel-Moore, R. H, Wilfley, D.E., Caldwell, M.B., Needham, M.L., & Brownell, K.D. (1996). Weight-related attitudes and behaviors of women who diet to lose weight: A comparison of Black dieters and White dieters. *Obesity Research, 4*, 109–116.

Stormer, S.M., & Thompson, J.K. (1998, November). An evaluation of a media-focused psychoeducational program for body image disturbance. Paper presented at the annual meeting of the Association for the Advancement of Behavior Therapy, Washington, DC.

Sylva K., & Lasser, R. (2001). Eating disorders in a disordered culture. *Exposure, 34*(1/2), 4–11.

Thompson, J.K., Heinberg, L .J., Altabe, M., & Tantleff-Dunn, S. (1999). *Exacting beauty: Theory, assessment, and treatment of body image disturbance*. Washington, DC: American Psychological Association.

Tiggemann, M., & Pickering, A.S. (1996). Role of television in adolescent women's body dissatisfaction and drive for thinness. *International Journal of Eating Disorders, 20*, 199–203.

VanLone, J.S. (2002). Social contagion of eating attitudes and behaviors among first year college women living in residence hall communities. Unpublished doctoral dissertation, West Virginia University.

Waller, G., Hamilton, K., & Shaw, J. (1992). Media influences on body size estimation in eating disorders and comparison subjects. *British Review of Bulimia and Anorexia Nervosa , 6*(2), 81–87.

Wertheim, E. H., Paxton, S. J., Schutz, H. K., & Muir, S .L. (1997). Why do adolescent girls watch their weight? An interview study examining sociocultural pressures to be thin. *Journal of Psychosomatic Research, 42*, 345–355.

Wiseman, C. V., Gray, J.J., Mosimann, J.E., & Athens, A.H. (1992). Cultural expectations of thinness in women: An update. *International Journal of Eating Disorders, 11*, 85–89.

Wiseman, C. V., Gunning, F.M., & Gray, J.J. (1993). Increasing pressures to be thin: 19 years of diet products in television commercials. *Eating Disorders: The Journal of Treatment and Prevention, 1* (1), 52–61.

8

—∞∞—

Prevention and Special Populations

I did not have a traumatic childhood. There were no major crises, no family members who were alcoholics, and no incidents of sexual abuse. I believe I became vulnerable to developing an eating disorder when the cumulative effect of a number of factors resulted in my experiencing emotional pain and stress as a level of intensity greater than I knew how to manage in a healthy way.

(Reiff, 1993, p. 198)

The prevention of eating disorders and eating disturbances is an especially important topic. In a report to the Congress of the United States of America, the Committee on Prevention of Mental Disorders of the Institute of Medicine indicated that "[t]here could be no wiser investment in our country than a commitment to foster the prevention of mental disorders and the promotion of mental health through vigorous research with the highest of methodological standards (Mrazek & Haggerty, 1994, p. xvii). Prevention is necessary to reduce the incidence of eating disorders because once eating disorders develop, they are debilitating and difficult to treat. Additionally, treatment resources are limited in most countries (even the United States) due to insufficient funds, insurance policies, and a lack of professional expertise. As well-known researchers in the eating disorders prevention field note, even if these were not disorders shrouded in anxiety, secrecy, and shame, there are simply not enough mental health professionals to meet the challenge (Levine & Smolak, 2001). Prevention is the only reasonable approach to eating disorders as a health care problem.

However, in spite of this recommendation, there has been little research on the factors that may prevent someone from developing an eating disorder (Crago, Shisslak, & Rubel, 2001; Levine & Smolak, 2001). Furthermore, eating disorder prevention efforts are complicated by a dilemma—there is an attempt to facilitate acceptance of one's body, whereas on the other hand, we recognize that obesity is a serious health problem in and of itself. It may be that some amount of body dissatisfaction is necessary to motivate people to participate in healthy exercise programs and eat in a healthy way. However, when body dissatisfaction is too high, eating disorders may develop. A thoughtful review of this dilemma is presented by Heinberg, Thompson and Matzon (2001), and concludes that the goal "albeit a sensitive one, is to encourage healthy self-esteem and a self-evaluation that is not dominated by appearance, while reinforcing the veracity of an overweight status and its concomitant body image dissatisfaction, with the goal of increasing healthy weight control strategies" (p. 228).

Prevention programs are designed to reduce the occurrence of eating disorders and disturbances; however, this is not as simple as it seems. First, there are three kinds or classes of prevention: primary or universal, secondary or targeted/indicated, and tertiary. Models for prevention programs are disease specific, nonspecific vulnerability-stressor, or empowerment-relational models, or some combination of these. Prevention can happen at different levels: macro, meso, and micro. Beginning with definitions of these terms is necessary to present the state-of-the-art in the prevention of eating disorders.

PRIMARY PREVENTION

Primary prevention, sometimes referred to as universal prevention, refers to efforts at reducing the incidence of eating disorders in individuals who have not yet developed any symptoms of a disorder (Levine & Smolak, 2001; Piran, Levine, & Steiner-Adair, 1999). This may be thought of as public health prevention and is aimed at the population at large. In other words, primary or universal prevention is designed to reduce the incidence of eating disorders (anorexia nervosa, bulimia nervosa, and eating disorders not otherwise specified) and eating disturbances, including dieting, vomiting, excessive exercise, and binge eating in the general population. This type of prevention program may include education and the nature and consequences of eating disorders, the negative effects of dieting and other unhealthy methods of weight control, and may also include some skill development to resist the pressure to diet. In addition, primary prevention may be developed based on enhancing healthy development from childhood through adolescence and adulthood. This aspect of the prevention program may be aimed at general factors such as self-esteem and coping.

Selective prevention is a kind of specialized prevention aimed at people who do not have any symptoms of eating problems but who are considered to be at high risk of developing an eating disorder. At this level, the participants do not have an eating disorder. They are considered to be at risk because they are in an environment that is competitive, perfectionistic, and focused on weight or shape (like a dancer in a ballet company; see Piran, 1999).

Many primary prevention have been designed to help girls to develop better body image and to reduce risk by teaching girls to resist the pressure to diet. It is difficult to do this in a climate that "glorifies thinness and vilifies failure to achieve thinness" (Striegel-Moore & Steiner-Adair, 1998, p. 13). Paradoxically, the sociocultural context facilitates the development of obesity by the overabundance of highly palatable, high-fat, highly sweet, and easily accessible food and the support of an increasingly sedentary lifestyle. In the social context of "a waist is a terrible thing to mind" and "you cannot be too rich or too thin," it is difficult to convince adolescents not to diet.

SECONDARY PREVENTION

Secondary prevention is aimed at early detection of a disease (Piran, Levine, & Steiner-Adair, 1999; Schoemaker, 1998). Secondary prevention is also called targeted or indicated prevention. Targeted or indicated prevention is used for people who are on their way to developing an eating disorder; they have attitudes and behaviors associated with eating disorders. The idea behind this level of prevention is to find the people who are beginning to experience an eating problem and provide an intervention that will stop the further development of the problem. It is important because early detection of the problem may make treatment more effective. (Consider the national effort to encourage women to seek mammograms as a screening test for cancer; if cancer is detected early, it is much more treatable.) In order to proceed with indicated prevention programs, first there must be a way to identify those individuals who are showing signs of the problem.

Screening and case finding are two approaches to identifying people who may be at the early stage of developing an eating disorder (Schoemaker, 1998). Screening is testing apparently healthy volunteers from the general population to identify those who might have early signs of a disorder. The goal of screening is early detection of a disease because treatment is either easier or more effective at an earlier stage of the problem. For example, a screening program might involve administering a set of questionnaires to a group of female high school students. Those who score above a certain point on the questionnaires may be good candidates for secondary prevention programs. According to Kashubeck-West, Mintz, and Saunders (2001), the Eating Attitudes Test (Garner, Olmstead, Bohr, & Garfinkel, 1982) and the Eating Disorders Inventory-II (Garner, 1991) are often used as tools to screen for eating disturbances and disorders.

Case finding is testing patients who have sought health care for disorders that may be unrelated to their chief complaint. For example, women who go to their gynecologist might be asked about their eating habits, and attitudes toward food and body image. In this case, the women did not seek treatment for any eating problem, but asking them about their eating attitudes and behaviors may result in finding eating problems that could be influenced with secondary prevention.

TERTIARY PREVENTION

Tertiary prevention involves the prompt identification of those who have an eating disorder and the treatment for the disorder. Because tertiary prevention is actually a synonym for treatment, it is discussed in chapter 9.

MODELS FOR PREVENTION PROGRAMS

There are several major models for guiding prevention programs: disease specific, nonspecific vulnerability-stressor, and empowerment-relational (Levine & Piran, 2001; Levine & Smolak, 2001). Each of these models comes with a set of assumptions that are linked to the kind of prevention program developed and the way in which the programs are evaluated. Although the models are described separately here, many prevention programs include components of more than one model.

The disease specific model emphasizes negative body image, shape and weight concerns, dieting, and sometimes negative affect. The prevention programs that are based on this model assume that there is a specific pathway from weight concerns and dieting to eating disorders. This assumption is consistent with an emphasis on attempts to reduce weight concerns and the intention to diet. Outcomes of these programs might include measures of body dissatisfaction and attitudes toward dieting.

The nonspecific vulnerability-stressor model focuses on the general relationships between poor adjustment, stress, poor health, lack of coping skills, and lack of social support. These programs do not have a primary focus on eating disturbances or disorders. Rather, they have a life skills approach focusing on general self-esteem and competence, which assumes that increasing resilience to stressors will reduce the development of eating problems. Prevention programs based on this model should help prevent anxiety, depression, and substance use that may accompany eating disorders. Outcome measures might include general adjustment and self-esteem, as well as measures of anxiety and depression.

The empowerment-relational model is based on the notion that girls and women are the best authorities about their own bodies. This type of program helps girls and women to "transform a strong sense of private insecurity, distress, and shame into a communal sense of injustice and thereby into plans for constructive action" (Levine & Smolak, 2001, p. 242). Empowerment-relational models often result in changes to the environment, as well as changes for the participants directly. Outcome measures might include assessment of the rules of the environment as well as measures of trust and self-esteem.

LEVELS OF PREVENTION

The levels of prevention include macro, meso, and micro; this refers to the people of groups targeted to receive the prevention program. Macro level prevention programs are designed to target larger societal values, institutions, and policies (such as the media). Meso level programs target specific societal institutions such as schools (there are many examples of school based prevention programs, some of which are presented in this chapter. Also, see www.nationaleatingdisorders.org). Micro level programs aim toward families or individuals. As you will see, prevention programs may fall into all of these categories.

PREVENTION RELATES TO DEVELOPMENT FROM CHILDHOOD THROUGH LATE ADOLESCENCE

Prevention programs should be designed with the developmental needs of the participants in mind. Developmental needs means that at certain times in the lives of children, adolescents, and adults, there are normal changes in the circumstances of life that present new challenges. A developmental transition is the period between the end of one stage of life and beginning of another stage. These developmental transitions are important in reference to the development of eating disturbances and eating disorders. They are times of special risk because they involve major changes in the lives of children becoming adolescents and adolescents becoming adults. (Other developmental transitions exist, but they are less relevant to eating issues.) Many of the changes are normal challenges and stressors, which involve increasing independence from family. During these times there can be major changes in personality and interpersonal relationships, as well as changes in social roles and cultural expectations. Generally, these changes result in healthy adaptations to the new life stage.

Sometimes a person may not adapt well to these changes. Maybe there is a lack of social support to cope with these changes. Or, maybe the person has low self-esteem or self-confidence. It is at these times that developmental challenges could result in the development of eating disorders, eating disturbances, or other psychological problems. Developmental psychologists are particularly concerned with the ways in which growing up may have positive or negative outcomes. Cytrybaum, Blum, Patrick, Stein, Wadner, & Wilk (1980) developed a model of transitions that was applied to eating problems by Smolak and Levine (1996). This kind of model can be used to organize questions about developmental transitions: Are some people particularly vulnerable during the developmental transitions? Do some people face more difficult transitions than others? What might lead to healthy or unhealthy outcomes from a transition?

Predispositions to developing an eating problem can be studied in terms of personality and social systems. Personality refers to all aspects of the self. For example, internalization of the thinness ideal is a part of the personality that is related to the development of a special vulnerability for developing an eating disturbance or disorder. Girls who internalize the thinness ideal may experience developmental transitions as problems, while those who have not internalized the thinness message may not have the same struggle. The nature of someone's personality may constitute either risk or protective factors for a person entering adolescence or adulthood. Social systems, which include family, peer, or other kinds of relationships, may either buffer (protect) or intensify (increase risk) the effects of developmental transitions.

It is critical to understand which factors are associated with the eating disturbances and eating disorders and which factors are associated with the reduction of risk (called protective factors), however, many risk and protective factors are not specific to eating disorders but rather are common to psychological adjustment in general (Crago, Shisslak, & Ruble, 2001). A *risk factor* is an attitude, behavior, belief, situation, or action that may put a group, organization, individual, or community at risk for problems. A *protective factor* is an attitude, behavior, belief, situation, or action that builds resilience in a group, organization, individual, or community. Protective factors contribute to development of resilience, which is defined as the ability to recover from, or cope successfully with, stress or adverse situations (Crago et al., 2001). Prevention may be thought of as a way to increase resilience, which can protect someone from developing an eating disorder.

The transition from late childhood to early adolescence is a period of high risk for the development of eating and body image problems (Levine & Smolak, 2001). Body image and dieting behaviors begin to emerge in girls between the ages of nine and eleven and increase in the transition to middle/junior high school. The change from being a child to an adolescent includes the period of puberty, one of the important transition points for developing an eating disorder. Early maturation and pubertal development are risk factors for eating disorders, which is not surprising because puberty is associated with a considerable increase in fat tissue. Avoidance of weight/fat is a major risk factor for developing eating disorders. As girls go through puberty, they become more dissatisfied with their weight and shape, and those who have developed earlier are more likely than their same-aged peers to diet and worry about their weight. Puberty is often thought of as a more difficult transition for girls than boys as girls experience losses in self-esteem, increases in depression, and less active roles in leadership. Of course, many girls make the change from being a child to being an adolescent without developing an eating disorder. As girls move into adolescence, they face changes in peer and family relationships, academic demands, and social role expectations that require different behavior, thoughts, and emotional understanding.

The later transition from high school age to college age is another important transition. Levenkron (2001) indicated that attending a residential college is an important transitional time with relevance to the development of eating disorders. As many as 19 percent of college students may have some kind of eating disorder. Levenkron challenges the assumption that all students who could be admitted to a live-away college should go to one. He indicates that a person with a history of an eating disorder or other emotional problems may not have the emotional maturity to go away from the family. Adolescents who are not ready to go without daily supervision, affection, and support should not go away. College students, especially in the first year, are susceptible to doing all the things that mommy and daddy wouldn't let them do, and they may drink too much or eat too little (or too much).

Other identifiable crisis junctures may happen during the junior year of high school (when exploring the option of leaving for college), during the senior year of high school (when preparing to leave home), during the freshman year of college (when girls are living out of the home), upon graduation from college (moving further from the dependence of family life), and at other profound positive or negative life-threatening moments that may occur in a young woman's life—marriage, childbirth, incest, or the loss of a best friend (Levenkron, 2001, p. 22).

EXAMPLES OF PREVENTION PROGRAMS

The next section of this chapter includes some brief examples of primary and secondary prevention programs used with elementary, middle, high school, and college students. Many resources address the topic of prevention of eating disorders. Two excellent books, *Preventing Eating Disorders* (Piran, Levine, & Steiner-Adair, 1999) and *The Prevention of Eating Disorders* (Vandereycken & Noordenbos, 1998) provide the basis for some of the information that follows. Additionally chapters in two newer books (Striegel-Moore & Smolak, 2001; Thompson & Smolak, 2001) address prevention issues. In Piran, Levine, and Steiner-Adair's (1999) seminal textbook on prevention of eating disorders, there are five examples of prevention programs in elementary schools and middle schools and five examples of programs used in high schools and college settings. The final chapters review the need for prevention with special populations such as athletes, dancers, and those with diabetes. In Vandereycken and Noordenbos's (1998) book, the chapters include the mass media, school-based prevention programs, and information about screening and work with physicians. The Internet also contains valuable resources, some of which are highlighted in a section here. See chapter 6 for the list of recommended sites for eating disorders prevention information.

An Example of a Prevention Program for Elementary School Age Children

Eating Smart, Eating for Me (Smolak, 1999; Smolak, Levine, & Schermer, 1998) is an excellent example of a program designed to be used with children in elementary school. The six goals of the program are

1. Explaining the importance of proper nutrition, including that fat is a nutrient, and to explain how to use the USDA Food Guide Pyramid to achieve healthy nutrition
2. Encouraging healthy, moderate exercise on a regular basis

3. Teaching students and parents about the diversity of body shape
4. Encouraging the development of a positive body image
5. Encouraging healthy eating rather than caloric-restrictive dieting
6. Encouraging critical evaluation of media messages about body shape and nutrition (Smolak et al., 1998, p. 153).

This program has been the subject of several studies, which were designed to assess the outcome of the prevention program with children aged nine to eleven years. In a study published in 2001, Smolak and Levine found that two years after 289 students participated in the Eating Smart, Eating for Me program, they were more knowledgeable, used fewer unhealthy weight management techniques, and had higher body esteem than adolescents of the same age in a different school. Interestingly, data collected from children in the same school but who did not participate in the prevention program had scores between those who were in the prevention program and those in the other school. This suggests that there may be a spillover effect from the children who did participate in the prevention program to their peers in school who were not part of the prevention program. This important finding means that there is a two-year benefit from this program and indicates that even people who do not participate may benefit from changes in those who do.

However, there are some caveats to these findings. First, findings are limited to Caucasian girls, because there has been little study of children from ethnic groups. Second, all of the data are self-report, which means that the girls complete questionnaires containing questions about their attitudes and behaviors. We cannot be sure that children understand what the researcher means by diet or exercising because children may have their own ideas about what these (and other) words mean. We don't know if children report what they hear from older girls and their mothers or if they really diet. Food diaries might be useful to confirm what is a diet.

An Example of a Prevention Program Used with Middle School and High School Age Adolescents

A school-based eating disorder prevention program developed and tested in middle and high school and college is described by Phelps, Dempsey, Sapia, and Nelson (1999). This program contains six sessions that focus on sociocultural pressures, that is, ways to enhance physical self-esteem, ideas to build personal competence, methods to reduce body dissatisfaction, and the provision of information about appropriate methods of weight control. In the final session, a person recovering from an eating disorder addresses the group.

In the middle school version, the first sessions focus on sociocultural pressures, which were described in this book in chapter 7. An exercise that is helpful in the sociocultural area is looking critically at magazines and discussing the images and the weight-control messages that appear. Magazines that are typically read by girls and boys differ; thus, this is an area in which the conversation might reveal interesting differences. The sessions focusing on physical self-esteem may allow participants to attend to the positive aspects of physical appearance. For example, they may be asked to find and comment on aspects of themselves that they do like, such as "I like my hair" or "I always liked my eyes." Physical fitness is described as healthy and strong, and participants are encouraged to find an activity that allows regular physical exercise. The sessions on building personal competence are focused on developing an internal locus of control, which means that people are encouraged to find answers within themselves rather than relying on external influences. It can be hard for adolescents to make decisions without relying on group pressure, but developing strong personal values may be helpful in preventing eating problems. The sessions on body dissatisfaction are designed to normalize the natural weight gain during puberty through comparing photos of normal weight teenagers to models of extreme thinness. The sessions on weight control highlight the negative aspects of dieting and weight reduction such as "yo-yo" dieting and starvation. Set-point theory can be used to persuade participants that people have a biogenetic disposition to a weight range that the body defends. In addition, these sessions may include information about healthy ways to control weight with a focus on moderate physical exercise and healthy eating. The Food Pyramid is a useful tool for addressing nutritional needs. The final session is one in which a person recovering from an eating disorder tells her story. This is usually engaging for adolescents, and they may be able to develop a deeper understanding of the serious nature of an eating disorder.

Phelps and her colleagues (1999) studied the effects of this program on 1,066 middle school aged girls and boys aged eleven to fifteen and a smaller sample of ninth to twelfth graders. Although the research did not find statistically significant changes in the middle school group, the researchers were encouraged by reductions in current use and future intent to use dieting, excessive exercise, purging and other unhealthy methods of weight control. Other changes were noted as well, but perhaps the most interesting finding was that although males were included in the program, they did not fully participate. Males "were unable to critically examine their beliefs about feminine beauty or scrutinize current sociocultural mores" (Phelps et al., 1999, p. 169). Therefore, they recommended that future implementations of the program be devoted to female participants only.

Among the high school students (only females were included based on the findings in the middle school study), this prevention program was effective in changing attitudes and beliefs about sociocultural influences, reduced willingness to engage in unhealthy eating behaviors, and reduced intention to engage in these behaviors in the future. Researchers reported that the participants in the program were quite interested and active in the program. A modified version of this program was also implemented in a college sample; two sororities were involved in the study. One sorority received the prevention program and the other served as a control group. Researchers indicated that the sorority members who participated in the program had less current use and future plans to use fasting, excessive exercise, purging, and a variety of other unhealthy weight control practices when compared to those who did not participate in the program. Feedback about the program from those who participated was very positive, and focused on the "opportunity to discuss openly the impact of peer and boyfriend pressures, as well as the constant inundation of media images portraying impossibly thin role models" (Phelps et al., 1999, p. 171).

Another example of a prevention program that has been developed is GO GIRLS!, which stands for "Giving Our Girls Inspiration and Resources for Lasting Self-esteem." GO GIRLS! was started by the national nonprofit organization, EDAP, Eating Disorders Awareness & Prevention, Inc. This organization is now part of the National Eating Disorders Organization and material appears on their Web site (www.nationaleatingdisorders.org). This program is designed to help adolescent girls learn about and challenge the current relationships between the media's construction and portrayal of the ideal woman, the business of marketing, and the resultant negative effects of the self-image, bodies, and spirit of many women.

GO GIRLS!™ focuses on the realities of young women in today's society through attention to crucial topics such as body image, media awareness, and the power of speaking out. Projects in the semester-long GO GIRLS! program include making presentations to executives at retail corporations, writing letters to national advertisers, participating in TV and radio interviews, and creating peer awareness campaigns in local high schools. The projects are designed to educate and empower participants to significantly change the way teens are portrayed in the media, the way they feel about themselves and, as one participant summed up her experience, learn "that one voice actually can make a difference."

Prevention Programs for High School and College Students

Hotelling (1999) described an integrated team work approach to preventing (and treating) eating disorders in college students. In a description of the Eating-Disorder Task Force at Northern Illinois University, Hotelling explained that psychologists, physicians, nutritionists, psychiatrists, athletic trainers, exercise physiologists, physical and health educators, advisors to sororities and fraternities, recreation center staff, housing and food service staff, counselors of student athletes, and students came together to address the prevention and treatment in a comprehensive manner. All these campus individuals may play a role in prevention of eating disorders on campuses. The group developed a list of goals; those relevant to prevention include: educating the staff on campus about eating disorders, providing a network for the faculty and staff interested in eating disorders, establishing services for prevention, and developing protocols for identification and referral for those with eating disturbances or disorders, and troubleshooting difficult situations with students suspected of having an eating disorder.

Primary prevention may be less useful on college campuses than in elementary school and middle schools (Hotelling, 1999). In the category of primary prevention, the work of the task force has focused on "policies or practices that may inadvertently undermine health by focusing on weight loss and appearance" (p. 212), such as weekly weigh-ins for student-athletes. Other primary prevention efforts include single presentations made to groups of students on topics such as self-esteem, stress reduction, and handling anger. These presentations are viewed as ways to increase resilience to eating disorders. Participation in the National Eating Disorder Awareness Week is another primary prevention effort (see below).

Secondary prevention may be more appropriate than primary at the college level (Hotelling, 1999) because many students enter college with either the beginnings of an eating disorder or have already been in treatment for an eating disorder. In her chapter, Hotelling advocated for developing a variety of strategies for identifying those with eating disturbances, such as targeting classes that may attract students who may have eating disorders (i.e., classes in health-related fields, education, nursing, dance). The Task Force uses information from residence life staff and the campus recreation center, who may notice signs of eating disturbances (cleaning staff in residence halls may report vomit in a certain bathroom on a regular basis, campus recreation staff may report people who overuse exercise equipment). This kind of comprehensive approach is designed to have an influence on all aspects of campus life.

In a related topic, Sigall (1999) presented the use of a Panhellenic Task Force on Eating Disorders. Because sororities have been identified as a group at risk of developing eating disorders, there have been prevention efforts targeting members of sororities. Some of these programs are peer-centered, meaning that members of the sororities participate in the development of the programs that are aimed at body image, healthy eating and weight, eating and emotions, and self-esteem. Members of each sorority select a representative to be a role model to promote healthy attitudes about body image and to participate in the planning and presenting of educational programs for her sorority.

NATIONAL EATING DISORDER AWARENESS WEEK

EDAP, Eating Disorders Awareness and Prevention, Inc., was a national nonprofit organization dedicated to the elimination of eating disorders and body dissatisfaction through prevention efforts, education, referral and support services, advocacy, training, and research. It is also now a part of the National Eating Disorders Organization. The sponsorship of National Eating Disorders Awareness Week is a major focus on this work. Eating Disorders Awareness Week is held each February. EDAW 2001 was celebrated in all fifty states and Canada, with over 550 educators and health professionals organizing more than 1,500 community outreach events. The toll-free information and resource telephone number (800–931–2237) is for educators, health professionals, friends and family members of people struggling with eating disorders, as well as the sufferers themselves.

INTERNET-BASED PREVENTION PROGRAMS

One example of an Internet-based prevention program is Girl Power! It is sponsored by the U.S. Department of Health and Human Services and is based on the Internet at www.girlpower.gov. The first page of this excellent resource says:

Welcome to the homepage for Girl Power!, the national public education campaign sponsored by the U.S. Department of Health and Human Services to help encourage and motivate 9- to 14-year-old girls to make the most of their lives. Girls at 8 or 9 typically have very strong attitudes about their health, so Girl Power! seeks to reinforce and sustain these positive values among girls ages 9–14 by targeting health messages to the unique needs, interests, and challenges of girls.

To help girls learn more, and feel better, about their bodies, the U.S. Department of Health and Human Services (HHS) has added a new area to its Girl Power! Web site. The area, called BodyWise, aims to teach girls about eating the right foods and staying active to maintain a healthy body size and a healthy self-image. To visit the site, go to www.health.org/gpower/bodywise. One of the Girl Power! campaign's most popular free products is a pocket diary, a small book to use to capture your thoughts, feelings, and ideas. The diary fits easily in a purse or backpack, and contains quotes from girls from around the country. You can order one by calling 1–800–729–6686 and asking for item GPDIR.

PREVENTION IN SPECIAL GROUPS

Some groups of individuals are thought to be at a higher risk to develop an eating disturbance or disorder. In this section of the chapter, two groups of people are discussed: athletes and those who have been sexually abused.

Eating Disorders in Athletes

As a freshman in high school I was on the gymnastics team. Everyone on the team, regardless of their size, had to be weighed on a regular basis. One day my coach weighed me in and declared that I "could afford to lose a few pounds" and at the very least I should watch my calories.

(Kano, 1993, p. 125)

Athletes represent a kind of special group as relates to eating disorders. Although many people know that participation in some sports may be associated with eating disorders, there are also some features of team participation that increase self-esteem among adolescents and may protect them from the development of eating problems. However, the majority of the data suggest that the prevalence of eating disorders and subclinical eating problems is larger in athletes than in nonathletes (Beals & Manore, 1999; Petrie & Rogers, 2001). To date, there is only one study that has used a clinical evaluation and used the DSM criteria to establish the prevalence of eating disorders and disturbances in athletes. In this study, Sundgot-Borgen (1993) found that the prevalence of "anorexia athletica" was 8.2 percent in a sample of Norwegian female athletes. Anorexia athletica was defined as a female athlete with intense fear of gaining weight even though she is underweight. Sundgot-Borgen also noted that disordered eating was significantly more prevalent among athletes participating in aesthetic and weight dependent sports (i.e., diving, figure skating, gymnastics, running).

Likewise, male athletes scored higher than male nonathletes on measures of bulimia, anorexia, and the drive for thinness, particularly when the men participated in aesthetic (e.g., gymnastic and diving) and weight-dependent sports (e.g., wrestling; Hausenblas & Caron, 1999). Female athletes reported more anorexic and bulimic behaviors, especially for female athletes who participated in aesthetic sports such as figure skating and gymnastics (Hausenblas & Caron, 1999).

The distinction between certain kinds of sports appears to be important. Some sports are more problematic for the development of eating disorders than others. "Lean sports" such as gymnastics, long distance running, dancing, and ice-skating (Ashley, Smith, Robinson, & Richardson, 1996) may be associated with eating disorders because success is linked to appearance or weight or both. Certain stereotypes about some of these sports prevail, such as "gymnasts should be 'tiny,' runners 'lanky,' and football players 'big'" (Petrie & Rogers, 2001, p. 747). Others distinguish between refereed sports (like basketball) and judged sports (like gymnastics) (Sundgot-Borgen, 1993).

Powers (1999) summarized issues in sports that increase risk for developing an eating disorder. She indicated that the research suggests that sports that reward a certain appearance such as gymnastics or body building increase risk. Judged sports like gymnastics, figure skating, and diving increase risk compared with referred sports like track and field or swimming. Endurance sports (running) increase risk. Sports with weight categories (like wrestling) increase risk. The lean (running) versus nonlean (tennis or swimming) also increase the risk of developing an eating problem. In addition, participation in individual versus team sports (running versus basketball) may also increase risk.

However, the news for athletes may not be all bad. Some researchers indicate that there are a number of factors associated with being an athlete that may actually protect a girl or women from developing an eating disorder (Smolak, Murnen, & Ruble, 2000; Zucker, Womble, Williamson, & Perrin, 1999). In the Zucker et al. study that compared nonathletes with athletes in refereed sports and athletes in judged sports, there were more individuals with a diagnosis of an eating disorder in those who participated in judged sports than in the other groups. In this study, the refereed sports were tennis, basketball, volleyball, and track, and the judged sports were diving, cheerleading, and gymnastics. The three groups did not differ in age or body mass index (a measure of weight and height), nor did they differ on a number of psychological tests of anxiety or depression.

However, those students who participated in referred sports had significantly less concern and dissatisfaction with body size and less of a drive for thinness as compared to both the athletes in judged sports and nonathletes. This finding is important because it demonstrates that participation in a referred sport may serve as a kind of protective factor against the development of eating disorders. Zucker and colleagues suggested that there are aspects of the team environment that may protect women from developing eating disorders, such as the supportive nature of teams and an emphasis on athleticism.

Participation in certain kinds of sports, therefore, seems to be a risk factor for the development of eating disturbances. However, because not all female athletes develop eating issues, it is worth considering what factors, along with participation in certain types of athletics, might be influential. Social pressure for thinness, athletic performance anxiety, and negative self-appraisal of athletic achievement may contribute to the problems by leading to an overconcern with body size and shape, thus making the person more vulnerable to the development of an eating disorder (Williamson, Netemeyer, Jackman, Anderson, Funsch, & Rabalais, 1995).

Female athletes with disordered eating are also at risk of developing amenorrhea and osteoporosis; this is referred to as the "female athlete triad" (Beals & Manore, 1999; Petrie & Rogers, 2001). Specifically, the triad refers to disordered eating, amenorrhea, and osteoporosis. Osteoporosis may result in bone fractures and permanent bone loss; this appears to be a problem for female athletes because as many as 66 percent of female athletes may be amennorheic (compared with 2 percent to 5 percent of nonathletes; Sanborn, Horea, Siemers, & Dieringers, 2000).

Thompson & Sherman (1999) wrote about the similarities between those with anorexia nervosa and "good athletes." A good athlete is a term that carries special meaning in this work. It refers to good athletic performance and the characteristics of the person that may contribute to better performance. They are not suggesting that good athletes are people who have anorexia nervosa but rather that many of the characteristics associated with anorexia nervosa may also be found in good athletes. Furthermore, these shared characteristics may be responsible for successful athletic performance. The similarity between those who have anorexia nervosa and good athletes may complicate the identification of those athletes who are at risk for developing disordered eating. Following are a few good athlete traits and the corresponding characteristic of anorexia nervosa: commitment to training/excessive exercise, pursuit of excellence/perfectionism, and coachability/overcompliance (see Thompson & Sherman, 1999). Taking these one at a time, commitment to training is essential for world-class athletes, and excellent athletes are known to do everything that they can, push their limits, and give maximal effort to their sport (Thompson & Sherman, 1999, p. 185). People with anorexia nervosa, who feel compelled to exercise, may exercise excessively in spite of their physical condition. "With their need for approval and tendency to be overly compliant, these individuals, if they are also athletes, are apt to train hard or over train to please their coaches or others who have an interest or investment in their performance" (Thompson & Sherman, 1999, p. 185).

The pursuit of excellence/perfectionism dyad refers to the high expectations that surround both athletic performance and anorexia nervosa. Coachability/overcompliance is related to the tendency for both athletes and people with anorexia nervosa to have strong needs for approval and a fear of displeasing others. Unselfishness/selflessness concerns the "there is no ME in TEAM" and the sense that those athletes with anorexia nervosa do not make decisions based on their own needs and desires. Anorexic athletes will put the needs of the coach and team before their own needs.

In summary, the research on athletes suggests that there may be an increase in the prevalence of eating disorders among participants of some kinds of athletics. It is possible that many of these athletes have eating disturbances; thus, these individuals are candidates for secondary prevention (Beals & Manore, 1999). Athletes may be at increased risk of poor nutritional status and health concerns, therefore, the secondary prevention programs should be aimed at limiting the progression of the problematic eating and exercise behaviors.

Sexual Abuse and Eating Disorders

The causal relationship between sexual abuse and eating disorders is a topic that has received a great deal of attention. This means that researchers have studied the relationship between sexual abuse and eating disorders to determine if sexual abuse may cause the development of eating disorders. A key question is: Does sexual abuse constitute a specific risk for eating disorders or is sexual abuse a risk for any psychiatric problem (Kearney-Cooke & Striegel-Moore, 1994; Smolak & Murnen, 2001)? Studies have shown that childhood sexual abuse is associated with increased risk for a variety of psychiatric problems, including eating disorders (Pope & Hudson, 1992). A study by Welch and Fairburn indicated that sexual abuse is not a risk factor specific to the development of bulimia. However, Kearney-Cooke and Striegel-Moore provide a strong argument in support of the specificity link that sexual abuse causes eating disorders. Overall, it is not clear if sexual abuse does cause eating disorders directly, but it is clear that there is a higher rate of eating disorders among those who have been sexually abused. Further, several psychological factors are associated with both eating disorders and sexual abuse, such as diminished self-esteem, self-blame, dissociation, issues with control, and personality disorders (Waller, Everill, & Calam, 1994). The issue of the link between sexual abuse and eating disorders, however, remains a topic of continued attention (Smolak & Murnen, 2001).

The model proposed by Kearney-Cooke and Striegel-Moore (1994) was recently tested by Tripp and Petrie (2001) in a study that was based on a sample of 330 female undergraduates. The model proposes that sexual abuse, shame, and body disparagement (a construct of affective, cognitive, and behavioral components that is associated with hating one's own body) are associated with eating disorders. Over 70 percent of the sample indicated that they had some kind of unwanted sexual contact, which ranged from being exposed to the sexual organs of a male to forced sexual encounters. Using more stringent criteria (included unwanted or forced touching of sexual organs or forced sexual contact), 60 percent still met the criteria. Only a minority experienced this abuse while children (21 percent). The data suggest that sexual abuse predicted higher levels of bodily shame that, in turn, predicted body disparagement, which predicted eating disorders. This study supports the association between sexual abuse and eating disorders.

A SUMMARY OF THE RESEARCH ON PREVENTION PROGRAMS

The research on prevention programs has been reviewed by Levine in recent book chapters (Levine & Piran, 2001; Levine & Smolak, 2001). The oldest prevention study was published in 1986, and the majority of research on this topic has been published after 1996. This field is developing rapidly as newer research builds on the knowledge derived from the most recent studies available.

Levine and Piran (2001) reviewed twenty-two studies, mostly of the disease specific prevention type. These studies, which included girls, boys, and women in the United States, Canada, and several other countries, led Levine and Piran (2001) to draw the following conclusions:

- Primary prevention programs are effective in changing the knowledge and attitudes of participants.

- It is difficult to know if changes in behavior occur as a result of prevention programs. Only three (of fifteen) studies that measured behavior change showed a positive behavior change.

- Secondary intervention programs are valuable in reducing the unhealthy attitudes and behaviors over the short term, while less is known about the long-term effects.

Levine and Smolak (2001) reviewed forty-two published and unpublished studies on prevention of negative body image or eating problems in elementary, middle, and high school students. In the ten studies on elementary school age children, some show positive changes on measures of eating attitudes, knowledge, and behaviors, and others show no differences. The studies of middle and high school age girls also show inconsistency in outcomes, though there have also been reports of increases in problematic attitudes and behaviors (in other words, sometimes outcomes show that more girls are trying to lose weight).

Austin's (2000) review of twenty-eight prevention programs over the last two decades draws some more pessimistic conclusions, that is, "the results of 20 interventions have been discouraging, with only four showing any type of positive behaviour change" and "four recording some worsening of symptoms post-intervention."

What seems clear from the prevention field is that this is a complex challenge (Levine & Smolak, 2001). Prevention is immensely complicated and challenging. The research is not yet sophisticated enough to draw conclusions about what kind of prevention programs works best for which participants. It remains necessary to continue to develop and evaluate prevention programs. "What this means is that mental health professionals, dedicated researchers, activists, parents, and a variety of professionals (e.g., school administrators, athletic directors, and teachers) must work together to extend, integrate, apply and carefully evaluate all of the three major models of prevention" (Levine & Smolak, 2001, p. 256).

REFERENCES

Ashley, C.D., Smith, J.F., Robinson, J.B., & Richardson, M.T. (1996). Disordered eating in female collegiate athletes and collegiate females in an advanced program of study: A preliminary investigation. *International Journal of Sport Nutrition*, 6, 391–401.

Austin, S.B. (2000). Prevention research in eating disorders: Theory and new directions. *Psychological Medicine*, 30, 1249–1260.

Beals, K. A., & Manore, M. M. (1999). Subclinical eating disorders in physically active women. *Topics in Clinical Nutrition, 14,* 14–29.

Crago, M., Shisslak, C. M., & Rubel, A. (2001). Protective factors in the development of eating disturbances. In R. H. Striegel-Moore & L. Smolak (Eds.), *Eating disorders: Innovative directions in research and practice* (pp. 75–89). Washington, DC: American Psychological Association.

Cytrybaum, S., Blum, L., Patrick, R., Stein, J., Wadner, D., & Wilk, C. (1980). Midlife development: A personality and social systems perspective. In L. Poon (Ed.), *Aging in the 1980's* (pp. 463–474). Washington, DC: American Psychological Association.

Garner, D. M. (1991). *Eating Disorders Inventory-2 Manual.* Odessa, FL: Psychological Assessment Resources.

Garner, D. M., Olmsted, M. P., Bohr., Y., & Garfinkel, P. E. (1982). The Eating Attitudes Test: Psychometric features and clinical correlates. *Psychological Medicine, 12,* 871–878.

Hausenblas, H., & Caron, A. (1999). Eating disorder indices and athletes: An integration. *Journal of Sport & Exercise Psychology, 21,* 230–258.

Heinberg, L. J., Thompson, J. K., & Matson, J. L. (2001). Body image dissatisfaction as a motivator for healthy lifestyle change: Is some distress beneficial? In R. H. Striegel-Moore & L. Smolak (Eds.), *Eating disorders: Innovative directions in research and practice* (pp. 215–232). Washington, DC: American Psychological Association.

Hotelling, K. (1999). An integrated prevention/intervention program for the university setting. In N. Piran, M. P. Levine, & C. Steiner-Adair (Eds.), *Preventing eating disorders: A handbook of interventions and special challenges* (pp. 208–221). Philadelphia, PA: Taylor & Francis.

Kano, S. (1993). Leap of faith. In L. Hall (Ed.), *Full lives: Women who have freed themselves from food and weight obsession* (pp. 110–127), Carlsbad, CA; Gurze Books.

Kashubeck-West, S., Mintz, L. B., & Saunders, K. J. (2001). Assessment of eating disorders in women. *The Counseling Psychologist, 29,* 662–694.

Kearney-Cooke, A., & Striegel-Moore, R. H. (1994). Treatment of childhood sexual abuse in anorexia nervosa and bulimia nervosa: A feminist psychodynamic approach. *International Journal of Eating Disorders, 15,* 305–319.

Levenkron, S. (2001). *Anatomy of anorexia.* New York: W. W. Norton.

Levine, M. P., & Piran, N. (2001). The prevention of eating disorders: Toward a participatory ecology of knowledge, action, and advocacy. In R. H. Striegel-Moore & L. Smolak (Eds.), *Eating disorders: Innovative directions in research and practice* (pp. 233–254). Washington, DC: American Psychological Association.

Levine, M. P., & Smolak, L. (2001). Primary prevention of body image disturbances and disordered eating in childhood and early adolescence. In J. K. Thompson & L. Smolak (Eds.), *Body image, eating disorders, and obesity in youth* (pp. 237–260). Washington, DC: American Psychological Association.

Mrazek, P. J., & Haggerty, R. J. (1994). *Reducing risks for mental disorders: Frontiers for prevention intervention research.* Washington, DC.: National Academy Press.

Petrie, T. A., & Rogers, R. (2001). Extending the discussion of eating disorders to include men and athletes. *The Counseling Psychologist, 29* (5), 743–753.

Phelps, L, Dempsey, M., Sapia, J., & Nelson, L. (1999). The efficacy of a school-based eating disorder prevention program: Building physical self-esteem and personal competencies. In N. Piran, M. P. Levine, & C. Steiner-Adair (Eds.), *Preventing eating disorders: A handbook of interventions and special challenges* (pp. 163–174). Philadelphia, PA: Taylor & Francis.

Piran, N. (1999). On the move from tertiary to secondary and primary prevention: Working with an elite dance school. In N. Piran, M. P. Levine, & C. Steiner-Adair (Eds.), *Preventing eating disorders: A handbook of interventions and special challenges* (pp. 256–269). Philadelphia, PA: Taylor & Francis.

Piran, N., Levine, M. P., & Steiner-Adair, C. (Eds.) (1999). *Preventing eating disorders: A handbook of interventions and special challenges*, Philadelphia, PA: Taylor & Francis.

Pope, H. G., Jr., & Hudson, J. I. (1992). Is childhood sexual abuse a risk factor for bulimia nervosa? *American Journal of Psychiatry, 149,* 455–463.

Powers, P. (1999). Athletes and eating disorders. *Eating Disorders: The Journal of Treatment and Prevention, 7,* 249–255.

Reiff, K. L. (1993). Perseverance overcomes. In L. Hall (Ed.), *Full lives: Women who have freed themselves from food and weight obsession* (pp. 197–214), Carlsbad, CA; Gurze Books.

Sanborn, C., Horea, M., Siemers, B., & Kieringer, K. (2000). Disordered eating and the female athlete triad. *Clinics in Sport Medicine, 19,* 199–213.

Schoemaker, C. (1998). The principles of screening for eating disorders. In W. Vandereycken & G. Noordenbos (Eds.), *The Prevention of Eating Disorders* (pp. 187–213), New York: New York University Press.

Sigall, B. A. (1999). The Panhellenic Task Force on eating disorders: A program of primary and secondary prevention for sororities. In N. Piran, M. P. Levine, & C. Steiner-Adair (Eds.), *Preventing eating disorders: A handbook of interventions and special challenges* (pp. 222–237). Philadelphia, PA: Taylor & Francis.

Smolak, L. (1999). Elementary school curricula for the primary prevention of eating problems. In N. Piran, M. P. Levine, & C. Steiner-Adair (Eds.), *Preventing eating disorders: A handbook of interventions and special challenges* (pp. 87–104). Philadelphia: Taylor & Francis.

Smolak, L., & Levine, M. P. (1996). Adolescent transitions and the development of eating problems. In L. Smolak, M. P. Levine, R. H. Striegel-Moore (Eds.), *The developmental psychopathology of eating disorders* (pp. 207–233). Mahwah, NJ: Lawrence Erlbaum.

Smolak, L. & Levine, M. P. (2001). A two-year follow-up of a primary prevention program for negative body image and unhealthy weight regulation. *Eating Disorders: The Journal of Treatment and Prevention, 9* (4), 313–325.

Smolak, L., & Murnen, S.K. (2001). Gender and eating problems. In R.H. Striegel-Moore & L. Smolak (Eds.), *Eating disorders: Innovative directions in research and practice* (pp. 91–110). Washington, DC: American Psychological Association.

Smolak, L., Levine, M.P., & Schermer, F. (1998). A controlled evaluation of an elementary school primary prevention program for eating problems. *Journal of Psychosomatic Research, 44*, 339–354.

Smolak, L., Murnen, S.K., & Ruble, A.E. (2000). Female athletes and eating problems: A meta-analysis. *International Journal of Eating Disorders, 27*, 371–380.

Striegel-Moore, R.H., & Smolak, L. (2001). *Eating disorders: Innovative directions in research and practice*. Washington, DC: American Psychological Association.

Striegel-Moore, R.H., & Steiner-Adair, C. (1998). Primary prevention of eating disorders: Further considerations from a feminist perspective. In W. Vandereycken & G. Noordenbos (Eds.), *The Prevention of Eating Disorders* (pp. 1–22). New York: New York University Press.

Sundgot-Borgen, J. (1993). Prevalence of eating disorders in elite female athletes. *International Journal of Sports Nutrition, 3*, 29–40.

Thompson, R.A., & Sherman, R.T. (1999). "Good athlete" traits and characteristics of Anorexia Nervosa: Are they similar? *Eating Disorders: The Journal of Treatment and Prevention, 7* (3), 181–190.

Thompson, J.K., & Smolak, L. (2001). *Body image, eating disorders, and obesity in youth*. Washington, DC: American Psychological Association.

Tripp, M.M., & Petrie, T.A. (2001). Sexual abuse and eating disorders: A test of a conceptual model. *Sex Roles, 44*, 17–32.

Vandereycken, W., & Noordenbos, G. (1998). *The prevention of eating disorders*. New York: New York University Press.

Waller, G., Everill, J., & Calam, R. (1994). Sexual abuse and the eating disorders. In L. Alexander-Mott & D.B. Lumsden (Eds.), *Understanding eating disorders: Anorexia nervosa, bulimia nervosa, and obesity* (pp. 77–97). Washington, DC: Taylor & Francis.

Williamson, D.A., Netemeyer, R.G., Jackman, L.P., Anderson, D.A., Funsch, C.K. & Rabalais, J.Y. (1995). Structural equation modeling of risk factors for the development of eating disorder symptoms in female athletes. *International Journal of Eating Disorders, 17* (4), 387–393.

Zucker, N.L., Womble, L.G., Williamson, D.A., & Perrin, L.A. (1999). Protective factors for eating disorders in female college athletes. *Eating Disorders: The Journal of Treatment and Prevention, 7*, 207–218.

9

——⚬⚬⚬——

Treatment

I used to diet and binge to comfort and protect myself, to assert my independence, to give myself an illusion of power and control, to give myself an excuse for not growing up and being responsible, to release tension and anxiety, and even to indulge myself. Now I know how to do all these things directly, healthfully, and much more effectively.

(Rubel, 1993, p. 50)

The only thing that will ever work is respecting the natural hungers of the body, treating ourselves with honor and respect, and learning to use our mouths to speak the truth as well as to eat the food.

(Roth, 1993, p. 250).

Anorexia, bulimia, and eating disorders not otherwise specified are disorders that have a lot in common, such as dissatisfaction with body shape and weight and disturbances in eating behavior. Fear about gaining weight and a negative attitude about weight and shape are also characteristics of eating disorders. Therefore, it makes sense that there are aspects of treatment that address these common themes regardless of the specific type of eating disorder. Treatment focused on body image is an example of a kind of therapy that makes sense for all individuals with eating disorders.

Because there are meaningful distinctions between the different types of eating disorders, there are also important differences in the treatment of these disorders. For example, the topic of weight is entirely different in treatment of anorexia and bulimia. In the treatment of bulimia, patients are informed that treatment generally has little or no effect on weight; therefore, they can eat much more than they think without gaining weight. Because weight gain is a major goal in the treatment of anorexia, however, this argument is not usable. When treating anorexia, the fear of weight gain must be addressed while the client is actually gaining weight. Restoring a healthy weight is part of the treatment of anorexia nervosa.

The American Psychiatric Association (2000) published an important paper called "Practice Guidelines for the Treatment of Patients with Eating Disorders." This paper is state-of-the-art for the treatment of eating disorders; it is based on 356 articles about the effects of treatment for people with anorexia, bulimia, and eating disorders not otherwise specified. More research is available to document the effectiveness of various treatment strategies for bulimia than for anorexia or eating disorders not otherwise specified. The recommendations made in the APA (2000) Practice Guidelines are presented in this chapter. The guidelines provide detailed information about treatment for each disorder separately. See the Appendix for the recommendations for each disorder.

It is important to note that eating disorders are psychological problems that often require collaboration between mental health professionals (psychologists, social workers, and counselors) and physicians (especially primary care practitioners, pediatricians, and psychiatrists). Physicians or dentists are often first to suspect that an eating disorder may be present, and they may refer the patient to a mental health professional who specializes in providing care for people with eating disorders. Physicians may see signs of eating problems when a regular patient loses a great deal of weight. Patients may report abdominal pain/bloating, constipation, irregular menses, or overall weakness. Sometimes, a doctor may notice swollen cheeks or glands. Dentists may see signs of changes in the teeth in those individuals who purge because vomiting erodes the enamel of the teeth (DiGioacchino, Keenan, & Sargent, 2000).

Mental health providers may refer individuals with eating disorders to physicians for an evaluation of physical health and nutritional status. At times, a client may not be willing to see a physician for an exam. However, it is a critical part of the treatment. Often a treatment team is formed to provide a comprehensive approach to the care of an individual person with an eating disorder; these teams may consist of a psychologist, psychiatrist, dietitian, and a social worker or counselor.

The importance of nutritional education and therapy in working with individuals who exhibit any eating issues cannot be overlooked (Thomas, 2000). The American Dietetic Association (2001) developed a position paper that emphasized the importance of registered dieticians in treatment of people with eating disorders:

It is the position of the American Dietetic Association (ADA) that nutrition education and nutritional intervention, by a registered dietitian, is an essential component of the team treatment of patients with anorexia nervosa, bulimia nervosa, and eating disorders not otherwise specified (EDNOS) during assessment and treatment across the continuum of care. (p. 810)

In *Eating Disorders: Nutrition Therapy in the Recovery Process,* Reiff and Reiff (2000) (a dietitian and psychologist team) emphasize the role of nutritional therapy in recovery from eating disorders and discuss such topics as metabolic rate and hunger. Basic information on nutrition as it applies to eating disorders and exercises that can be used to discover the impact of nutrition are also included. Because the impact of nutrition on eating behavior and health is not typically part of the educational experience of the majority of mental health professionals, registered dieticians are a part of the treatment team (Thomas, 2000). Registered dietitians work with clients to ensure that treatment issues relevant to health and nutritional status are addressed. Rock (1999) indicates that for individuals with bulimia the role of the nutritional intervention is to normalize the eating pattern, which is often chaotic and replete with rigid foods and dieting, interspersed with binge eating and purging. For anorexia, the nutritional intervention focuses primarily on weight restoration. Interestingly, individuals with eating disorders often collect and read literature about food, calories, and energy consumption. Interest in dietary issues is often high.

A particular issue likely to be faced by mental health counselors as well as medical professionals working with individuals with eating problems is denial of the seriousness of the problem. Some people with eating disorders refuse treatment. This is particularly common in the treatment of anorexia. When someone is diagnosed with anorexia, the first reaction may be feeling caught, trapped, discovered, or cornered (Levenkron, 2001). They may not be ready to be patients, but the nature of anorexia does not allow medical doctors and mental health practitioners to wait. Because people with anorexia may get sicker and sicker as they lose weight, treatment often may need to begin before the patient is ready. Boskind-White (Boskind-White & White, 2000) tells her new patients with anorexia that the first job faced by the therapist and client is to determine if outpatient treatment is safe or if the person will need to be hospitalized. Therapists may tell patients who are so ill that they can be hospitalized against their will so that the patients can preserve their dignity by cooperating with voluntary admission to the hospital (Levenkron,

2001). When patients begin treatment reluctantly, they may be likely to stop attending. Sometimes patients refuse to accept the part of treatment that concerns weight gain, but they may initially be willing to attend individual counseling or family therapy. Psycho-educational interventions (see chapter 6; also Garner, 1997) may be less threatening than traditional counseling. Psycho-education is used to provide accurate information about the consequences of food restriction, binge eating and methods of purging, along with the effects of starvation. Psycho-education may be a place to start with resistant clients. Self-help books may be another way to provide help to clients who may be unwilling to commit to counseling.

STEPPED CARE TREATMENT

Stepped care treatment (Stein, Saelens, Dounchis, Lewczyk, Swenson, & Wilfley, 2001; Wilson, Vitousek, & Loeb, 2000) is a plan that can be used to start treatment for a person with an eating disorder. In a stepped care treatment plan, the lowest step is used first. The lowest step is the one that is simplest, least costly, and least intrusive. For example, a low step care could involve self-help or guided self-help (in which a professional meets with the client to assist in the use of self-help materials). If the person does not improve with the care provided in a lower step, the next step care is provided. The next steps include psycho-educational groups and other brief forms of counseling. As these steps fail to meet the needs of the client, additional treatment options are available. The most intensive step is inpatient hospitalization. Evidence suggests that the stepped care treatment approach to providing help for eating disorders may be most effective with bulimia and eating disorders not otherwise specified. The lower steps may not be appropriate for anorexia, especially if the person is in need of urgent medical care.

In bulimia and some eating disorders not otherwise specified, there is no reason to believe that there would be negative effects from starting with a treatment too low in the steps of care. When a step doesn't help the client, there is another strategy to try. However, in anorexia, a person may need to start at a higher step because they are medically unstable. Another reason for being concerned about starting people with anorexia at a step that is too low is that compared to persons with bulimia, anorexia patients are less often motivated to make changes, and they may participate in treatment with less commitment (Wilson et al., 2000). People with bulimia who seek treatment want to improve so that they can have some relief from their eating disorder symptoms. When one step fails, it is useful to frame the next step as a continued investment in recovery. Because individuals with anorexia may be less motivated to change (in fact part of the criteria that define anorexia is the fear of gaining weight), if a step that is too low is tried and the client fails to improve, she may want to decline offers for additional kinds of treatment.

A variety of treatments are available for individuals with eating disorders. The psychologist, psychiatrist, or other mental health worker who is providing the care selects the appropriate treatment. Treatment for eating disorders may include self-help, psycho-education, various types of individual counseling (such as cognitive-behavioral therapy or interpersonal therapy), family counseling, group therapy, medication, nutritional therapy, and partial or inpatient hospitalization.

Another model for making decisions about what kind of treatment is best for a person with an eating problem is presented by Garner and Needleman (1997). They created a flowchart that can be used to select the most appropriate treatment. For example, a person who does not meet the weight criteria for anorexia, has no immediate physical complications and does not have a severe disorder of either anorexia, bulimia or eating disorder not otherwise specified may be best helped with self-help or psycho-education. If the symptoms are more severe and include regular bingeing and purging, cognitive-behavioral therapy (a description of which follows in this chapter) is recommended. A patient who is emaciated (very thin; meets weight standards for anorexia), experiencing physical complications, or who is at risk of committing suicide should be hospitalized for psychological treatment, medical stabilization, and weight restoration.

The American Psychiatric Association (2000) Practice Guidelines also specify levels of treatment, which include outpatient, intensive outpatient, partial hospitalization, residential treatment center, and inpatient hospitalization. The majority of this chapter focuses on the outpatient levels of treatment. In the United States, there seems to be an emphasis on outpatient treatment of eating disorders (Peterson & Mitchell, 1999), probably due to insurance company policies that push for less expensive treatment (Levenkron, 2001). Partial hospitalization, which is often called day treatment, and inpatient hospitalization programs are also described. It is noteworthy that in the inpatient settings, one is likely to find the same kind of therapy provided to outpatients, but in the day treatment or inpatient hospitalization programs, the staff is able to control access to food and monitor medical issues closely.

Self-Help

Self-help is a first step because it is easily available to clients and not as expensive as intensive psychotherapy. In this context, self-help means using a book, tape, or other source of information to help control the eating disorder. Many resources are available in the self-help category. In several national studies of psychologists who work with individuals who have eating disorders and eating disturbances, these books were rated as helpful to clients (Norcross, Santrock, Campbell, Smith, Sommer, & Zuckerman, 2000) as are written for people struggling with eating disorders and disturbances.

Fairburn, C.G. (1995). *Overcoming Binge Eating*. New York: Guilford Press.

The Twelve Steps and Twelve Traditions of Overeaters Anonymous. (1995). Rio Rancho, NM: Overeaters Anonymous.

Hollis, J. (1996). *Fat Is a Family Affair*. Cedar City, MN: Hazelden.

Migliore, M.A. with Ross, P. (1998). *The Hunger Within: A Twelve-Week Guided Journey from Compulsive Eating to Recovery*. New York: Main Street.

Price, D. (1998). *Healing the Hungry Self: The Diet-Free Solution to Lifelong Weight Management*. New York: Plume.

Roth, G. (1989). *Why Weight? A Guide to Ending Compulsive Eating*. New York: Plume.

Roth, G. (1991). *When Food Is Love*. New York: Dutton.

Sacker, I.M., & Zimmer, M.A. (1987). *Dying to Be Thin: Understanding and Defeating Anorexia Nervosa and Bulimia: A Practical, Lifesaving Guide*. New York: Warner.

Two additional books, not contained on the above list, written by Thomas Cash, are also recommended. The first, *What Do You See When You Look in the Mirror? Helping Yourself to a Positive Body Image*, (1995) is an excellent book full of information along with short exercises designed to help people create a healthy body image. In 1997, he published a workbook based on the 1995 book. *The Body Image Workbook: An 8-Step Program for Learning to Like Your Looks* (1997) provides the material in a format that allows people to experience the exercises fully and integrate a better body image into daily life.

The Internet is also a valuable source of information about eating disorders. Not all eating disorder Web sites provide reputable information; some excellent reputable Web site addresses are listed in chapter 6.

Because some people with an eating disorder do not want to seek treatment, these self-help options are a first step toward recovery. Many people will discover that they need more help than a self-help book can provide. Guided self-help books are used in conjunction with meetings with a professional. A review of several studies of the effectiveness of guided self-help indicated that as many as 30 percent of individuals with bulimia who use a self-help manual improve, this also means that 70 percent do not improve (Wilson et al., 2000). In one study, even more than 30 percent improved; Cooper, Coker, and Fleming (1996) found that over half of individuals with bulimia who were treated with a self-help manual stopped bulimic episodes and vomiting. However, those individuals who do not improve using self-help materials are in need of additional options for treatment. It may be that reading a self-help book and doing some of the exercises that appear in these books prepares the person for counseling or psychotherapy treatment.

In addition to self-help manuals and the Internet, there are support or self-help groups for eating disorders. Support groups are usually free of charge, held in a nontherapy setting, and are often led by persons who have recovered from an eating problem rather than a mental health professional (Fairburn & Carter, 1997; Garvin, Striegel-Moore, Kaplan, & Wonderlich, 2001). Many self-help groups are associated with national organizations: a list of Web sites is included at the end of this chapter. These organizations may provide newsletters, telephone hotlines, and consultation to parents and professionals. Tremendous variation exists on the kinds of support groups offered and there is little evidence to indicate which kinds of groups are most beneficial with various kinds of eating problems. Referrals to support groups may be useful, however, as an adjunct to counseling or as continued support after formal therapy has ended.

Psycho-Education

Psycho-education is the next step in the stepped plan of care. At this level, psycho-education is used for people who are having problems with eating and body image to learn about eating disorders, the symptoms of eating disorders, and the problems that may develop when someone has an eating disorder. Psycho-education includes information that is presented in chapter 6 of this book. The goal is to change attitudes and behaviors that are likely to lead a person to have more eating and body image issues. Psycho-education is designed to reduce eating problems, but it is not counseling or therapy. It is more like a small group in which there is a leader who talks about a topic and provides information. Some psycho-educational programs are presented through computer programs. Through psycho-education, people with eating disorders are provided accurate information to challenge the misinformation and myths that those with eating problems may hold. These bits of misinformation may keep those who have an eating disorder from changing their behavior. For example, they may believe that the purging is safe, or they may be convinced that throwing up rids their body of all the calories they consumed in the binge. These statements are not true, so it is important for those with eating problems to learn more about the body and how it works.

Computers are an excellent vehicle for providing psycho-educational interventions. A computer-based psycho-educational program can be used as an adjunct to treatment with individuals who have an eating disorder or as a way to present information on issues related to eating disorders for young women who may be at risk of developing an eating problem. In one example the use of a psycho-educational computer-based program (Andrewes, Say, & McLennan, 1995), a young woman who developed an eating disorder was described. The program provided information about eating disorders, dieting, exercise, nutrition, and risk factors for eating disorders. Individuals using the computer program were guided through questions about eating disorders and quizzed on the information presented. In a study of this short psycho-educational computer program, those who used the program learned more about dieting and eating disorders than those who used a computer program without the eating program. However, the program did not change attitudes about eating and body images ("I consider my body's weight and shape to be more important than my health" and "I think that my thighs are too large"). Participants said that they liked using the program. Thus, it seems that a short time using a computer program can result in changed knowledge about eating issues. It is not effective in changing attitudes, which suggests they are much harder to change than knowledge. This type of education is most promising as prevention for eating disorders rather than an intervention for those already exhibiting symptoms (Andrewes et al., 1995).

Two other recent studies have assessed the use of computer programs along with e-mail support via the Internet as ways to provide psycho-educational materials to young women at risk for developing eating problems (Celio, Winzelberg, Taylor, Wilfley, Eppstein-Herald, Springer, & Dev, 2000; Winzelberg, Eppstein, Eldredge, Wilfley, Dasmahapatra, Dev, & Taylor, 2000). When a computer program called Student Bodies, which addresses body image dissatisfaction, weight concerns, and dieting, was used along with an e-mail support group, participants showed reduced negative attitudes and behaviors associated with the development of eating disorders and decreased negative feelings about bodies in college-aged women. Student Bodies contains information on eating disorders, healthy weight regulation, nutrition, and exercise and includes audio and video presentations that are designed to capture the interest of the users. This is encouraging as a way to reduce risk for individuals who may be demonstrating some of the early signs of problem attitudes and behaviors.

For some people at risk for developing eating disorders, this kind of information may be enough to lead to a significant change in behavior and a reduction in eating related symptoms. Some people with bulimia improve (reduce their binge eating and purging) substantially after participating in five sessions of group psycho-education. However, individuals with more severe eating problems may not respond as well to this kind of treatment. Because psycho-education is less expensive and less intrusive than counseling or psychotherapy, and knowledge about food may be enough to help someone overcome an eating problem, it is a step that can be used with people who have an eating disorder. However, even though people who participated in group psycho-education reduce their binge eating and purging, only a few reduced their binge eating and purging to the point that these behaviors were completely absent. In other words, group psycho-education may help some people, but many people will need the next steps. Most often, individuals need additional psychological therapy to recover from eating disorders.

COGNITIVE-BEHAVIORAL THERAPY

Cognitive-behavioral therapy is described as the treatment of choice for bulimia; it is a gold-standard, meaning that it may be the best treatment available for this disorder (Chambless et al., 1998; Stein et al., 2001; Wilson, Fairburn, & Agras, 1997). Most researchers have concluded that cognitive behavioral therapy is the most extensively researched and supported treatment for bulimia (Stein et al., 2001; Richards, Baldwin, Frost, Clark-Sly, Berrett, & Hardman, 2000). Agras (2001) also indicates that it is less expensive and more effective than medication-based treatments. A ten-year follow-up of women who had treatment with cognitive behavioral therapy (with or without an antidepressant) or a placebo indicated that participants who were treated with either cognitive behavioral therapy or an antidepressant had improved social adjustment compared to those who had only the placebo treatment (Keel, Mitchell, Davis, & Crow, 2002). Cognitive behavioral therapy is superior to other forms of therapy, such as supportive counseling, behavior therapy, and psychodynamic therapy (Richards et al., 2000); comparisons between these treatments in controlled research trials supports the finding that cognitive behavioral therapy works better to reduce symptoms of bulimia than the alternative treatments tested.

Cognitive is a word that means thought, and this treatment focuses on the thoughts and behaviors present in people with eating disorders. With modifications, cognitive-behavioral therapy may be used to treat eating disorders not otherwise specified, especially binge-eating disorder.

Cognitive behavioral therapy has also been used to treat anorexia, though there is little research on this topic. The cognitive behavioral therapy program for anorexia contains some of the same components of the program for treatment of bulimia and addresses issues specific to anorexia, such as the effects of starvation and the need for weight gain (Bowers, 2001). For example, a cognitive behavioral program for people with anorexia may place a primary focus on identifying and targeting automatic thoughts about weight and shape.

Cognitive behavioral therapy is based on a treatment manual that guides the nineteen to twenty sessions that are spaced out over four or five months. (Several manuals are available; the material that follows is based on Wilson, Fairburn, & Agras, 1997, which is well-researched and accepted by professionals in the field.) The treatment is problem oriented (focused on the eating problem), focused on the present and future (rather than the past), and based on a collaborative working relationship between the therapist and client. Homework assignments are a part of the treatment. A book called *Overcoming Binge Eating* (Fairburn, 1995) is often used along with cognitive behavioral therapy to provide more information about binge eating.

There are three stages of treatment. During the beginning of treatment, the therapist works to establish a good relationship with the client. The focus of the first eight sessions is on changing behavior. The problematic behaviors are binge eating and purging/use of laxatives or other drugs. The therapist uses these sessions to teach the client about the need for changes of behaviors and thoughts associated with body image and food issues. Weekly weigh in is a part of treatment, but the client is advised not to weigh in at other times during the week. The client learns about weight regulation, the effects of dieting, and the physical consequences of binge eating, vomiting, and laxative abuse. It is important to reduce the frequency of binge eating by introducing a pattern of regular eating.

The concept of self-monitoring is an important part of cognitive behavioral therapy. Clients are asked to write down all the food they eat on monitoring forms that include information about the time of the day, what was eaten, if it was a meal, snack, or a binge, whether it led to purging, and the feelings and thoughts associated with the food. The monitoring sheets are not designed for counting calories or grams of fat, and this behavior is discouraged. The reason for this self-monitoring is to provide a detailed description of the eating problem and the circumstances associated with it. Increasing the person's understanding of what she eats and how this is related to certain events, thoughts, or feelings helps regain control of eating.

The prescription of regular eating habits is an important part of recovering from bulimia. In this aspect of treatment, the person with bulimia is taught to eat three meals a day and two snacks. Meal skipping is discouraged because highly restrictive eating may be a trigger for binges. When clients begin to eat in a more regular pattern, they can successfully reduce the number of binges and the number of calories consumed. Even though there is often a fear of gaining weight, when people begin eating normal meals the binges decrease, so people do not usually gain weight. Identifying high-risk situations for binges is another part of this phase of treatment. Planning for avoiding some of these high-risk situations, or planning out how to behave in these high-risk events can help prevent the binges.

In Stage 2 (sessions 9–16), the focus is on eliminating dieting, problem-solving skills, and cognitive restructuring. Clients are encouraged to stop limiting their food intake and to begin to eat some of the foods that were forbidden as part of their eating disorder. Because restricting food often leads to cravings and then binges, this is especially important. The problem solving skills are included to help the client to identify the specific situations that may lead to binge eating. The steps in problem solving include: (1) identifying the problem, (2) figuring out different ways to cope with the problem, (3) rating the effectiveness and feasibility of the possible ways of coping, (4) picking one and planning how to do it, (5) following through with this plan, and (6) evaluating how well the plan worked. It can take several sessions of discussion to work through problem-solving plans.

Cognitive restructuring refers to a part of treatment designed to target the kinds of thoughts that people with eating disorders often have that may contribute to their problems with food and body image in an attempt to alter these thought processes. An example of this type of thinking is called dichotomous or all-or-nothing thinking. This means that a person sees things as all good or all bad. A day may be all good if there is no binge eating, and all bad if a forbidden food is eaten. This kind of thinking influences many aspects of daily living and makes it difficult to see positive changes as they are made. A quote from *Full Lives* provides an example of how these cognitive changes impact recovery: "I've learned to challenge black-and-white thinking. Rarely is something as simple as right or wrong, good or bad, wildly successful or a total flop. I've learned to spot shades of gray and to always include something positive with a negative judgment. For example, I no longer tell myself that I'm the dumbest, stupidest person on the face of the earth when I make a mistake" (Rubel, 1993, p. 46).

Other helpful strategies used in this stage of treatment may focus on body image. Some people with bulimia avoid letting people see their bodies by wearing "fat clothes," which are loose fitting and generally shapeless. These individuals are asked to start to wear more flattering and revealing clothes, to look at their bodies in the mirror, go swimming, and get comfortable revealing more of their bodies. On the other hand, there are some people with bulimia who are too focused on their bodies, often spending long hours observing and studying themselves in detail. It is suggested that people who are too focused on their bodies experiment with stopping this excessive focus on the body; for example, they can stop making comparisons between themselves and others.

In the last stage of treatment, a plan is developed to prevent returning to old patterns after the end of treatment. This is called relapse prevention. During this final phase of treatment, sessions may be held every other week, rather than weekly. The work is designed to talk about situations that might be difficult and prepare for ways to cope with them. In some ways, this brings together all aspects of treatment and to review the progress made so far. Because people with bulimia may be vulnerable to relapse, especially under times of stress, this part of treatment is important. Learning that setbacks do happen occasionally and how to handle them may keep someone from a complete reversal to bulimia. A written plan is part of this last phase of treatment.

As indicated earlier, cognitive behavioral therapy has been demonstrated to be the most effective treatment for bulimia. Roughly 40 to 50 percent achieve a complete remission from binge eating and purging with cognitive behavioral therapy (Wilson et al., 2000). Many others show partial but not complete improvement. However, there are still some people who do not improve with cognitive behavioral therapy. Some people seem unable to commit to the cognitive behavioral therapy package; they seem to have a longer history with disordered eating, excessive laxative abuse, more depression, and more dissatisfaction with their bodies than those who did engage in the cognitive behavioral therapy (Coker, Vize, Wade, & Cooper, 1993). When cognitive behavioral therapy fails to help the patient, the next step might be the use of other psychological interventions.

INTERPERSONAL PSYCHOTHERAPY

Interpersonal psychotherapy (Fairburn, Jones, Peveler, Hope, & O'Connor, 1993; Fairburn, 1997) focuses on helping clients understand their relationships with people. The material that follows here is a description of Fairburn's interpersonal psychotherapy and is written in his many publications on interpersonal therapy (Fairburn, 1997). It usually requires fifteen to twenty sessions over four or five months. Interpersonal psychotherapy is based on the idea that understanding the interpersonal context (relationships that include family and friends) within which the eating disorder developed and has been maintained is necessary for the person to change their eating disordered behavior (Fairburn et al., 1997). In other words, in order to help people stop their eating problems, it is necessary to find out and understand fully what is keeping it going. As an example, many binges are associated with an interpersonal trigger, such as an argument with a friend or family member or feelings of loneliness. Interestingly, in interpersonal psychotherapy there is no attention or direct discussion about eating habits or behavior. Instead, the therapist helps the client to study their past and present relationships and to understand how these relationships might be related to the eating disorder.

In the beginning of treatment, the therapist works with the client to study four different histories: (1) the eating problem (how it started, dates of first binge, purge); (2) relationships (family, friends, peers), (3) other life events that may have been talked about in relation to the development of the eating problems and in the context of relationships with others (might include a move, parental divorce, starting college), and (4) specific problems with self-esteem and depression. This information is used to create a life chart that shows how the eating problem, relationships, life events, and self-esteem/depression are related in the life of a person. The information obtained in the life chart forms the basis for the discussion in sessions with the therapist.

Four major interpersonal issues arise in life charts. Presented in order of the frequency in which they occur, they are interpersonal role disputes (64 percent), role transitions (36 percent), interpersonal deficits (16 percent), and grief (12 percent) (Fairburn, 1997). Interpersonal role disputes are problems that occur when a client has difficulty with someone who is important and powerful. This could include a parent, spouse or partner (if the person is older and married or involved in a significant relationship), children, friends, or employers. In interpersonal psychotherapy, the goal is to resolve the individual's interpersonal problems by clarifying the problem in the relationship, considering the possibilities for changes, and helping the client to make positive changes in these relationships. In role transitions, the issue is usually one of establishing independence from parents. Other transitions include beginning or ending college, changing jobs, getting married, or becoming a parent. In interpersonal psychotherapy, the therapist works with the client to understand the changes that go along with these transitions in life. For individuals who are working to establish independence from parents, the therapist might explore the kind of relationship the person wants to have with parents and help to guide the development of healthy independence.

Less common problems are interpersonal deficits and grief. Interpersonal deficits refer to problems that an individual may have in developing and keeping relationships with people. Sometimes, a client describes a history of being isolated and not having close friends. In this case, the therapist helps the client to understand the reason she might be having trouble forming or keeping relationships. Sometimes the relationship between the client and the therapist can be used as a way to understand the development of important relationships. Grief is an issue that arises when someone important in the client's life has died. Facing the loss requires the client to express feelings about losing an important person and to adjust to life without the person who is gone. As the individual can be less focused on the past, it is easier to develop new interests and relationships.

During the sessions focused on the interpersonal problems, few clients bring up their eating disorder. They rarely describe binge eating or purging or body image issues. However, in the last few sessions, it is more common for clients to talk about their eating problems as they plan for the end of formal counseling. Therapists often tell clients that eating problems may be a kind of Achilles heel, meaning that the eating problems may recur in times of emotional stress. Thus, the final sessions are planned to solidify the interpersonal changes that have been made during the process of psychotherapy and to reduce the risk of relapse.

Although studies of cognitive behavioral therapy have dominated the research literature, there have been a number of studies assessing the effectiveness of interpersonal psychotherapy for bulimia. This research shows that interpersonal psychotherapy is an effective treatment for bulimia (Chambless et al., 1998). Although a simultaneous integration of cognitive behavioral and interpersonal psychotherapy is not possible (one focuses directly on eating related symptoms and the other does not), interpersonal psychotherapy could be used when individuals do not respond well to cognitive behavioral therapy.

OTHER KINDS OF PSYCHOTHERAPY

Other kinds of individual psychotherapy may be useful as an alternative treatment for eating disorders when cognitive-behavioral and interpersonal therapies prove ineffective. Long-term psychodynamic therapy is one example. Psychodynamic therapy focuses on the conscious and unconscious motivation for behavior, conflicts, psychological defenses, and is strongly based on childhood experiences. Psychodynamic therapy for eating disorders may take from six months to many years. It focuses on fostering an emotional experience that corrects underlying deficits in self-identity. Group-oriented psychodynamic therapy may be used to help patients reexperience past experiences and reexamine the ways to resolve these problems. However, this therapy for eating disorders has not been scientifically validated (Chambless et al., 1998). Additionally, there are currently no controlled studies comparing long-term psychodynamic therapy and other short-term therapies, such as cognitive-behavioral therapy. Therefore, psychodynamic therapies may be implemented in cases when current empirically validated therapies have failed.

FAMILY THERAPY

Family therapy may be useful for individuals with eating disorders because much of the eating disordered behavior influences the entire family. This is especially true for younger adolescents who live at home with parents when they develop an eating disorder, particularly anorexia (Garner & Needleman, 1997). Stein et al. (2001) indicate that family therapy for anorexia is more widely researched than cognitive behavioral therapy for anorexia and believe that it may be the most efficacious treatment. A group of researchers working at the Maudsley Hospital in London have demonstrated that an intensive family therapy program, consisting of fifteen sessions over eight to fourteen months, has been effective for about a third of the patients who have participated (Dare & Eisler, 1997). In their book, the authors describe a program that works toward weight restoration and improved parent-adolescent relationships (Lock, le Grange, Agras, & Dare, 2000). The program focuses on the entire family and their concern about the person with anorexia. During this phase, the parents are responsible for controlling the food intake of the person with anorexia. After sufficient weight has been gained, control is changed to the person with anorexia, and the family issues not related to eating are discussed. The final sessions focus on relapse prevention, establishing healthy family roles and boundaries.

According to Dare and Eisler (1997), families of individuals with anorexia may have characteristics of enmeshment, overprotectiveness, and rigidity. Enmeshment and overprotectiveness refer to boundaries that are not well established and often leave the person with anorexia feeling as though she cannot separate herself from her family. Rigidity within the family system involves the persistence in behaviors that are not adaptive. There are also issues around conflict, typically involving the family's inability to tolerate disagreement and avoidance of topics that are likely to spark controversy.

In family therapy, it is essential to treat the entire family as a unit, rather than allowing the individual with anorexia to be the identified patient. Families are often in a great deal of distress over the low weight and food refusal of the person with anorexia. Because consistent weight gain is an important part of treatment for anorexia, this aspect of treatment must be addressed with the entire family. Although it is the responsibility of the person with anorexia to gain weight, parents and family are encouraged to assist by allowing her to eat foods of her choosing.

Although it is difficult to make generalizations, Levenkron (2001) noted that in his work with over 300 people with anorexia, he observed typical responses to a daughter who develops anorexia. The mother often feels guilty and scared and overwhelmed by the development of anorexia in her daughter. She may become angry when the daughter refuses to eat but then feel guilty about being angry. The father is often confused, resentful and worried about his daughter. Siblings may be angry and frustrated as well and disappointed in the sister with anorexia. Siblings may be afraid that the sister with anorexia may take parental attention away from them as the person with anorexia becomes the focus of the family. Sometimes siblings react by trying to be the best siblings and stay out of trouble, while others become jealous of the sister with anorexia.

GROUP THERAPY

Groups of various types are widely used to treat individuals with eating disorders and disturbances. Counseling groups provide a promising kind of treatment for bulimia and eating disorders not otherwise specified. Not only do groups provide cost-effective prevention and treatment that reaches large numbers of people (an important feature because eating issues appear to be increasing for both men and women), they are a highly effective method of providing prevention and treatment (Fettes & Peters, 1992; Polivy & Federoff, 1997). Groups reduce the secrecy and shame associated with eating problems, supply a place for talking about the kinds of distorted beliefs and self-perceptions with others who are also facing eating disorders, and provide an interpersonal context to facilitate links between eating disorders and relationships (Laberg, Tornkvist, & Andersson, 2001). Laberg, Tornkvist, and Andersson (2001) interviewed the participants in a group treatment for bulimia and found that there were many aspects of the group experience that were important to the members. Many of these aspects are unique to group treatment, such as connecting with others who are struggling with the same problem, feeling the support of members of the group, and learning to trust each other.

There are many different kinds of groups for eating disorders; some are based on the cognitive behavioral therapy program and the interpersonal therapy programs described above. Most researchers have concluded that cognitive behavioral therapy is the most extensively researched and supported treatment for bulimia (Richards et al., 2000; Stein et al., 2001), and there have been a number of studies demonstrating the effectiveness of interpersonal psychotherapy (Fairburn, Jones, Peveler, Hope, & O'Connor, 1993; Wilfley et al., 1993). Other groups may be more like a support group, psycho-educational, or based on a family kind of approach. Generally, groups focus on the eating disordered behaviors, attitudes, and feelings. Group treatment in combination with additional therapy may be more effective than group therapy alone. No particular type of group treatment has consistently demonstrated better results than other types (Polivy & Federoff, 1997).

Because of difficulties doing group work with individuals who have anorexia, considerably less is known about these group interventions. There has been very little written about group therapy with people who have anorexia. Some therapists do not use group approaches at all for the treatment of anorexia.

There is a growing body of literature on the use of groups with individuals who do not have anorexia, bulimia, or eating disorder not otherwise specified, but do have a problem related to body shape and weight. Some of these groups are designed as prevention groups, such as one described for college women that focuses on improving body image and decreasing dieting (Nicolino, Martz, & Curtin, 2001).

Short stories may be used as an effective group level intervention for people who have eating disorders and disturbances. Stories are especially useful in addressing disordered eating attitudes and behaviors because they allow group members to confront their eating problems in a non-threatening way. Shifting the focus from the individuals in the group to a neutral character in a story may allow individuals to more openly process issues related to eating and body image disturbance. When a group leader presents a story that symbolically represents the act of binge eating (such as "all-or-nothing" behaviors), group members may identify with the story and then they can participate and share with others in the group. Using a short story in groups may be an effective intervention because it allows members enough distance from a particular eating disturbance to feel comfortable engaging in the group process. For example, one story, "Pulling Weeds and Planting Flowers," describes a person who is removing self-defeating behavior and learning to replace it with more healthy and adaptive behavior (Andersen, 1994). Questions like "Can we plant flowers at the same time we are pulling weeds?" and "Where do you think this group is right now in taking care of our gardens?" can be used to raise a useful discussion about the destructive nature of eating disordered behaviors. More information about short stories in groups focused on eating disorders can be found in Van Lone, Kalodner, and Coughlin's (2002) article, "Using Short Stories to Address Eating Disturbances in Groups."

MEDICATION

Medication should not be the exclusive mode of treatment for eating disorders. "Drug therapy has never been seen as the sole treatment but as an ancillary to other types of interventions, primarily inpatient or outpatient counseling" (Mitchell, 2001, p. 205). You cannot go to a doctor and get a prescription that will make the eating disorder go away.

There is no evidence that antidepressants or other medications are effective treatments for anorexia (APA, 2000; Wilson et al., 2000). Mitchell (2001) provides some explanation about this statement about anorexia. People with anorexia usually require many different kinds of interventions, which makes it very difficult to know the effects of any single aspect of treatment; therefore, we can not be sure if medication is effective if it is part of a package of treatment. Also, many patients with anorexia do not appreciate the severity of their physical condition, and they may not cooperate with taking medication as directed, which makes conducting research on the use of medication with anorexia difficult. Finally, Mitchell (2001) suggests that because there are few people with anorexia, it takes a long time to collect enough data for meaningful research conclusions to be drawn. A kind of antidepressant called serotonin reuptake inhibitors (SSRIs) may be helpful in preventing relapse in those with anorexia; however, people of very low body weight may not respond to SSRIs.

Most of the research on medications for bulimia indicate that there is some degree of improvement of eating symptoms or mood or both associated with antidepressant medication use (Mitchell, 2001). Fluoxetine (an antidepressant) is the only FDA-approved drug for bulimia. However, the best outcomes are associated with a psychological therapy like cognitive behavioral therapy in combination with medication. Thus, medication, along with counseling, might be a part of treatment for someone with bulimia. Medication alone is generally less effective than cognitive behavioral therapy, more intrusive, and less acceptable to many patients than counseling. Medication should be viewed as a part of a comprehensive treatment package and should not be prescribed without attention to psychological issues that are addressed in individual, group, or family therapy.

HOSPITALIZATION

Hospitalization is more often needed for individuals with anorexia who reach a body weight that causes physical complications, although individuals suffering from bulimia who are unresponsive to psychological treatment may also be hospitalized. The issue of inpatient hospitalization versus outpatient care is especially important in anorexia. Refeeding in a hospital setting is necessary when a patient is severely malnourished and medically unstable. When health issues require medical monitoring, an inpatient treatment facility is needed. However, many patients resist hospitalization. Perhaps they resist because they know that in the hospital, weight gain is much easier to accomplish. Other reasons that patients try to avoid hospitalization is fear of losing control, giving up power, and not wanting to give up identity as a person with an eating disorder. Some patients do not want to recover. Various feeding strategies such as use of intravenous fluids or nasogastric tube feedings make weight gain in the hospital possible, even if the patient does not eat. The length of stay in the hospital may vary from less than twenty-eight days (an important number because many insurance plans will only pay for twenty-eight days of inpatient care a year) to much longer stays. Six months or more used to be commonplace in the inpatient treatment of anorexia. However, changes in the insurance industry include lowered reimbursements for physical and psychiatric treatment that has been especially problematic for treatment of anorexia (Levenkron, 2001). Eating disorders are quite expensive to treat, especially in an inpatient treatment format. Regardless, inpatient hospitalizations may be warranted for the following reasons:

- to manage medical emergencies such as severe weight loss, electrolyte imbalances, and hypotension
- to prevent increased weight loss by interrupting patterns of bingeing, purging, and the use of laxatives
- to manage associated psychological complications such as depression, family crises, risk of self-harm, and substance abuse disorders

Day treatment programs have increased in popularity, in part, in response to changes in the insurance companies reimbursement policies (Levenkron, 2001). Day treatment means that the patient comes for treatment and stays all day but returns home to sleep. Many day treatment programs operate five days a week. Day treatment programs provide an economical alternative to inpatient hospitalization, allowing clients medical monitoring, intensive psychotherapy, and structured meal programs without removing clients from home. Such programs may also provide a transition from inpatient treatment to outpatient treatment.

THE COSTS OF TREATMENT

As indicated earlier, treatment of eating disorders is quite expensive. A study of a database of an insurance company's claims of almost 2 million male and over 2 million female patients indicated that just over 1 percent of all claims for mental disorder treatment were for an eating disorder (Striegel-Moore, Leslie, Petrill, Garvin, & Rosenheck, 2000). Data were available from 517 women and 49 men treated for anorexia, 725 women and 41 men treated for bulimia, and 756 women and 176 men treated for eating disorder not otherwise specified. Patients with anorexia were hospitalized more often than those with other eating disorders (20 percent of those with anorexia were hospitalized compared with 13 percent of those with bulimia and 11 percent of those with eating disorder not otherwise specified). The females with anorexia were in the hospital an average of 26 days, with a cost of $17,384 (there were not enough data to analyze this for male inpatients). Those individuals with bulimia who were hospitalized stayed an average of 14.7 days, with a cost of $9,088, and those with eating disorder not otherwise specified who were hospitalized stayed an average of 20 days with a cost of $13,297. It is interesting that those with eating disorder not otherwise specified stayed in the hospital longer than those with bulimia; thus, the cost of treatment of eating disorder not otherwise specified in this group was more costly than the treatment for bulimia. This may be because some people diagnosed with eating disorders not otherwise specified may be very similar to those who have anorexia, and the treatment provided is like the treatment for anorexia. You may recall research described in the chapter on anorexia indicated that 75 percent of people who are diagnosed with eating disorders not otherwise specified could be reclassified as people with anorexia if the criteria for anorexia were readjusted. Data for the outpatient setting indicated that those costs associated were greatest for anorexia ($2,344 for 17 sessions), less for bulimia ($1,882 for 15.6 sessions), and least for eating disorder not otherwise specified ($1,582 for 13.7 sessions).

These costs have been compared with the cost associated with the treatment of other psychiatric disorders, such as schizophrenia and obsessive-compulsive disorder, which are viewed as the most expensive and chronic psychiatric disorders. It is as costly to treat anorexia as it is to treat schizophrenia (the average cost of treatment for schizophrenia from the study was $4,824). Bulimia costs less to treat than schizophrenia but more than obsessive-compulsive disorder (which cost $1,930).

The costs of treatment may be able to be reduced if hospitalization can be avoided (but sometimes it is not possible to treat a person outside of the hospital). In addition, early identification of an eating disorder may prevent the disorder from becoming chronic; thus, the best way to reduce treatment costs is through prevention.

WHAT KIND OF TREATMENT IS PREFERRED?

It is important to understand the patient's perspective of the treatment for eating disorders. It is rare in research to ask patients what they think was helpful about treatment. Although this is a small study of only 21 individuals (10 had anorexia; 11 had bulimia) recovering from an eating disorder, detailed information about their views on the helpfulness of various aspects of counseling was collected in interviews (le Grange & Gelman, 1998). The younger patients with anorexia who were living at home with their parents received family counseling. This approach focuses on united parental control over the adolescent's eating while supporting the parents and absolving them from blame for the child's illness. The patients with anorexia also received individual sessions that focused on support, education, and their symptoms of the eating disorder. The older clients with anorexia and all the clients with bulimia received cognitive behavioral therapy.

There were 14 clients who received the cognitive behavioral therapy treatment. Ten of the 14 believed that the therapy was helpful, and 4 reported that it was not. Looking at the specific interventions that were viewed as helpful, behavioral strategies (8/14), supportive/understanding environment (8/14), changing dysfunctional beliefs (7/14), and psychoeducation (5/14) were mentioned. Interestingly, behavioral strategies were also described as unhelpful by many patients (8/14). Some patients indicated that the behavioral strategies were both helpful and unhelpful, depending on the circumstances. Food monitoring was mentioned as unhelpful especially when the symptoms of the eating disorder were overpowering. This means that when patients were unable to control their binge or purge behaviors, they viewed the behavioral strategies as not powerful enough to help them. Other unhelpful aspects of treatment included inadequate addressing of causes (6/14) and neglect of personal problems/feelings (4/14). The lack of attention to the cause of an eating disorder is part of cognitive behavioral therapy, but many patients responded that they wanted to understand why they had developed an eating disorder. The neglect of personal problems was described by one patient as a lack of attention to the emotional side of the eating disorder. Of the 14 patients who received cognitive behavioral therapy, 10 thought that they had improved, but formal outcome data suggest that 6 had improved and that 8 were unchanged.

Turning to the 7 people who received the family counseling treatment, 6 indicated that treatment was helpful. The assessment of actual recovery indicated that 5 had improved and 2 were unchanged. They rated supportive/understanding environment (5/7), changing dysfunctional beliefs (4/7), psycho-education (5/7), and the watchdog role of the therapist (4/7) as helpful. Unhelpful aspects of treatment included inadequate addressing of causes (4/7) and neglect of personal problems/feelings (2/7).

Again, the formal rating of patients and their self-assessment of progress did not match. For the most part, there were more people who thought they had improved than the formal assessment criteria indicated. However, the authors indicated that the formal criteria were quite strict, and it may be that the patients are better judges of their eating disorder than judges using criteria.

Cognitive behavioral therapy does not give a great deal of attention to the underlying causes of the problems. Family counseling is also not focused on understanding the intrapsychic causes of eating disorders. However, it is clear that for almost half of the patients treated in this study, they wanted greater attention to the causes of the eating disorder. Because the causes of eating disorders are complicated and differ on a case-by-case basis, it can be difficult to address the direct cause of an eating disorder in treatment. It is worth noting that greater attention might be necessary for patients to develop an understanding of the problems, even if it is not necessary for their recovery (le Grange & Gelman, 1998).

One issue of importance in inpatient treatment of anorexia is nasogastric feeding, which involves placing a tube into the nose where it is passed through the esophagus and into the stomach. Nasogastric tubes are used to provide nutrition to patients who refuse to eat and have dangerously low weight or who can not absorb nutrition due to the effects of starvation. This is the most commonly used approach to providing nutrition to people who are hospitalized for anorexia (Neiderman, Farley, Richardson, & Lask, 2001).

A study of the attitudes and effects of nasogastric feeding revealed that there may be significant resistance to the use of this type of forced feeding by patients with anorexia, although the parents provided consent for the procedure because they viewed it as a way to prevent the death of their child (Neiderman, Farley, Richardson, & Lask, 2001). This was a study of 58 people (21 patients, 21 mothers, 13 fathers, and 3 from parents responding jointly). Of the 21 patients who answered the question about consenting to the nasogastric tube, only 7 (29 percent) indicated that they agreed to the tube, whereas 17 (71 percent) said they did not consent to the tube. One patient who agreed to the placement of the tube said that she "wanted things to be taken out of my control." Of those who objected, they refused because they thought it would be painful, they didn't want to gain weight, and they didn't want to lose control over their intake of calories. However, the parents of these patients all agreed to provide consent for the nasogastric tube because they wanted to prevent their child from dying due to starvation or dehydration, and they recognized that there may be no other way to feed their child. Reactions to the tube varied significantly from those patients who hated it to those who acknowledged that it was necessary. A slight majority (66 percent) realized that the nasogastric tube was a necessary part of their recovery. The other 44 percent reported that they hated it when it was used, and they still felt that it was not helpful in their recovery. The parents were more positive in their evaluation of the use of the tube; 73 percent felt this was a "regrettable necessity," and 27 percent indicated that there were some problems with the use of the tube (i.e., negated child's rights).

Another way to provide nutrition is through intravenous parenteral hyperalimentation, which is feeding through a vein. In one case, a person with anorexia was able to use this system for feeding while living at home rather than in the hospital (Latzer, Eysen-Eylat, & Tabenkin, 2000). The patient was unwilling to eat food but did assist in the use of intravenous parenteral hyperalimentation, and she gained twenty-two pounds over seven months of use.

In Apostolides' (1998, p. 158) book on eating disorders, she suggests that treatment will be easier for people with eating disorders if they keep some of these ideas in mind:

- There is no "right" therapy combination. You must choose among the therapies and decide which ones will best help *you* heal. You can always add some therapies and drop others to find what works for you.

- Individual psychotherapy is the only type of therapy that all people with an eating disorder should have as part of treatment. Shop around until you find the right therapist for you.

- Therapy takes time and money, but you are worth the sacrifice. This is the most important investment you can make.

- Part of the frustration of treatment is the inevitable "slipping back" into old behaviors. Both progress and relapse are part of letting go.

It is important to note that Apostolides (1998) writes from the perspective of a person who recovered from an eating disorder and is provided here as evidence of the kind of treatment that is preferred by patients.

CONCLUSIONS

Treatment recommendations are limited by the research that evaluates the effectiveness of the treatments for individuals with eating disorders. There are some problems with this research. First, most of the research is based on shorter-term treatment and the short-term effectiveness of treatment. Because eating disorders tend to be long-term problems, the research does not really tell us if people get better and stay better. There have not been enough studies of the long-term effects of treatment for persons with each of the eating disorders.

Another problem is the definition of recovery. For bulimia, recovery is usually described in terms of reductions in the frequency or severity of binge eating, purging or other problematic behaviors, or the proportion of people who stopped or reduced these behaviors. For anorexia, recovery is framed as the amount of weight gained or the proportion of individuals who achieved a weight that is a percentage of ideal weight. The return of menstruation in women is another outcome measure of the success of treatment. What is missed in this assessment of change is the change in attitudes about body image. In anorexia, this includes the "intense fear of gaining weight or becoming fat" and "disturbance in the way in which one's body weight or shape is experienced, undue influence of body weight or shape on self-evaluation, or denial of the seriousness of the current low body weight." In bulimia, this includes the notion that self-evaluation is unduly influenced by body shape and weight (APA, 2000). Also, associated issues, such as depression, anxiety, and other psychological adjustment, are rarely reported.

Other issues that influence the type of treatment selected and the outcome of treatment are the other psychological problems that a person has.

Substance abuse/dependence, mood (depression), and anxiety disorders (especially obsessive-compulsive disorder) are examples of other psychological problems that may be present in individuals with eating disorders. These issues complicate treatment of the eating disorders because they are issues that also require attention. It is difficult to help a person with an eating disorder who is also dependent on alcohol or other drugs. Likewise, when a person has an eating disorder and depression or an anxiety disorder, the treatment must attend to both problems. Severe depression can impact the patient's ability to work in psychotherapy.

The research on the effectiveness of treatment for anorexia is much less developed than for bulimia. This means that we do not know which treatments are most effective, and there is a great need for additional research to identify effective treatments. What we do know is that the lower levels of stepped care, such as self-help and group psycho-education, are not likely to be sufficient to treat anorexia. It is difficult to complete research studies on anorexia because it can be difficult to have enough participants to conduct large studies, and long follow-ups are necessary to determine the success of a treatment.

REFERENCES

Agras, W. S. (2001). The consequences and costs of the eating disorders. *The Psychiatric Clinics of North America, 24* (2), 371–379.

American Dietetic Association (2001). Position of the American Dietetic Association: Nutrition intervention in the treatment of anorexia nervosa, bulimia nervosa, and eating disorders not otherwise specified (EDNOS). *Journal of the American Dietetic Association, 101*, 810–819.

American Psychiatric Association (2000). *Practice guidelines for the treatment of patients with eating disorders* (2nd ed.). Washington, DC: Author.

Andersen, A. (1994). Stories I tell my patients: Pulling weeds and planting flowers. *Eating Disorders: The Journal of Prevention and Treatment, 2*, 184–185.

Andrewes, D., Say, S., & McLennan, J. (1995). A self-administered computer-based educational program about eating-disorder risk factors. *Australian Psychologist, 30* (3), 210–212.

Apostolides, M. (1998). *Inner hunger.* New York: W.W. Norton & Company.

Boskind-White, M., & White, W. C. (2000). *Bulimia/anorexia.* New York: W. W. Norton.

Bowers, W. A. (2001). Basic principles for applying cognitive-behavioral therapy to anorexia nervosa. *The Psychiatric Clinics of North America, 24*, 293–303.

Cash, T. F. (1995). *What do you see when you look in the mirror? Helping yourself to a positive body image.* New York: Bantam Books.

Cash, T. F. (1997). *The body image workbook: An 8-step program for learning to like your looks.* Oakland, CA: New Harbinger Publications.

Celio, A. A., Winzelberg, A. J., Taylor, C. B., Wilfley, D. E., Eppstein-Herald, D., Springer, E. A., & Dev, P. (2000). Reducing risk factors for eating disorders: Comparison of an Internet- and a classroom-delivered psychoeducational program. *Journal of Consulting and Clinical Psychology, 68*, 650–657.

Chambless, D. L., Baker, M. J., Baucom, D. H., Beutler, L. E., Calhoun, K. S., Crits-Christoph, P., Daiuto, A., DeRebeis, R., Detweiler, J., Haaga, D.A.F., Bennett-Johnson, S., McCurry, S., Muesser, K. T., Pope, K. S., Sanderson, W. C., Shoham, V., Stickle, T., Williams, D. A., & Woody, S. R. (1998). Update on empirically validated therapies, II. *The Clinical Psychologist, 51*(1), 3–16.

Coker, S., Vize, C., Wade, T., & Cooper, P. J. (1993). Patients with bulimia nervosa who fail to engage in cognitive behavior therapy. *International Journal of Eating Disorders, 13* (1), 35–40.

Cooper, P. J., Coker, S., & Fleming, C. (1996). An evaluation of the efficacy of supervised cognitive behavioral self-help for bulimia nervosa. *Journal of Psychosomatic Research, 40*, 281–287.

Dare, C., & Eisler, I. (1997). Family therapy for anorexia nervosa. In D. M. Garner & P. E. Garfinkel (Eds.), *Handbook of psychotherapy for anorexia nervosa and bulimia* (pp. 307–324). New York: Guilford Press.

DiGioacchino, R. F., Keenan, M. F., & Sargent, R. (2000). Assessment of dental practitioners in the secondary and tertiary prevention of eating disorders. *Eating Behaviors, 1* (1), 79–91.

Fairburn, C. G. (1995). *Overcoming binge eating*. New York: Guilford Press.

Fairburn, C. G. (1997). Interpersonal psychotherapy for bulimia nervosa. In D. M. Garner & P. E. Garfinkel (Eds.), *Handbook of treatment for eating disorders* (2nd ed., pp. 278–294). New York: Guilford Press.

Fairburn, C. G., & Carter, J. C. (1997). Self-help and guided self-help for binge-eating problems. In D. M. Garner & P. E. Garfinkel (Eds.), *Handbook of treatment for eating disorders* (2nd ed., pp. 494–499). New York: Guilford Press.

Fairburn, C. G., Jones, R., Peveler, R. C., Hope, R., & O'Connor, M. E. (1993). Psychotherapy and bulimia nervosa: The longer-term effects of interpersonal psychotherapy, behavior therapy, and cognitive behavior therapy. *Archives of General Psychology, 50*, 419–428.

Fettes, P. A., & Peters, J. M. (1992). A meta-analysis of group treatments for bulimia nervosa. *International Journal of Eating Disorders, 11*, 97–110.

Garner, D. M. (1997). Psychoeducational principles in treatment. In D. M. Garner & P. E. Garfinkel (Eds.), *Handbook of treatment for eating disorders* (2nd ed., pp. 145–177). New York: Guilford Press.

Garner, D. M., & Needleman, L. D. (1997). Sequencing and integreation of treatments. In D. M. Garner & P. E. Garfinkel (Eds.), *Handbook of treatment for eating disorders* (2nd ed., pp. 50–63). New York: Guilford Press.

Garvin, V., Striegel-Moore, R. H., Kaplan, A., & Wonderlich, S. A. (2001). Health services research for eating disorders in the United States: A status report and a call to action. In R. H. Striegel-Moore & L. Smolak (Eds.), *Eating disorders: Innovative directions in research and practice* (pp. 153–172). Washington, DC: APA.

Hollis, J. (1996). *Fat Is a Family Affair.* Cedar City, MN: Hazelden.

Keel, P. K., Mitchell, J. E., Davis, T. L., & Crow, S. J. (2002). Long-term impact of treatment in women diagnosed with bulimia nervosa. *International Journal of Eating Disorders, 31*, 151–158.

Laberg, S., Tornkvist, A., & Andersson, G. (2001). Group therapy: Qualitative study of eating disorders. *Scandinavian Journal of Behavior Therapy, 30*, 161–178.

Latzer, Y., Eysen-Eylat, D., & Tabenkin, H. (2000). A case report: Treatment of severe anorexia nervosa with home total parental hyperalimentation. *International Journal of Eating Disorders, 27*, 115–118.

le Grange, D., & Gelman, T. (1998). Patients' perspective of treatment in eating disorders: A preliminary study. *South African Journal of Psychology, 28* (3), 182–186.

Levenkron, S. (2001). *Anatomy of anorexia.* New York: W. W. Norton.

Lock, J., le Grange, D., Agras, W. S., & Dare, C. (2000). *Treatment manual for anorexia nervosa: A family-based approach.*

Migliore, M. A. with Ross, P. (1998). *The Hunger Within: A Twelve-Week Guided Journey from Compulsive Eating to Recovery.* New York: Main Street.

Mitchell, J. E. (2001). Psychopharmacology of eating disorders: Current knowledge and future directions. In R. H. Striegel-Moore & L. Smolak (Eds.), *Eating disorders: Innovative directions in research and practice* (pp. 197–212). Washington, DC: American Psychiatric Association.

Neiderman, M., Farley, A., Richardson, J., & Lask, B. (2001). Nasogastric feeding in children and adolescents with eating disorders: Toward good practice. *International Journal of Eating Disorders, 29*, 441–448.

Nicolino, J. C., Martz, D. M., & Curtin, L. (2001). Evaluation of a cognitive-behavioral therapy intervention to improve body image and decrease dieting in college women. *Eating Behaviors, 2*, 353–362.

Norcross, J. C., Santrock, J. W., Campbell, L. F., Smith, T. P., Sommer, R., & Zuckerman, E. L. (2000). *Authoritative guide to self-help resources in mental health.* New York: Guilford.

Peterson, C. B., & Mitchell, J. E. (1999). Psychosocial and pharmacological treatment of eating disorders: A review of research findings. *Journal of Clinical Psychology, 55*, 685–697.

Polivy, J., & Federoff, I. (1997). Group psychotherapy. In D. M. Garner & P. E. Garfinkel (Eds.), *Handbook of treatment for eating disorders* (2nd ed., pp. 462–475). New York: Guilford Press.

Price, D. (1998). *Healing the Hungry Self: The Diet-Free Solution to Lifelong Weight Management.* New York: Plume.

Reiff, D., & Reiff, K. K. (2000). *Eating disorders: Nutrition therapy in the recovery process.*

Richards, P.S., Baldwin, B.M., Frost, H.A., Clark-Sly, J.B., Berrett, M.E., & Hardman, R.K. (2000). What works for treating eating disorders? Conclusions of 28 outcome reviews. *Eating Disorders: The Journal of Treatment and Prevention, 8* (3), 189–206.

Rock, C.L. (1999). Nutritional and medical assessment and management of eating disorders. *Nutrition in Clinical Care, 2,* 332–343.

Roth, G. (1989). *Why Weight? A Guide to Ending Compulsive Eating.* New York: Plume.

Roth, G. (1991). *When Food Is Love.* New York: Dutton.

Roth, G. (1993). Dessert. In L. Hall (Ed.), *Full lives: Women who have freed themselves from food and weight obsession* (pp. 247–254), Carlsbad, CA; Gurze Books.

Rubel, J. (1993). Are you finding what you need? In L. Hall (Ed.), *Full lives: Women who have freed themselves from food and weight obsession* (pp. 32–51), Carlsbad, CA; Gurze Books.

Sacker, I.M., & Zimmer, M.A. (1987). *Dying to Be Thin: Understanding and Defeating Anorexia Nervosa and Bulimia: A Practical, Lifesaving Guide.* New York: Warner.

Stein, R.I., Saelens, B.E., Dounchis, J.Z., Lewczyk, C.M., Swenson, A.K., & Wilfley, D.E. (2001). Treatment of eating disorders in women. *The Counseling Psychologist, 29* (5), 695–732.

Striegel-Moore, R., Leslie, D., Petrill, S.A., Garvin, S.A., & Rosenheck, S.A. (2000). One-year use and cost of inpatient and outpatient services among female and male patients with an eating disorder: Evidence from a national database of health insurance forms. *International Journal of Eating Disorders, 27,* 381–389.

Thomas, D. (2000). The dietitian's role in the treatment of eating disorders. *British Nutrition Foundation Bulletin, 25,* 55–60.

The Twelve Steps and Twelve Traditions of Overeaters Anonymous. (1995). Rio Rancho, NM: Overeaters Anonymous.

Van Lone, J.L., Kalodner, C.R., & Coughlin, J.W. (2002). Using short stories to address eating disturbances in groups. *Journal for Specialists in Group Work, 27,* 59–77.

Wilfley, D.E., Agras, A.W., Telch, F.C., Rossiter, M., Schneider, J.A., Cole, A.B., Sifford, L.A., & Raeburn, S.D. (1993). Group cognitive-behavioral therapy and group interpersonal psychotherapy for the nonpurging bulimic individual: A controlled comparison. *Journal of Consulting and Clinical Psychology, 61,* 296–305.

Wilson, G.T., Fairburn, C.G., & Agras, W.S. (1997). Cognitive-behavioral therapy for bulimia nervosa. In D.M. Garner & P.E. Garfinkel (Eds.), *Handbook of treatment for eating disorders* (2nd ed., pp. 67–93). New York: Guilford Press.

Wilson, G. T., Vitousek, K. M., & Loeb, K. L. (2000). Stepped care treatment for eating disorders. *Journal of Consulting and Clinical Psychology, 68* (4), 564–572.

Winzelberg, A. J., Eppstein, D., Eldredge, K. L., Wifley, D., Dasmahapatra, R., Dev, P., & Taylor, C. B. (2000). Effectiveness of an Internet-based program for reducing risk factors for eating disorders. *Journal of Consulting and Clinical Psychology, 68* (2), 346–350.

Appendix

The following pages review the current recommendations by the APA (2000) for the treatment of the specific types of eating disorders.

ANOREXIA NERVOSA

Anorexia nervosa is a complex, serious, and often chronic condition that may require a variety of treatment modalities at different stages of illness and recovery. These goals are met via three major components of treatment: nutritional rehabilitation, psychosocial interventions, and medications.

The specific aims of treatment for patients with anorexia are

- To restore patients to healthy weight (at which menses and normal ovulation in females, normal sex drive and hormone levels in males, and normal physical and sexual growth and development in children and adolescents are restored)
- Treat physical complications
- Enhance patients' motivations to cooperate in the restoration of healthy eating patterns and to participate in treatment
- Provide education regarding healthy nutrition and eating patterns
- Correct core maladaptive thoughts, attitudes, and feelings related to the eating disorder

- Treat associated psychiatric conditions, including defects in mood regulation, self-esteem, and behavior
- Enlist family support and provide family counseling and therapy where appropriate
- Prevent relapse

Nutritional Rehabilitation

Nutritional rehabilitation is a crucial element of treatment for anorexia. The goals of this aspect of treatment are to restore weight to normal, normalize eating patterns, help the patient recognize when she is hungry and when she is full, and to correct the effects of malnutrition. Because these goals are of primary importance, they take precedence over other aspects of treatment, especially in the early stages. As weight increases, some of the eating disorder symptoms will also become less problematic. For example, as weight is regained, food choices increase, hoarding decreases, and obsessions about food decrease in intensity and frequency. The effects of starvation may explain these changes (see description of the Keys study of the effects of starvation in chapter 6). A dietitian is an important player on the treatment team. However, as the patient with anorexia nervosa gains weight, he or she may become quite anxious and depressed. A psychologist on the team is equipped to respond to these feelings. If the patient has stopped using laxatives and diuretics, there may be fluid retention (edema and bloating). It is important to note that these changes are temporary as the body adjusts to improvement in electrolytes, heart and kidney function.

Psychosocial Interventions

Treatments of a psychosocial nature are used to help patients to (1) understand and cooperate in their nutritional and physical rehabilitation, (2) understand and change the behaviors and dysfunctional attitudes related to their eating disorder, (3) improve their interpersonal and social functioning, and (4) address psychological conflicts that reinforce or maintain eating disorder behaviors. Through individual counseling and behavioral interventions, along with family counseling and support groups, these goals may be addressed.

Medication

Medication does not appear to be helpful in the treatment of anorexia and is not recommended. When a person also has depression or an anxiety disorder, medication may be used. However, malnourished individuals with anorexia are more prone to the side effects of antidepressant medications than depressed patients of normal weight. Therefore, antidepressant medication should only be used carefully.

Hospitalization

The issue of inpatient versus outpatient care is important in anorexia. Refeeding in a hospital setting is necessary when a patient is severely malnourished and medically unstable. When health issues require medical monitoring, an inpatient treatment facility is needed. In the hospital setting, it is possible to produce weight gain through various feeding strategies such as use of intravenous fluids or nasogastric tube feedings.

BULIMIA NERVOSA

Treatment for bulimia nervosa includes (1) nutritional counseling and rehabilitation, (2) psychosocial interventions in individual, group or family formats, and (3) medications.

Nutritional Counseling and Rehabilitation

The nutritional component of treatment for bulimia focuses on the reduction of binge eating and purging. Most people with bulimia are of normal weight; thus, there is not a need to focus on weight gain as a treatment goal (as in anorexia). It is necessary to develop a pattern of regular nonbinge meals, with increasing the calories and nutrients in the foods. Nutritional counseling can be very helpful to minimize food restriction (forbidden foods), correct nutritional deficiencies, increase the variety of foods eaten, and encourage healthy but not excessive exercise habits.

Almost all treatment for bulimia includes nutritional education. This refers to the need to provide accurate information to challenge the misinformation and myths that those with this type of eating problem may hold. These bits of misinformation, or erroneous beliefs, may keep those who have an eating disorder from changing their behavior. It is important for those with eating problems to learn more about the body and how it works. For some people, information may be enough to lead to a significant change in behavior and a reduction in eating-related symptoms.

Psychosocial Intervention

The goals of the psychosocial aspect of treatment may overlap with the nutritional goals. These goals are accomplished through individual, group, family, and/or marital treatment. Support groups may also be a part of treatment for bulimia. The goals are

- Reduction in, or elimination of, binge eating and purging behaviors
- Improvement in attitudes related to the eating disorder
- Minimization of food restriction
- Increasing the variety of food eaten
- Encouragement of healthy but not excessive exercise patterns
- Treatment of comorbid conditions and clinical features associated with eating disorders
- Addressing themes that may underlie eating disorder behaviors such as developmental issues, identity formation, body image concerns, self-esteem in areas outside of those related to weight and shape, sexual and aggressive difficulties, affect regulation, gender role expectations, family dysfunction, coping styles, and problem solving

Medications

Medications, primarily antidepressants, are used in patients with bulimia. While they should not be the only treatment provided, antidepressants can be helpful in reducing disturbed eating behaviors such as binge eating and vomiting. Additionally, antidepressants reduce depression, which occurs in a significant number of individuals with bulimia.

BINGE EATING DISORDER

APA (2000) specifies that there are three aspects of treatment for binge eating disorder: nutritional rehabilitation and counseling, psychosocial treatments, and medications.

Nutritional Rehabilitation and Counseling

Working with individuals who have a binge eating disorder requires a focus on weight because many of the people diagnosed with this disorder are overweight. Some research on very-low-calorie diets (under strict medical supervision) has indicated that some people are able to lose substantial amounts of weight and maintain weight loss. However, for some individuals, the focus on weight loss and dieting may make their eating disorder worse. Some therapists focus on self-acceptance, improving body image along with an emphasis on better nutrition and exercise. These nondieting approaches have been used with obese individuals without binge eating disorder as well.

Psychosocial Treatments

Many of the treatments for binge eating disorder have been adopted from those for bulimia. Cognitive behavioral therapy, behavior therapy, and interpersonal psychotherapy have been used successfully with people with binge eating disorder. However, long-term success rates have not been maintained well by any of these forms of therapy. One study of patients with binge eating disorder found that 57 percent had good outcomes, 35 percent had intermediate outcomes, 6 percent had poor outcomes, and 1 percent died.

Medications

Antidepressant medications have been used in the treatment of binge eating disorder with some notable success. In several studies, reductions of binge eating from 63 percent to 90 percent were found with antidepressant medications. Other types of medications have been used, such as various forms of appetite suppressants. However, fenfluramine and phentermine (Fen-Phen) that was used as a treatment for obesity, was linked with the development of pulmonary hypertension, which may cause death. Fenfluramine has since been removed from the market.

TREATMENT FOR EATING DISORDERS NOT OTHERWISE SPECIFIED

Except for binge eating disorder, there is little literature to guide recommendations for treatment for the various types of eating disorder not otherwise specified. The APA says, "in general, the nature and intensity of treatment depends on the symptom profile and severity of impairment, not the DSM-IV diagnosis" (2000, p. 25). This indicates that the type of eating disorder not otherwise specified is an important determinant of the kind of treatment that can be used. Because APA does not provide further guidance on this issue, following are suggestions based on the similarity of the type of eating disorder not otherwise specified (Walsh & Garner, 1997). Eating disorder not otherwise specified type one includes females who meet all the criteria for anorexia except individual has regular menses. For example, people who fit into this category are very similar to those who have anorexia and should be treated as if they have anorexia. Type two is for people who meet all criteria for anorexia except that, despite significant weight loss, the individual's weight is in the normal range. Sometimes, these individuals were previously obese, and have lost a great deal of weight. They may remain preoccupied with weight as is seen in anorexia. They may see themselves as recovered from obesity and can describe health improvement as a result of their weight loss. However, the amount of attention to weight and body image is not healthy, although the patient sees it as important to prevent weight gain. These individuals can be treated by focusing on the degree of psychosocial and physical impairment as a result of the eating disorder symptoms.

Type three includes people who meet all criteria for bulimia except that binge eating and purging or other way to control weight gain occur at a frequency of less than twice a week or for less than three months. This is very similar to bulimia nervosa and should be treated as bulimia nervosa. In type four, individuals of normal weight vomit after eating a small amount of food or use other inappropriate compensatory behavior. These individuals may be so terrified of weight gain that they cannot tolerate any food in their stomachs. This type can also be treated like bulimia, with a special focus on the method of compensation. Type five is for people who repeatedly chew and spit out food (they do not swallow it). This is a small minority of the people who present with eating disorder not otherwise specified, and it should be treated as anorexia.

REFERENCES

American Psychiatric Association (2000). *Practice guidelines for the treatment of patients with eating disorders* (2nd ed.). Washington, DC: Author.

Walsh, B. T., & Garner, D. M. (1997). Diagnostic issues. In D. M. Garner & P. E. Garfinkel (Eds.), *Handbook of treatment for eating disorders* (2nd ed., pp. 25–33). New York: Guilford Press.

Index

About the Author

CYNTHIA R. KALODNER, Ph.D., is director of the Counseling Psychology program at Towson University and a licensed psychologist in the state of Maryland. She has written extensively about eating disorders and disturbances and has made presentations across the country. Dr. Kalodner is known for her group counseling with girls and women who have eating disturbances and has been featured in a videotape about eating disturbances called *In Search for Acceptance: The High Cost of Looking Good*.